Hannah's Dress

For Kaspar and Taddeo – the street of your childhood

Pascale Hugues

Hannah's Dress

Berlin 1904–2014

Translated by C. Jon Delogu
With passages from the German translated by Nick Somers

polity

First published in French as *La robe de Hannah*, © Éditions des Arènes, Paris, 2014

This English edition © Polity Press, 2017
This paperback edition © Polity Press 2018

Polity Press
65 Bridge Street
Cambridge CB2 1UR, UK

Polity Press
101 Station Landing
Suite 300
Medford, MA 02155, USA

ISBN-13: 978-1-5095-0981-2
ISBN-13: 978-1-5095-0982-9(pb)

A catalogue record for this book is available from the British Library.

Library of Congress Cataloging-in-Publication Data

Names: Hugues, Pascale, author.
Title: Hannah's dress : Berlin 1904-2014 / Pascale Hugues.
Other titles: Robe de Hannah. English
Description: English edition. I Malden, MA : Polity Press, [2017]
Identifiers: LCCN 2016038265 (print) I LCCN 2016038429 (ebook) I ISBN 9781509509812 (hardback) I ISBN 9781509509850 (Epub) I ISBN 9781509509843 (mobi)
Subjects: LCSH: Streets--Germany--Berlin--History--20th century. I Schöneberg (Berlin, Germany)--History--20th century. I Schöneberg (Berlin, Germany)--Social life and customs--20th century. I Schöneberg (Berlin, Germany)--Biography. I Berlin (Germany)--History--20th century. I Berlin (Germany)--Biography.
Classification: LCC DD887 .H8413 2017 (print) I LCC DD887 (ebook) I DDC 943/.1554--dc23LC record available at https://lccn.loc.gov/2016038265

Typeset in 9.75 on 15pt Meridien by
Servis Filmsetting Limited, Stockport, Cheshire
Printed and bound in United Kingdom by Clays Ltd, Elcograf S.p.A.

The publisher has used its best endeavours to ensure that the URLs for external websites referred to in this book are correct and active at the time of going to press. However, the publisher has no responsibility for the websites and can make no guarantee that a site will remain live or that the content is or will remain appropriate.

Every effort has been made to trace all copyright holders, but if any have been overlooked the publisher will be pleased to include any necessary credits in any subsequent reprint or edition.

For further information on Polity, visit our website: politybooks.com

Contents

Acknowledgements

Thank you to all my neighbours past and present who took me into their confidence and shared with me the history of their lives. This return to the past was often painful. I admire your courage. And if any of you still doubt the interest of your 'little ordinary lives', I hope that this book justifies the initiative and actions of the person who listened to you, rapt in attention, for hours and hours.

Thanks to Barbara Wenner, my literary agent in Berlin, who accompanied me and shared in every discovery.

Thanks to Polity Press for taking interest in the story of a simple Berlin street, and to Anthony Giddens for his enthusiasm.

Thanks to C. Jon Delogu for his light and artful translation of the French text into English.

Thanks to Hermann Simon of the Centrum Judaicum who put me on the trail of the Jewish emigrants from my street and was with me in spirit during my travels; to the historian Gundrun Blankenburg, who knows better than anyone how to tell the story of the succession of constructions in my neighbourhood, building by building, between yesterday and today; to the archivist Axel Schröder, the guardian of the memory of my street, who held me firmly by the hand so as to keep me from getting lost in the dizzying labyrinth of the Landesarchiv-Berlin; and to Martin Luchterhandt, the archive director, who pointed me to the exit. Without him, I would still be ferreting about among all those enormous folders. Thanks also to Hannelore Emmerich and Veronika Liebau of the Tempelhof-Schöneberg Archives for never giving up despite my barrage of nit-picky questions. And thanks to Elga Abramovitz, Harald Bodenschatz, Werner and Birgit Simon, and Christian Wülfken for their expert re-reading of the manuscript.

Thanks, finally, to Ingeborg and Georg Ullrich for allowing me to often take refuge in their house in Oderbruch and write far away from my street.

1

Quiet Street in Nice Neighbourhood

I don't know why I came to live here. Why this street rather than another? Choosing a street is rather arbitrary when you first arrive in a city you don't know. The procedure for avoiding unpleasant surprises is always the same: unfold a large-scale map, pore over it to get one's bearings amid the dense network of streets, intersections, bridges, squares and rail lines, then get out a pencil to circle and label key items – *park, underground, rail and bus stations, nice neighbourhood*. Then list and rank the areas in descending order of preference – from *perfect* to *it will do*, from *if I must* to *no way*.

What was the deciding factor that suddenly led me to make my choice? The central location. The proximity of a market and an underground stop. The outdoor cafés in the neighbouring streets. The evening calm. The peaceful shade of the chestnut trees that lined the pavements. Wasn't I also feeling under pressure to get settled somewhere as soon as possible with no time to spend weeks searching for the ideal location? Maybe it was just a chance harmonic convergence: a flat became available just as I was looking for one. A promising classified ad in the paper announced '*Ruhige innerstädtische Strasse mit Altbausubstanz in guter Wohnlage'* – 'Quiet central street, renovated older building, nice neighbourhood'. What more could one ask for? I don't think I hesitated long. It was my lucky day.

Visiting the flat, I was charmed right away by the ceiling mouldings – garlands of leaves with chestnuts danced above my head. Then by the high sliding panel doors in the living room, the oval panes of old glass above other doors, the shiny wooden floor creaking under my feet, the big hundred-year-old cast-iron radiators hidden discreetly behind ornate covers, the delicate brass window handles, and the little terrace with its forged iron railing all bathed in sunlight. To go back down I took the old elevator, to which only residents of the building had a key – a droll, twisted little key. The compartment of dark wood jerked abruptly between the second and first floors but finally returned me to the garnet-coloured marble entrance hall on the ground floor.

The estate agent who managed the building – a sturdy woman with a cultured pearl necklace, over-spilling F-cup bosom, seventies-style French twist, and a fake-friendly smile – met me again at the front door to tell me of the *'ex-cep-tion-al'* fringe benefits that came with the place: a meticulous concierge, a team of women who cleaned the common areas *thoroughly* every week from top to bottom (she pronounced the word *thoroughly* with such vigour that I had no difficulty imagining this Amazon leading a horde of intrepid women in the battle against dust and dirt), and neighbours with standing – *mit Niveau* – a term she let slide over her lips like a caramel. There were also private concerts, bridge parties in the afternoon with German champagne and petits fours, as well as chic cocktail parties. And thank goodness there was no pub at street level turning schnapps-soaked drunkards onto the pavement in the middle of the night. There were, however, good schools for children within a quarter-mile radius, she said, while looking me up and down and judging the curve of my tummy but withholding the question that she was clearly dying to ask. Finally, the knockdown argument: the department store KaDeWe was only five minutes away, she exulted, and here was the bus stop directly out front!

KaDeWe – she spoke these three syllables with deference, her eyes sparkling just like the window displays of this mythical store at Christmas time. Fully conscious of holding my destiny in her hands, the estate agent quickly examined my file – the identity of my employer, pay slips, and other papers were flipped through in rapid succession. She had the habit of placing people on a particular rung within her little house hierarchy. I had no title – one demerit; I was French – did this raise my score a little or cause me to sink even lower? I never found out. We said goodbye at the doorstep. She slipped on her beige leather gloves and with a little honk and brisk acceleration she was off, behind the wheel of her convertible Mercedes that matched her gloves and her handbag, returning to the more distinguished neighbourhood where she herself lived.

Alone on the pavement, I inspected the street for a good long while. It was rather short. It begins at an underground stop built below a red brick, neo-gothic church with three spires, and goes straight until it crosses a small square of scruffy grass lined with a few wooden benches (perhaps what earned it the name 'park' according to the map) where the neighbourhood's drunkards and dog owners congregate. It then crosses another square bordered with plane trees until it runs up against a ham-coloured high-rise of 1970s-era council housing. This meaty block clashes with the grey and beige austerity of the other facades. Satellite TV dishes jut out from the balconies. On the ground floor is the kitchen of Call-a-Pizza. Tins of Marco Polo red peppers are stacked beside the door. Out back along the wall is a little pyramid of cigarette butts that pile up over time when the cook comes to take his break. Motor scooters and a Fiesta used to make deliveries are parked along a low wall next to the garbage bins. Cars cannot go any further. Only pedestrians can slip through *the mouse hole* – a narrow arch and windswept passageway – that links the street to a major road on the other side. So cars have to turn around. The street is part of an impossible labyrinth for taxi drivers who don't know the twisted layout of these blocks. No, it's not even a street – it's a cul-de-sac.

The displacement of the city centre after the Wall came down pushed the street to the margins of the new Berlin, far from the chic neighbourhoods, far from all that's shiny and hopping and humming. In my street one can sleep peacefully. Young people from around the world are not partying below late into the night. Tourists never set foot here. My street has conserved a rumpled look that I find moving. Unperturbed, it keeps its distance. It refuses to yield to all the new fashions, and I admire its tenacity. 'Ah, so you live in the former West Berlin!' cluck the disdainful bobos who live in the *Mitte* neighbourhood. Only in the last few years has there been a timid gentrification in my area, as rising rents, higher prices for those who wish to buy, and an overall shortage of housing stock, especially of older units, have caused it to be looked on more favourably again.

The post-war architects, those plastic surgeons of urban planning charged with restoring some kind of face to disfig-ured German cities, did not help matters. Blocks of four-storey structures with flat roofs stand alongside the few remaining Wilhelminian buildings with voluminous red-brick roofs that survived the bombings, though with extensive damage. They are the vestiges of an earlier bourgeois era. Never would the architects who worked like dogs at the beginning of the previous century to construct this classy street destined for a bright future have imagined for an instant that its history could turn out this way – a street in tatters, rundown, almost pitiful. A street made of patches and repairs. All these buildings squeezed tightly together seem to be holding each other up to keep from falling down. With no shared proportions and no unity of style or time-period, the street's zigzag roof line testifies to its troubled past. To measure the destruction caused by the hail of bombs that annihilated my street, one has to look at this aerial photo taken in 1928 from a Zeppelin flying over the blue sky of Berlin that day. One sees a clear straight line with stout buildings on either side and tall mature trees – a far cry from its present, halting outline. Several rows of buildings were completely demolished and never replaced. These holes are immediately recognizable, like missing teeth in the middle of a smile. A plaque covered in graffiti says that the so-called park is named after an obscure, Jewish suffragette teacher who died in New York in 1948 – *an eminent representative of the bourgeois feminist movement.* This is a remnant of the 1990s battle for equality of the sexes, but in the neighbourhood everyone calls it the *Pennerpark;* i.e., the hobo park.

Keep dogs on a leash! No barbecues! Keep entry clear! Put rubbish in the bins! No noise between 8 p.m. and 7 a.m.! No smoking or consumption of alcohol! Looking around, these signs at the beginning of the path for pedestrians and cyclists seem to have been posted with the sole purpose of offering everyone the joy of breaking the rules. The slides and swings of the small playground show signs of abandonment. The mothers in the area have clearly put out the word themselves: This area is 'Off limits!' The ones using the playground are too working class, or in other ways the wrong kind of people, and it stinks of urine! A syringe was supposedly found in the little house where kids can play make-believe, and they say a toddler in its oral phase nearly swallowed a cigarette butt. One cool autumn night, three individuals high on something are said to have tried to burn a bench to stay warm. Among the dead leaves that surround a second bench one can see beer caps and empty mini-bottles of *Kräuterfreunde, 40%*. The park has its regulars: a man with an apostle's beard who stirs the contents of the rubbish bins with a stick and places his booty in a shopping trolley; a woman dressed all in black who wanders about the shrubbery in winter. I followed her one day and discovered her secret rites. She suspends sacks of seeds in branches for the birds. She even constructed a little shelter for them out of a shoebox waterproofed with strips of tape. But the strangest encounter occurred some years ago under a birch tree near the playground. I was watching my children going down the small slide when an elderly woman approached me and suddenly recounted how she had been raped when the Russians arrived. It was a momentary loss of composure no doubt, a slip of the tongue, for then she pulled herself together and continued on her way leaving me alone and in shock. I never saw her again. But I wonder how many women in my street lived this nightmare and have never talked about it.

In the middle of the eighties the old buildings suddenly grew one storey higher. Hemmed in on its little island of land since the war, Berlin did not have the luxury of sprawling out and so it sprouted up. The beamy angled attics where renters until then had stored their unused furniture and piled up old magazines and newspapers were transformed into sunny penthouse lofts with fireplaces, marble bathrooms, tiled patios, lush flowering gardens, and large bay windows – in sum, all the signs and symbols of a higher social standing. Placed like a futurist lid over a porcelain tureen of old Meissen, the lofts obliterated the past of these buildings for good. They were foreign add-ons that ended up destroying the unity of the volumes underneath. More chic and much more expensive than the flats on the lower floors, these un-humble abodes that touched the sky became the living quarters of a new aristocracy. The loft clearly marked the beginning of the gentrification of my street.

I grew up in Strasbourg in a Renaissance house built in 1586, where every gable, decoration, oriel window, archway, and stone was original. It had passed through the centuries without a scratch. What a shock to find myself in Berlin on a street that bore so many scars! I have to admit, my Berlin street is rather ugly and very worn out. It has none of the perfectly prescribed regularity and unbroken flow one sees in the facades of Paris streets. Here there are craters and buildings with no style. That architectural harmony in Paris astonishes me every time. Of course, it was never bombed. It wasn't destroyed during the war. True, there were a few scandalous urban planning blunders, some fires, and some demolitions to make way for a wide avenue, the *périphérique*, or a shopping centre – but mostly the streets of Paris have not changed much. It's easy to guess at their former appearance, imagine their past life, and think of passers-by in period clothes filing naturally in and out of the tall Haussmannian flat blocks. The streets of Paris have gently traversed time and tide, and have arrived in our own era having suffered almost no damage. Nothing of the sort can be said about my street. It's a hotch-potch reassembled after fractures and brutal teardowns with one period built over another such that the later version effaces almost all traces of what existed before. On the pavement in front of number 11, pedestrians still trip over *the marble hole*, a depression of the surface caused by a heavy shell that fell there during the last fighting in April 1945. In the 1950s the kids in the neighbourhood would store their marbles in it. Not long ago, maybe only five years or so, one could still see bullet holes in certain facades. And before the elevator in my building was refurbished and freshly painted two years ago, you could still see shrapnel marks on its walls.

But these imperfections don't matter. My street is one of those places one ends up loving warts and all. My affection is the quiet kind that one extends to people and things that have no need to prove anything to us. It's a love nourished by habit and solidified by simple daily living without hue and cry. Day by day, my street and those around it have remained the constant witnesses of our lives – of births and deaths, love and rejection, holidays and birthdays, boredom and high drama, inscrutable emotions, fleeting nostalgia – and the days have turned into years that have gone by without our noticing their passing. Yes, in a way these streets have become a part of who we are. They were the setting of colourless days passing in single file, of life's bits of nothing, its blank hours, all the insignificant moments and microscopic events that in time are erased one by one from our memory. It would be so easy to mock these banal streets, although they are fully aware of their modest standing and never pretend to rise above their social station. Their open vulnerability is touching really, and compels a certain sympathetic loyalty.

My street has none of the pretensions of the prestigious grand avenues such as the Wilhelmstrasse and the Kurfürstendamm, which overflow with horrors and frivolity. Until 1945, the Wilhelmstrasse was the address of the Chancellery of the Third Reich. The Kurfürstendamm was the leading nightspot during the 1920s and later functioned as the West's ostentatious showroom during the Cold War. There are no world historical events attached to my street. I've found only one photo depicting an event that someone wanted to remember. It is dated 8 May 1911 and shows the guild of the master bakers of Schöneberg on parade. The canvas awnings lowered over some balconies give the facades a certain Mediterranean look. The street is brand new, as one can tell from the young trees that have just been planted along the pavements and stand protected by iron corsets. Curious locals have come down to get a closer look. They are watching this rare show on their street that is usually so calm. One can see girls in white ruffled dresses holding on to their mothers' arms, and boys in the sailor suits made popular by Wilhelm II, the *Flottenkaiser* who was so enamoured with the naval power of his country. The children follow behind the formation of bakers each in his frock coat and top hat and sporting the extravagant upturned moustache that they all copied from the Emperor. Each also has a light-coloured sash across his torso, and a fancy ribbon pinned over his heart, a sign of Berlin's mania for decorations and medals during the Empire. One fellow near the front is holding a flag, but it's impossible to make out the inscription on its cloth as the photo has faded with age. The men go by with chests straight but no smiles as they stare into the photographer's lens. In three years they would go off to war and many would never return. Was my street used regularly for these sorts of parades that the Empire so admired? It's unlikely. I imagine it was rather just a chance occurrence, the outcome of the parade organisers wanting to use it as a convenient shortcut to join up with the large neighbouring avenues.

Come to think of it, I hope my street is aware of its responsibility toward me, since, for a foreigner especially, one's place of residence is like a shortcut into the country, a miniature mirror of its customs and character traits. It offers the possibility of a manageable field study – a synecdoche that's small enough to be easily covered yet vast enough to offer representative parts that can stand for the whole. I have spent lots of time observing my street and thinking about my adopted country through its lens. It has taught me how the Germans relate to nature, order, authority, and to their difficult past. Living here, I have observed how their democracy functions, what being in a community means to them, and their vision of social justice. Also the way they resist or allow themselves to be carried along by the acceleration of time. Yes, all that is readable in my street. This microcosm helps me understand the entire country. I don't think it fully appreciates the weight that rests on its shoulders.

My street has no outstanding features, just the usual stuff: streetlamps, advertising columns, circuit boxes, manhole covers, the gaping entrances to cellars and underground parking lots, and the homeopathic medicine sign planted in the front garden of number 26. There are pergolas covered with ivy or other vines to hide the ugliness of a row of rubbish bins. The paving stones and granite slabs of the pavements are laid out in the customary pattern. Customary as well are the signs in modern hieroglyphic code listing all the undesirables: dogs, bikes, ball playing, and pedlars. And then there are the other improvised signs stapled to the plane trees, such as the one advertising 'Math tutoring', or this innocent plea to a chance benefactor: 'Young married couple, kind and discreet, hoping to find three-room flat in older building with sunny balcony – contact us!' Of course there are also pictures of lost dogs and cats and below them crude pronouncements – *Call now! Reward Guaranteed!* – that suggest a child's hope against hope. In the last few years a new ornament has begun to take over our street: brass-topped cobblestones placed in the pavement in front of blocks of flats from which Jews were deported. I have counted eight. Sometimes in the middle of the afternoon a penitent ceremony blocks the entryway into a building. Standing in a semi-circle or prostrate with eyes on the ground, today's Germans struggle with their past. Someone places a rose. Kind words are spoken about 'our Jewish fellow citizens' – *unsere jüdischen Mitmenschen.*

There is also the usual cast of characters: the majestic platoon of dustcarts that pull up at dawn with all their lights on, including the rotating roof light that sends long stripes of orange over the still sleeping street. Later on comes the postman, pushing his post cart in front of him like a carefree dandy walking an important dog. And there is the snow-plough man in winter and the sweepers all year round. My favourite is the tall African-looking one who appears on Mondays folded up like a wooden ruler inside the tiny compartment of his sweeper-vacuum machine. This Sisyphus is condemned to endlessly suck dog poo from the pavements with its long plastic trunk and make it disappear inside the vehicle. Passers-by scrunch up their faces in disgust while giving him a wide berth to pass on, but he always nods respectfully and gives way to them. There are package delivery vans, door-to-door salesmen, Jehovah's Witnesses and other pedlars of some higher law, groups of kids disguised as vampires on Halloween night, a procession of lantern-holders on the night of Saint Martin, Romanian accordion players with gold incisors serenading under street balconies on Sunday afternoons, graffiti artists spraying a furtive 'Fuck you!' or *'Nazis raus!'* on some facade in the middle of the night, rousing the loud indignant swearing of the building's owners the next morning, travellers dragging suitcases with rumbling rolling wheels loud enough to wake the dead, and the thin voice of the Pakistani distributing flyers who yells 'Advertising' into the intercom to get you to open the door. A few businesses are gathered together at the end of the street near the entrance to the underground, from which one can occasionally hear some sad violin music rise up. Among the stores there's a copy shop, a speciality shop for snowboarders, a hardware shop, a café-bar where Berliner retirees meet up in small groups for ham and beer at around five on a Sunday afternoon, a co-op day-care centre – and that's it. At the other end of the street there's a restaurant that has changed hands many times and gone from Greek to Australian-Asian, to Italian. The mainstays of daily city life – post office, newspaper kiosk, bakery, supermarket – are all missing. It's a purely residential street.

My street has its gossip and odd characters. A burlesque dancer who was a recluse lived on the top floor at number 3 for years. Found dead dressed in black tights, this person had left marks from many *pas de bourrée* all over the wood parquet. There was a suicide victim discovered with open veins in a bathtub, and a cabinet-maker at number 15 who in the late seventies took his wife down into his basement workshop and sawed her head off. There was even an article about it at the time in the *Berliner Morgenpost*. There's also the story about some roommates who, having neglected to take their rubbish down to the back court-yard for several weeks, finally did so and discovered that their potatoes had grown sprouts several metres in length.

When it comes down to it, I know fairly little about my neighbours. Who is that couple that often walks up the street holding hands? He's dark, tall and stiff; she's short with dyed blond hair. They hold onto each other like Hansel and Gretel walking through a dark forest. And who is that stocky man who always wears his green felt hat with a little feather and never goes out without his German Shepherd? And what about the elderly lady who sets off in small nervous steps each morning to make the interminable expedition to the supermarket? And the short man in his tweed jacket who tips his cap at me when we meet? (An old-fashioned gesture that makes me melt each time.) Who's the couple with the three children at number 5 ... newcomers? I haven't seen the handsome man at number 25 for weeks now – why? Has he gone on holiday in his sports car? I would also like to know who the self-appointed policeman is who two times now has stuck a little note on my windshield to say 'You suck at parking!' I imagine him leaving his place at night with a stack of such notes in his pocket. I can see him in the dark handing out his special citations to every vehicle not perfectly parked and thus, with this modest gesture, relieving the frustrations of his day. How I'd like to meet him in broad daylight and give him a piece of my mind – 'Rigid bastard! Parking Nazi!' But I do hope he's given out one of his 'You suck at parking!' cards to the BMW with Munich licence plates that once a month is parked for several hours right on the pavement in front of number 26.

My street bears the dull habits of a middle-class community of people thrown together and forced to get along. Neighbours who live on the same floor might let out at most a brusque *Morgen!* between clenched teeth, give a slight nod when sharing the elevator compartment, or perhaps initiate a curt exchange, most likely a lamentation about the weather (bad) or the times (tough). Between one floor and another, one might borrow an egg, sign for a parcel, water the plants or feed the mice or cats during the holidays, but also go up and complain about excessive noise. That's all.

It's an ordinary street. A street like hundreds throughout Germany that were built in the early years of the twentieth century and then mostly destroyed during the war. In a way it is completely interchangeable with its earlier incarnations, and in fact it has kept the same name since it was built. Even in 1945, no one saw a need for any palimpsest. It never gave passing honour to any great man of the past. It never bowed to any discredited despot after a change in regime. My street's name is so insignificant that it's not even worth mentioning. Its fate is an exemplum that could serve to illustrate many others. It's easy to go by it without even really paying attention. Easy to pass its facades without even raising one's head – hurrying on, absorbed in one's own thoughts. At first glance, it looks like a street with no history, for who could imagine the stories woven behind those smooth stone surfaces? Who could guess the underground tremors that would shake the apparent stillness of it all?

2

Built to Last

My street was born in 1904. The same year as Salvador Dali and Pablo Neruda, Count Basie and Glenn Miller, Jean Gabin, Cary Grant and Johnny Weissmuller, alias Tarzan. 1904 – so distant and so dense with history. In France, Alfred Dreyfus won the right, on appeal, to have his case re-examined, and Prime Minister Émile Combes closed private schools affiliated with religious congregations. The city of Baltimore was destroyed by fire, and a collision at the La Chapelle station in Paris between express trains arriving from Boulogne and Lille killed fourteen people. The first underground line in New York began service and for the first and last time the potato sack race was one of the competitive sports at the summer Olympic Games in St Louis, Missouri. The FIFA football organization was created in Paris and *Madame Butterfly* opened at La Scala in Milan. Grape-picking began early in the north of France and Pope Pius X forbade the wearing of low-cut evening gowns. Among the Nobel Prize winners that year there was Ivan Petrovich Pavlov, for his research into the physiology of digestion, and Frédéric Mistral, for his novels set in Provence. There were also inventions including Monopoly, the bracelet-watch, the kenotron (an ancestor of the semiconductor diode), the telemobiloscope (an early type of radar), the disposable razor and the ice cream cone.

When one sorts through this pile of events and ranks them from most to least important, from the nuttiest to the most tragic, one notices that this year already contained the seeds of the First World War. In 1904, faced with the increasingly aggressive Weltpolitik of the young German empire, Great Britain and her 'hereditary enemy' France signed the Entente Cordiale. The very Francophile Edward VII, 'King of the United Kingdom of Great Britain and Ireland and of the British Dominions, Emperor of India', and the French president of the Third Republic Émile Loubet agreed on the boundaries of their respective spheres of influence in North Africa and Asia, thereby slowing the industrial progress and naval ambitions of Wilhelm II. This was the beginning of the isolation of Germany. In 1904, in the German colony of South-West Africa, the revolt of the indigenous Herero and Nama peoples was violently crushed by General Lothar von Trotha in the Battle of Waterberg. This was the first genocide of the twentieth century. Also in 1904, Kaiser Wilhelm II recorded a brief speech about the virtues of discretion and modesty on one of the phonographic cylinders invented by Thomas Edison. It is the first ever political recording. *Put up with pain, do not seek what is unattainable or without value, be satisfied with each day as it comes, look for the good in each thing as it presents itself, and take pleasure in nature and in man as they are ...* A crackly voice can be heard in this recording as though someone is speaking over the noise of raindrops falling on a tin roof during a storm. On that day the last German Emperor sounds more like a Tibetan monk offering soothing wisdom and less like the warrior in his eagle helmet who ten years later would lead his country and the entire world into a devastating war. Amidst all the brouhaha of these grand historical events, barely audible, one can hear the first shovelfuls of dirt being moved about to begin building my street.

On certain nights out on the balcony, carried on the evening breeze, one can detect the scent of hay and pines coming from the vast plains of Brandenburg. It reminds me that my street was built on farm land. In 1870 Prussia defeats France at the Battle of Sedan. Bismarck is able to unify Germany. A powerful empire in the heart of Europe is proclaimed on 18 January 1871 in the Hall of Mirrors at the Palace of Versailles. Berlin becomes an imperial capital and the new German nation industrializes. A remarkable economic boom and the wish to have a capital corresponding to the political ambition of possessing a 'place in the sun' led to the rapid transformation of the modest Prussian capital into a monumental imperial city. The German power elite have only one word on their lips: *Representation*. During this period of peace and prosperity, opportunities and optimism, Berlin makes pathetic efforts to compete with Paris, Vienna and London – each a splendid metropolis sure of its high rank and attractive features. Berlin even overreaches a bit. *Metropolinchen*, 'Metropolette', is the mocking diminutive earned by this bragging pursuit of superlatives: the largest luxury hotels, the largest of the large department stores of Europe, a disproportionately large cathedral, a Siegesallee or 'Victory Avenue', lined with the marble statues of kings, margraves and prince-electors of Prussia, which Berliners deride as the Puppenallee or 'Avenue of Dolls'. In similar fashion, Berlin women wear the largest and most extravagant hats and Berlin men sport the longest moustaches. Moreover, at this time Berlin has become one of the largest industrial cities of Europe, famous for its *Mietskasernen* ('rental barracks') – rabbit-hutch-style living quarters with unsanitary back courtyards that stretched out forever – and small, overcrowded flats rife with tuberculosis, alcoholism and incest. The population explodes. Civil servants, soldiers and officers of the imperial army, employees of new companies, salesmen, builders, new industrial workers – suddenly the new gigantic city has to house all these folks.

Building new living quarters has to happen as fast as possible. Speculation in the real estate market is red hot. The property developers of the day (*Terraingesellschaften*) pop up like mushrooms in a forest in autumn. There is the chance to make a lot of money, and also the risk of losing everything. In the stock market crash of 1873, many Terraingesellschaften went bankrupt. Others, such as the Berlinische Boden-Gesellschaft run by the Jewish businessman Salomon Haberland and his son Georg, prospered. The Haberlands made a fortune in textiles and then switched to buying and developing building sites.

Their activities were a godsend to the little village of Schöneberg, located on meagre soil but strategically well-positioned at number 1 Reichsstrasse, the main avenue that led from the castle at the centre of Berlin to Potsdam, the symbol of imperial glory. The Berlinische Boden-Gesellschaft undertakes to build a whole new neighbourhood, the *Bayerisches Viertel*, or Bavarian District, intended for *higher-income households*. It is to be a purely residential neighbourhood, erected at some distance from the noise and bustle of central Berlin and yet not in a distant suburb far from everything. In 1904 my street is still on the edge of Berlin, but little by little as the capital grows out and beyond it, it comes to be considered more a part of the centre, in the heart of Berlin-West.

Farmers and gardeners in Schöneberg, among them Georg and Gustav Mette, Max Willmann, Louise Bergemann, Werner Munk and Wenzel Marie, sold Georg Haberland the acres that eventually turned into my street. The Berlinische Boden-Gesellschaft turned these parcels of land into ready-to-build lots and resold them to *solvent individuals* or to *housing developers*. Georg Haberland refused to be compared to the land speculators who gained a bad reputation at the turn of the century. He had stern words for *the miserly individuals who are not interested in carrying out a building project and only want to live off the building loans they've obtained.*

The buyers who acquired these housing lots agreed to build blocks of flats. It was considered a safer and more profitable investment than a stock portfolio, and the runaway inflation of the 1920s would prove them right. The Berlinische Boden-Gesellschaft is a major player when it comes to deciding on the general urban plan and the installation of the basic infrastructure: streets with *front gardens and shade trees*, sewers and gutters, lighting thanks to electric streetlamps – *a wonderful bonus for residents since the neighbouring streets were only lit with gas*, notes Georg Haberland in a celebratory booklet published on the fortieth anniversary of his company. The road network is composed of residential streets and wider access roads. Commercial activities are prohibited in the residential streets except at intersections where they cross other streets. The train line between Berlin and Potsdam traverses Schöneberg. The new neighbourhood is linked to the rest of the city by trams and omnibuses, and in 1913 it obtains its own underground line. Polluting factories are also banned, and in marked contrast Georg Haberland designs a purely 'Decorative Square' with massive geometric forms, a lawn, a ring of trees, narrow gravel pathways and a fountain.

The whole was strikingly different from the narrow streets and suffocating atmosphere of the old pre-existing neighbourhoods.

In only a few years, the village of Schöneberg, which had been the bucolic destination for Berliners on Sunday excursions, was transformed into custom-made residences for Berlin's wealthier bourgeoisie. In 1898 Schöneberg became its own town and shortly thereafter would erect a magnificent town hall thanks to the support of wealthy donors.

I often dream of a genie coming out of an oil lamp to grant me a wish. I would not hesitate for a second about what to wish for: a day, an entire day to walk about in Berlin as it existed before the war and in my street as it was then. When I discovered my street in some of the large volumes stored at the *Landesarchiv Berlin*, I thought for an instant that my wish had come true. This austere building, which hardly looks like it could contain magic at first glance, is a converted munitions factory in Reinickendorf, just after a tunnel at the end of a highway exit. From a raised platform in the reading room, a watchman keeps his silent vigil. Here time slows down, history advances in small steps at the pace of the librarians pushing carts among rows of shelves. Over time layers of dust have settled under the high windows. One hears the regular sound of turning pages, the rustle of papers, the wheels of microfiche reading machines off in a side room. Occasionally the sudden whoosh of air created by a large weighty volume being slammed shut. Sometimes too a conversation in low tones, a clearing of the throat, a persistent cough, a stifled laugh or a sigh ... *O, how sad* ...

Outside the buzz of the city; inside an orderly hive as calm as a monastery. Leaning over our files with arched backs, fifteen or so of us take a singular pleasure in the stubborn pursuit of our research and pay no mind as the hours go by and nightfall arrives little by little outside. We've plunged into the thick forest of the arid reports that the multiple administrative services of our city have always produced. We pass through a wrinkle in time and change eras. Time stops in the reading room even though it marches on outside.

On the cover page to some of the files pertaining to construction in my street I sometimes see the name of the last person to consult it. I get the feeling he or she maybe wandered in there by mistake and quickly backtracked. Most of the time I'm the first to consult each volume. It's true, who besides me would take an interest in these mundane facts classified with meticulous care in chronological order and bound together with little cotton strings? Who else would care about page after page of the book-keeping and blueprints related to staircases, circular stairwells, mansard-level flats, attics, wardrobes, workshops, garages and storage rooms?

Who wants to wade through the convoluted wording of a construction permit issued by the municipal department of public works stating that *after examination of a copy of the construction plans and the site, there is no reason to object to the construction project as presented so long as it complies with the general policies set out in our correspondence dated 12 February 1900, g. 831 and 14 October 1903, VIII.b.2627?*

Or this 'certificate of major work completed' sent in 1905 by the expert-inspector Klaus Schneider to the general contractor of Barth number 6: *The building site has been completely inspected and the following observations can be made: walls dry, lower floor inhabitable, ventilation of sanitary installations correct, fireplaces and chimneys installed, sealant applied to wooden partition walls and ceilings, stairwells and banisters in place, metal grills covering cellar windows*?

Or this notification to renters: Mr Duds at number 23 *is informed that due to the irregular availability of hot water, the following sums will be reimbursed to renters or deducted from their next month's rent*?

Or this complaint from an irate renter: *About three weeks ago I alerted my landlord, Mr Robert Baer, at number 11, as well as the doorman Mohaupt, to the fact that the plaster framing around certain of my windows risked falling at any moment. Mr Baer has still made no reply. The porter immediately accompanied me to my residence and was able to confirm the truth of my claim, but without taking any action for now. Today, at half past seven this morning, a horizontal portion of plaster fell into the garden, and it was only by a stroke of good fortune that the occupants of the ground floor flat were not on their balcony at that instant*?

Or these requests by flustered independent business owners? I melt reading these polite, innocent pleas: on 14 February 1927, at number 19, Frieda Heiter, a seller of soaps and perfumes, writes in her elongated handwriting to the royal director of public works to ask permission to affix an advertising sign *identical to the enclosed drawing* to the building's facade. *My soap shop is already heavily penalized by its poorly visible location; it hardly earns me enough to pay my monthly rent; this is why I'm forced to resort to advertising and plead with you to consider favourably my request.* Her neighbour, Anton Singer – a dealer in tyres, vulcanization, automobile oils, greases and other accessories – wishes to place a large sign that reads Continental Tyres above the entrance to his shop. And in 1936, Herr Scheffell, the gourmet baker at number 19, objects to having been refused the right to attach to the garden fence in front of his shop a cloth sign reading *Drink*

Milk! – while noting that butchers and ice-cream sellers have been granted permission to do so. He contests *the acceptability of this decision that has reduced his sales of dairy products. Heil Hitler!*

And what ought one to say about these announcements of new norms following repeated sanitation inspections of the Kaiser-Barbarossa Pharmacy? Absolutely delicious descriptions! *Smallpox registers* are to be kept. *Vials of veratrine* are to be thrown out. Bottles of *Folia digitalis* are to be resealed. Volatile substances, dyes and empty bottles are to be removed from the stockroom. A morphine scale whose delivery was delayed finally arrives. The syrup of *Althaea officinalis* is to be kept away from humidity; and the *Ol. foeniculi, Ol. eucalypti* and *Ol. juniperi* are to be kept out of direct sunlight.

And then, overturning these occult lists and the arid language of bureaucrats, I suddenly fall on these exceedingly polite formulations: *We have the distinct honour to turn our attention to your missive of 10 August. We beseech you again with utmost respect ... Mister General Engineer of the Imperial Court ... I would be infinitely grateful ...* The pompous *Hochachtungsvoll* is replaced in the 1930s by *Heil Hitler!* with its sharp exclamation point, or by the nationalist fanfare of *Mit deutschen Grüssen*, 'German salutations'. Later, in the post-war Federal Republic era, one comes across *Mit freundlichen Grüssen*, 'With friendly salutations', which, in trying for an abolition of distance, seems to be confusing respect and friendship.

This exercise is a bit like walking alone over new-fallen snow – step by step, one page at a time. I cautiously grasp each loose page. One syllable at a time I try to decode these compositions in archaic German. But most often I'm not even capable of making out the letters of these texts that resemble the flat-lining of an electrocardiogram when the heart has stopped beating. What a relief when I come across the clear shapes of typed characters made by the blue ink of an official stamp. Sometimes there's a scribble in the margin – a note, a passing thought, a reverie perhaps. The thicket of twisted stick marks remains a mystery to me. I take care not to damage the pages as I turn them. The memory of these streets is so fragile. God knows what a miracle it is that these documents survived bombardments, fires and the general chaos of 1945, as well as the succession of wilful erasures, moves, humidity, rats, the tidiness instinct of some new chief of urban planning, the zeal of a librarian eager to make room on the shelves for the new histories being written, and the simple passage of time. The pages have a slightly sweet, almost milky odour. Sometimes there's a whiff of vinegar or mildew, but also the scent of old leather, and even tobacco. Stains from dampness leave strange shapes on certain warped leaves. The edges of overly dry paper crumble and fall on the carpet. I spend hours exploring, my hands dusty, my eyes peeled, my heart beating excitedly. I am becoming acquainted with my neighbours from earlier decades, from long before I was born, from long before I moved to my street. I am discovering a world that would have disappeared had it not been for the arduous dedication of an archivist who must have spent hours sorting and arranging this massive quantity of documents as best as possible. In fact, I regularly have the impression of being in over my head, that a gigantic surf is pulling me under.

What a childlike joy, therefore, when I discover a familiar name: H. Eller, the neighbourhood chimneysweep. And look here, at number 19, the *Hauptmann* (Captain) C. Tippenhauer, *a former army officer, and as such constrained by the turn of these last years to create for himself a new source of revenue*, who throughout

the year 1921 fought to get permission to install a small chocolate factory in the basement of his building. The Hauptmann
regularly bursts forth out of these files like an impish jack-in-
the-box springing out of his container.

As I gradually put all these futile-seeming pieces of information together, and clear a passageway through the fog of ordinary incidents and the murmurings of pavement conversations,
the past life of my street softly appears, though without my
being able to influence in the least the rhythm of this reconstitution. I observe the whole thing with humility as the past
reattaches itself to the present.

In 1904, many developers had bought building sites from the
Berlinische Boden-Gesellschaft and were getting ready to start
erecting their brand new block of flats. They submit their blueprints to the royal director of public works for Schöneberg,
pleading for the director *to have the high good graces to approve
them.*

A note recording that *the wished for buildable surface area is indicated here by red hash marks* is written in black ink on onion skin
tracing paper. The honorary royal geometer, W. v. Frankenberg,
authorized expert for Berlin, has added his round blue stamp.
On the side of the plans W. v. Frankenberg has written in by
hand the surface area determined by his calculations. The first
letter of the words *blueprints* and *location* is ornamented with
interlacing ivy as though it were the incipit of a fairy tale. And
it's true, the story of my street begins like a fairy tale. Once
upon a time there were a handful of businessmen as vain as
peacocks who wanted to leave their mark in this lowly material
world and at the same time invest their newly earned piles of
money in piles of stones. Over a roughly two-year period, they

constructed blocks of flats with cellars, a ground floor, four additional floors composed of two flats each, attics and high-angled roofs that guaranteed a comfortable temperature on the highest floor. The flats each have seven or eight rooms, but sometimes as many as ten in a dizzying succession: living room or salon, reception room, dining room, boudoir, balcony, smoking room, bay window, bedroom, bathroom, children's bedroom (1.50 x 3.92 metres), larder. The buildings are each custom designed to accommodate in the same flat the masters and their living quarters in front, then the bedrooms, the kitchen and the servants' quarters in the rear. There are no smaller quarters facing onto the back courtyard for lower-income renters.

The architecture of the flats respects this horizontal hierarchy: luxury in front, simplicity out back. As one advances toward the rear, the rooms become progressively smaller, the ceilings lower, and the light dimmer. High double windows can be found in the front rooms, small simple windows in the back rooms. Ceiling mouldings decorate the front rooms, basic white plaster appears in the back. Waxed oak flooring is laid out in the front, white pine boards nailed and oiled are out back. The cook and the nanny live cramped together next to the kitchen at the back of the flat, in a small narrow room that looks more like a walk-in wardrobe. A small service stairwell is reserved for their use. It descends to the back courtyard, a dark and damp spot where the rubbish bins are stored and there is a bar for beating rugs at the proper hour. The *Berliner Zimmer*, or 'Berlin room', constitutes a solid barrier between these two distinct areas and marks the border between the public space and the private. My street's bourgeoisie became poorer during the years of high inflation. The maids were let go. No one knew what to do with all these rooms any more. When the global economic crisis of the 1930s hit, the owners finally asked the housing authorities for permission to split these enormous flats in two, since no one could afford to rent the entire space anyway.

The buildings have an incomparably high level of comforts, including the most modern conveniences: bathrooms, flush toilets, venetian blinds, painted metal lambrequins, double-glazed windows to protect against cold, but also against excessive heat, noise and dust, electric lighting, lifts, central heating and central vacuuming. The little front gardens along the facade – *which must be bordered by tasteful iron fencing mounted on a low wall at most fifty centimetres high, and as ornamental gardens must be carefully planned and maintained* – allow the building's residents to be just that little bit further from the street, thus sending the clear signal that we do not mix with the common people passing by on the pavement and we certainly do not tolerate any coal delivery men in the back courtyard. A *Portier*, as the building's doorman was known at the time, bestowed a final chic touch on these blocks of flats. His title, borrowed from the French, conferred an air of distinction on this modest post. From his ground floor room equipped with kitchen nook, alcove and running water, the porter watched over all comings and goings. After all, one couldn't let people walk into these buildings like one walks into a bar.

After spending hours in their company, I developed quite a fondness for the real estate investors who built my street. The merchant Robert Bär at number 17; the industrialist Richard Barth at number 6; the Huguenot Max Emile George Moniac at number 26, president of the company Grün&Moniac, founded in 1881 and specializing in the design, construction and installation of water and gasworks for central heating systems; Carl Hausmann at number 2, president of a supply company for fireproof cement, stone or cement archways, and floor and wall tiling; the architects Robert Zetschke at number 22, Paul Jatzow at numbers 17 and 26, Walter Zander at number 6, and Carl Graf who bought the last plot nearest the square. These gentlemen were parvenus who had become wealthy almost overnight thanks to the unprecedented boom of the *Gründerjahre*, the first years of the Empire's founding. Did my investors profit from the war reparations paid by France to the new Empire? There's no doubt that manna served to erect the new capital. My street is perhaps a French street to a certain extent, and even indirectly financed by my ancestors. This hypothesis lends a certain legitimacy to my presence here.

The property investors competed amongst each other. Georg Haberland writes that *it was difficult for the owner of a plot to have his say over the facades or the layout of each building. The majority of the investors were themselves architects and naturally tried to orient the progress on the buildings according to their aesthetic tastes.* The street was a runway for presenting their facades. On the saffron-coloured plans of rough canvas, I discover the gables, the turrets, the cornices and the festoons of sculpted leaves under the windows. So many ornaments hardly any of which survive today. The facades all resemble each other and yet none is the exact replica of any other. Each developer added his personal touch, a slight variation here and there: an oval oeil-de-boeuf, a frieze, a rosette, a floral motif, a column, a baroque piece, a mythological figure protecting itself from the rain under a balcony, two putti with rounded bottoms stretched out over the arch of an entryway.

But it was especially in the front hallways, called in a Germanified French *Entré*, in the masculine with no second 'e', or *Vestibül*, that each building manager let his imagination run wild. Walls tiled in dark-coloured marble were decorated with mirrors, plant motifs and antique heads. The most sumptuous *Entré* is certainly the one at number 3 – entirely covered in white marble with mirrors, a caisson ceiling, a little fireplace and sculpted women's heads on the walls. A marble bench offers the elderly a chance to catch their breath before they take on ascending to the floors above. And then there are the swallows nesting under the gutters, the ivy climbing up the waterspouts, and the new renters arriving with their complicated titles, *Doktor* and *Professor*, their military ranks, and their stock portfolios and influential acquaintances. The Berlin directory for 1907 confirms the high degree of social homogeneity along my street. Among the most frequently listed professions, businessmen, whose money it is safe to say is fairly new, far outnumber the various rentiers, pensioners, civil servants, proxyholders, lawyers, as well as the veritable regiment of military officers. There are a handful of doctors and pharmacists, several directors, architects, and accountants, and many widows (I counted eight and the two wars hardly lowered their number in my street) and old maids of indeterminate age. At the time, each building tolerated certain tradespeople on the premises: a woman who did ironing, two soap sellers, a hardware seller, a master cobbler, a master blacksmith, a dairyman, a midwife, a dressmaker, a restaurant maître d', a tramway attendant, and a certain A. Königsmann, a podiatrist and remover of corns. My street was also home to some minor artists whose names, as far as I know, have been lost to posterity. A sign of a certain amount of wealth is the large number of those who possess a telephone, indicated with a boldface capital T next to their name in the directory. In 1907, there was still a faithful correspondence between the stone facades and the residents, between the habitations and their inhabitants – the former mirroring the success of the latter.

The movers carry up heavy dressers, colossal armoires, pianos, rolled up carpets, drapes, chandeliers, standing lamps, leather easy chairs, smoker's tables, vanities with their stools, beds with horsehair mattresses, oil paintings – often copies of old masters. Curtains of white tulle protect the privacy of those inside from the discreet glances of those down in the street. On their imposing bookshelves the new occupants place many volumes of canonical German literature, alongside all twenty-four volumes of the great Meyer encyclopaedic dictionary.

The real estate developers built this street for eternity. They believed in progress and technological innovation. They did not imagine for an instant that their good fortune would soon abandon them. My street seemed immune to the ravages of time, the destructive passions that would engulf Europe twice, the unforeseen sides of the human condition. As though the bricks, rafters and roof tiles had the power to protect everyone and everything inside from misfortune! And yet the property boom came to a halt suddenly in 1914, when the tradesmen were called to war. Many of the master craftsmen who had worked on building sites in the street in 1904 would not return from the battlefields of the Somme and Verdun. Little by little, over the years of financial crisis, inflation and unemployment between the two wars, the buildings of the imperial era deteriorated. Facades showed chips and cracks, mouldings went unrepaired. Between the wars, Bauhaus enthusiasts were already mocking them as hopelessly outdated and encumbered. Too much finery! Too much of everything! Between 1943 and 1945, Allied bombardments exploded any remaining illusions into millions of pieces. It took two years to build my street and two years to destroy it. But in 1904 no one saw their future as black.

3

Lilli Ernsthaft: Our Doyenne

Of all the residents on our street, Lilli Ernsthaft was unusual in more ways than one. Her husband – a wealthy Austrian, the head of a beer import/export business, Ernsthaft & Co., a former Viennese opera singer, the owner of a Benz and the employer of a driver as well as two maids and a piano tuner – was the street's first renter. In 1905, Heinrich Ernsthaft moved into the second floor flat at number 3. A vast space divided into seven rooms, it was far too big for him. The walls still smelled of fresh paint. The street was unfinished; in fact it was still one big construction site.

Some years later, on a rainy Friday the thirteenth in September 1922, Lilli Doller married Heinrich Ernsthaft at eight in the morning at the Schöneberg town hall. After the ceremony, the newlyweds returned by taxi to Heinrich's flat. As she stepped out of the car, Lilli realized that she had left her umbrella behind. But she didn't get upset. *We were hardly superstitious people, as our choice of wedding date shows, so we just went back to the office to retrieve the umbrella.*

It was a simple love story. They had first met at the home of some friends and then later each morning at the tramway stop of the 62 line. Lilli was a stenographer-typist. Heinrich a businessman. On the way to work, Heinrich's *singing won him a place in Lilli's heart.* He asked her to marry him. A meal for a few friends was laid out in the groom's dining room with its new velvet-covered walls. That evening the young and frightened Lilli lay down for the first time in the large marriage bed. On 7 August 2001, in that same bed, one month before September 11, an ambulance came to collect her little shrivelled body. She had lived seventy-nine years at the same address. For many years, until her death at the distinguished age of ninety-nine and nine months, she was the doyenne of our little community. Three months later and she would have been our centenarian.

Lilli Ernsthaft broke all records. She was never particularly proud, nor even really aware of the privileged place she occupied in the honorary hierarchy of our street. Confined to her bed in her dimly lit Berlin room during the last months of her life, this very old woman with her snow-white hair and deeply creased face was the last survivor from a world that had disappeared forever. Yes, it can be said, even if it might seem a bit maudlin: she had been the living memory of our street.

To the many regular visitors who called on her, Lilli Ernsthaft liked to prattle on about the golden age of our modest street, even though, as she never tired of pointing out herself, it couldn't hold a candle to the truly opulent avenues of the great European cities. Her favourite was Unter den Linden, *at least as it was at the time the Emperor and Crown Prince still lived there,* followed closely by the Champs-Élysées – *each of these showcase avenues being of course designed to affirm the prestige of their respective countries, notably on the occasion of the many parades that filed down them.* The bakers' parade in my street, it's true, was but a ridiculous simulation of those grand events.

Lilli Ernsthaft would talk about life at the beginning of the last century. Such as the little Chinaman who continuously bowed stiffly in the window of the Chinese shop located just behind the big new department store Wertheim's in Leipziger Strasse. Larger than Harrod's! Larger than the Galeries Lafayette! The new capital often sought to outdazzle older European metropolises, and did. Lilli liked to speak of the showroom of the Persian carpet wholesalers and of the paintings and bronzes of her father, an Austrian Jew born in Lemberg, present-day Lviv in Ukraine. Or about the first electric tramway, built the year she was born, or the above-ground line that crossed Nollendorfplatz and that became an underground line when she was six or seven. Just before the Winterfeldplatz it disappeared into a tunnel. *A real show!* She talked about her portrait in a sailor suit that a certain Hoffmann displayed in the window of his photography shop. *'Later, he became Hitler's official photographer!'* I never knew if that recollection horrified her or was intended as more self-flattery. She could always recite by heart – eighty years later – the verses that Herr Brockmüller v. Bremen, her suitor at the thermal spa in Bad Oeynhausen, composed and placed in a little cup that he gave to her as a present:

From this cup, my beautiful child,
Try each morning just to savour
A mocha as hot as love is wild
So your happiness will never waiver
Especially if you think of the friend
Who at the spa learned you had no flaws
And who each day brings a cup
To his lips that desire yours

Herr Brockmüller was not the only unrequited lover. According to those I spoke to who remembered her when she was still young, Lilly Ernsthaft had classic features and was the most beautiful woman on our street.

There were many of them in my street before the war, these princesses from good families who were so ill-equipped to cope with the hard times that fate put their way. They often had fragile constitutions, wore shoes with champagne-coloured laces, poplin dresses with little tulle collars, and wide-brimmed straw hats, and would bow with knees bent to pay respects to the friends of their mothers. Their lives were a gay ribbon of walks in the park at thermal spas, piano lessons and tennis, tea dances with an orchestra between five and seven, and evenings of light opera such as *Walzertraum* and *Wiener Blut*.

It was Frau Klemm, the last chemist before the Kaiser-Barbarossa pharmacy at number 26 closed its doors, who first spoke to me about her old friend Frau Ernsthaft. Once a week, Frau Klemm would cross the street to play Gin Rummy with Frau Ernsthaft at number 3. Frau Klemm would bring cakes. Frau Ernsthaft provided coffee and a small glass of liqueur for ladies.

For some time, my flat building had been in an uproar. The psychoanalyst on the first floor was trying to win the support of the renters to have a commemorative plaque in a wooden frame mounted in the entryway that would bear the names of the thirteen Jews deported from the building. Over the course of several months, there was a little war of memories going on between one floor and another. The psychoanalyst warned: *When one forgets even the names, nothing is left!* The renter on the third floor stopped speaking to her neighbours: *It sickens me to live in a building where it was possible to send thirteen Jews to their death because of the indifference of the other residents! I am ashamed of those among us who are refusing to participate in this initiative and who thereby are directly carrying on the legacy of the Nazi collaborators!* The concierge was outspoken in expressing his concern: *A plaque will endanger the entire building. Imagine the neo-Nazi graffiti when they discover what's going on here!* The grumpy man on the fourth floor had slammed his door: *I'm not giving a penny!* Some accused others of repressing the past: *So we draw the curtains and go on like before!* Others reproached some for their moralizing tone and the accusatory finger they would raise toward heaven like a righteous spear from morning to night. I had just arrived in Berlin at the time, and this quarrel illustrated to me the insolvable problem that the Germans have with Germany. On the day of the ceremony to unveil the plaque, Frau Klemm nudged Frau Ernsthaft to the front while local municipal representatives were effusive with their repetitions of *Never forget* and *Never again*. My landlord apologized for not being able to be present that day and sent his respects. The psychoanalyst laid down a wreath saying, *We hope that these discreet watchwords will incite those who glance at them as they go by to undertake the work of salutary mourning.* Then, like after a funeral, everyone filed down to the Greek restaurant at the corner for a drink.

No one in the street would have guessed that the little old lady at number 3 who was always so impeccably dressed was herself Jewish. *She never let it come forward*, observed a neighbour who nevertheless was aware that *Frau Ernsthaft kept a Jewish candleholder in her living room*. Or did everyone know or had always known it after the war? Maybe they preferred to avoid such an embarrassing subject. Lilli Ernsthaft was the last surviving member of the German-Jewish bourgeoisie in my street. A miraculous survivor. We might have given out another medal to her, just as we honour those who manage to swim across the English Channel or who plant their flag at the top of Mount Everest. So, with a bouquet of roses and a baby in my arms, I went to knock on the old woman's door. She welcomed us, my son and I, with little cries of ecstasy. *Oh, ein Baby! Ein Baby bei Ernsthaft!* ('A baby in the Ernsthaft home').

Lilli Ernsthaft's flat seemed not to have changed one bit since the 1920s. *A real antique shop*, Frau Klemm had warned me. The art nouveau stained-glass at the balcony, the built-in pearl-coloured shelving in the den, the Chippendale chairs, and the wobbly round side-table were all steeped with an odour of old age. The armoires still contained the remnants of a wardrobe from a past life – cocktail dresses, summer dresses, mid-season dresses. Entire communities of gloves were boarding in the front hall cupboard. For each handbag there was a matching pair. When she had me over for *Kaffee*, I went back in time sitting beside her. Lilli Ernsthaft chattered away while offering me dry cakes and strawberry biscuits – her stories embroidered with polite old-fashioned formulas as though she were decorating the trim of a lace tablecloth. *One or two delicacies, dear neighbour? Tout le plaisir est pour moi, Madame!* (she was particularly proud to offer me that sentence in French). *Frau Ernsthaft speaks the German of the Weimar Republic,* Frau Klemm used to chuckle. She often wore a light turquoise dress with flowing sleeves that made her resemble a butterfly in flight as she poured boiling water over the Nescafé powder at the bottom of our cups. She would apologize for trembling too much and not seeing well enough to risk making real coffee. And she was always in high heels. Once a week, a talkative woman would come to give her a manicure and a veritable fireworks display of conversation. Kunigunde Fritze applied a raspberry polish to the fingernails of Lille Ernsthaft to cheer up the old woman's hands, which were covered with thick, ink coloured veins.

When she had company, Lilli Ernsthaft could now and then give the impression of reliving the old Sunday meals from the late 1920s, when the Ernsthafts and their son Harry would have lunch with Mr and Mrs Kutschera and their children Gert and Karin. The Kutscheras were the owners of the Café Wien on the Kurfürstendamm, a comfortable establishment with a billiard room on the upper floor, an orchestra on the band-stand, a magnificent garden, and the *Filmbühne Wien* right next door as well as the Zigeunerkeller, or 'Gypsy Cellar', a Berlin attraction where Hungarian violinists accompanied diners as they ate heartily. Karl Kutschera, a Hungarian Jew, and his Viennese wife Josephine, known to all as Pipi, were fabulously wealthy. *He owned a splendid villa in Kladow overlooking the Havel. The Kutscheras' property was immense, with many greenhouses, fruit trees, rows of asparagus, raspberry bushes, stables and sties – it extended all the way from Sakrower Landstrasse to the banks of the Havel,* Lilli Ernsthaft would declare with particular pride at having these distinguished friends.

We would then go into the living room to have our coffee. The children would play kneeling on the carpet. The women would chat amongst themselves while the men would smoke cigars. Lilli Ernsthaft said to me one day between two small bites of strawberry cookies, in a voice as nearly normal as one could imagine, that Gert and Karin *did not come back from Poland, that only their parents survived, and that they had never gotten over it, you can well imagine, the poor things, but you'll have a little more coffee, won't you dear neighbour?* A shadow passed across the little music

salon where she proposed we sit that day, next to the large
Bechstein piano which, since it had not been tuned in a long
time, made itself useful by serving as a giant tray table for little
bottles of liqueur. My hostess suddenly appeared so frail. I felt
awkward. Ought I to lower my eyes? Ask for details? Brusquely
interrupt the joyful babbling of anecdotes and the tinkle of our
little forks on the porcelain plates to inform her that all she had
said up until now was superfluous drivel of no importance and
that, yes, the fate of Gert and Karin interested me more than all
these sepia-coloured, kitschy images from her roaring twenties?
But Lilli Ernsthaft did not allow the big heavy storm clouds that
were gathering on the horizon of her memory to enter the room
and darken the feathery afternoon and the few hours of tranquil happiness that my visit had provided. Instead she hurried
to shoo them off with recollections of other memories as bubbly
as the champagne served at the grand New Year's Eve ball at
the Café Wien, when she swirled in the arms of Heinrich to the
new music arriving from across the Atlantic. Onestep, Twostep,
Quickstep – all learned at the Fleischmann dance school – and
in the evening, Heinrich and Lilli would repeat the new steps in
their large living room.

One day, on the dresser behind Lilli Ernsthaft, I discovered a
portrait of the two children – Karin with a bow in her hair and a
joyful sparkle in her eyes, and a sweet-smiling boy that was Gert.
The Kutschera children continued to live on, snugly sheltered
among other photos from the good times. Lilli Ernsthaft had not
forgotten them. But rather than dwell on what became of them,
she continued to leaf through her address book, run through
a mental list of the acquaintances and friendships of a married
woman who lived between the two wars, and recall celebrities
she had known or seen from a distance decorated with medals,

titles and honours. Lawyers, spouses of diplomats and foreign counsellors, company presidents and board members, the niece of the famous writer Oskar Blumental, Dr Lahmann, the director of the *Weisser Hirsch* sanatorium in Dresden – *very famous at the time!* – where Heinrich would go to have a spa treatment each year in May, Baron von Tucher, the owner of the beer brand of the same name, the tenor Franz Völker and his son the *Kammersänger* Georg Völker, Frau Doktor Steiner, the sister of the painter Georg Grosz – all these figures circulated through the rich and multifaceted lives of Lilli and Heinrich Ernsthaft. She even had the flattering privilege, during a final stop on her honeymoon at the Hotel Fürstenhof in Nuremberg, to bathe in the same tub with golden fixtures that the Emperor Wilhelm had used some years before. Clearly vanity rather than disgust was uppermost in her mind when she recalled this shared physical intimacy in soapy water with an aged flabby-skinned ruler.

But Lilli Ernsthaft's most beautiful trophy was Fritz Aschinger, one of her husband's best clients. They had *become better acquainted at the Weinhaus Rheingold* – the most fashionable restaurant in the city, on Bellevuestrasse near Potsdamer Platz. Fritz Aschinger was the owner of the largest hotel and restaurant chain in Europe. Lilli recounted the ingenious idea their friend had had: *Hundreds of big affordable brasseries where one could drink standing up and for ten pfennigs have an open-faced sandwich or for slightly more a bowl of delicious pea soup served with as much bread as you liked. The best quality at the best price!* – that was the slogan of the Aschinger chain and it meshed perfectly with the new accelerated rhythms of the capital. Workers no longer went home for lunch. They had to eat fast, inexpensively, and go back to work feeling full. *But the Aschinger empire also included some of the most luxurious hotels in Berlin, including the Bristol on the avenue Unter den Linden, the Palast-Hotel on the Potsdamer Platz, the Hotel Kaiserhof and the Fürstenhof opposite the Haus Vaterland. After having become acquainted,* recalled Lilli, *we would dine together every Saturday at the Hotel Fürstenhof and we'd always have caviar as an appetizer and for dessert flaming crêpes Suzette flambéed and served right at our table.*

Lilli Ernsthaft told me about a trip to Montreux where they stayed at a very chic hotel with a balcony overlooking Lake Geneva. *We all met for breakfast – that is Fritz Aschinger and his sister who lived in Italy, Madame the attaché Elisabeth Kermektchiew, and my husband and I – in the suite of the business consultant Lohnert and his wife. When the bellboy had set out the breakfast things, our host locked the door and took a suitcase out of an armoire that contained, believe it or not, several Aschinger-brand dried sausages. He next drew a whetstone from his pocket and began sharpening one of the hotel knives before cutting us each a large piece of sausage.*

But the most beautiful episode of all these dizzying excursions was their stay with the Aschingers in a suite at the Hotel Claridge Paris, *the most distinguished hotel on the Champs-Élysées.* The hotel director received her like a princess. *When we arrived, there were flowers in every room, a giant sweet jar for the women and cigars for the men. When we left, there was no bill to pay, probably because of the Aschinger name, which was known throughout the world in gastronomic circles. In reply to this magnanimous gesture, our three gentlemen, Aschinger, Lohnert and Ernsthaft, made an equally sumptuous gift: they ordered the jeweller Hülse in Berlin to make a golden tobacco case with little diamonds set in it that spelled the initials of the hotel director.*

All these names that she dropped into the cooking pot of her story formed a scintillating mist that obscured the tragedies of her life. The black clouds dissipated. I saw them depart through the high windows. I saw them rise far, far into the pure sky overarching our peaceful afternoons together. And I did not dare to call them back, not even for an instant; and although questions burned my lips, I didn't take the risk of asking them.

This was how she was. Lilli Ernsthaft resembled more her laughing first name than the austere surname of her husband who was thirty-three years her senior. She did not like tarrying lugubriously over misfortunes. Here was her account of Germany's declaration of war on Russia on 1 August 1914: *One beautiful summer day, my parents took me to Potsdam. We crossed the magnificent park until we reached the shore and the restaurant where we were to have lunch. We were led to a large semi-circular outdoor terrace with a view of the Havel. We had just placed our order when a newspaper salesman burst into the restaurant and shouted out to those on the terrace, 'Germany has declared war on Russia!' At that moment, my father paid for what we had ordered and to my great disappointment we quickly left the restaurant without eating a single mouthful. This is how our summer excursion to the magnificent destination of Potsdam came to an end. At twelve years old, one is not yet able to measure the significance of such an event.* And if she didn't mention in passing that she used to eat with her parents at the soup kitchen set up in the square at the end of our street, you could forget amid the rest of her narrative that Germans suffered from hunger during the war. With a little pale metal box, Lilli would also go around collecting money for wounded soldiers to make her contribution to the war effort. *My favourite cousin never came back from the front. He fell for the 'Vaterland' – a homeland that twenty-five years later no longer wanted us.* She evoked hastily the abdication of the adored Emperor, whom she would go see with her father on Sunday mornings *as he descended the Unter den Linden avenue down to the Brandenburg Gate accompanied by the Empress Augusta-Victoria and without any police escort or bodyguards. The people cheered as they passed and we too waved our hands and hailed them!* She also recalled the proclamation of the Republic, the Spartacist Uprising, the murder of Rosa Luxemburg and Karl Liebknecht, the Kapp Putsch and other events that, all told, meant that *unfortunately we did not get to have a truly pacific post-war period.* On the terrible inflation of the 1920s, a financial storm that led to so many bankruptcies, upset life on the street, and filled it with people out of work and even beggars: *It was a crisis that probably affected me less than it did most Germans since, as a young woman, my head was in the skies and I was much more interested in Austrian cuisine which of course I knew well since it had been a part of my family, but which I did not take up myself, neither at my parents' home nor at my new home, because there an experienced steward supervised everything in the house including the cooking.*

Even the memory of Adolf Hitler's coming to power on 30 January 1933 is just one more bothersome event in this Weimar Republic that changes governments like a man changes his starched shirts. *The political horizon darkened. At that moment we were in Karlsbad with some friends. One morning we were peacefully having coffee when suddenly the resounding voice of Hitler reached us through an open window on the first floor. That voice alone was enough to fill us with a certain anxiety, even if of course we had no idea what this man's rule would mean for us. From 1933 on things got steadily worse. We were pariahs.* However, she never talked about the *atrocious period* that she survived. She did not feel *the same obsession that made German television feel obliged to warm up the Holocaust again every day. Each time, it reawakens my pain.* In the early 1990s, alone in her living room, she would watch the news on television – *but never police shows or pornography! Occasionally I'll put up with a talk-show* – and she'd see the hordes of skinheads parading in the streets of the former East Germany and become frightened. And what if it were to begin all over again?

The only record she made of the 1930s, the war, and the way she, her husband Heinrich, and their son Harry survived the Third Reich is contained in a leather-bound notebook entitled *My Life*. Her niece Elga showed up one morning with her typewriter under her arm and a lively smile on her face.

'Aunt Lilli, it's time now to write down your memories!'

'Who will be interested in them besides yourself?'

'Starting now, I will come each week and you will tell me your memories and I'll type them up.'

Elga, an editor at Aufbau Verlag, a large West German publishing house, had a feeling that aunt Lilli's testimony was particularly important. Elga was sixteen when Harry showed up one morning at her parents' house in Johannisthal. He had just ripped the yellow star from his coat and fled from Clou, an old dance club in Friedrichstrasse where Jews had been held on 27 February 1943 as part of the round-up of the last forced workers in Berlin, known as the *Fabrik Aktion*, before their deportation to Poland.

Every week one could hear the tap, tap, tap of the typewriter on the second floor. Tap, tap, tap it went with pauses and irregular beats, jumps, sudden gaps, and long stretches of steady clickety-clack sounds. Elga's fingers sprinted and stumbled over the keyboard. She was in a hurry. She was afraid she wouldn't be able to keep pace with the gush of memories that were pouring out of aunt Lilli for the first time. Tap, tap, tap. The rise to power of the Nazis: *In 1937, given the political situation, Heinrich is required to sell his business to one of his associates for next to nothing. The money was placed in an account that was then frozen, I remember, and he could make no withdrawals.* The *Anschluss* with Austria in March 1938: *We were declared German citizens and were therefore entirely under the authority of the Germans such that all the horrible measures put in place against the Jews applied to us too at that point.*

She told of the jewellery and the three full boxes of silverware that she was forced to bring to a certain collection centre, including her necklace of real pearls! Of her platinum watch encrusted with little diamonds and sapphires and the bracelet with its five segments of alternating white and black pearls! Her golden handbag with the sapphire clasp! Heinrich's golden cufflinks made out of four Louis d'Or coins! And his golden cigarette cases! Two silver confectionary bowls sculpted in the shape of a chariot and a sled, and a full Chippendale silverware service for twelve, complete with a soup ladle, two special knives and forks for carving meat, serving spoons for vegetables and sauces, and special butter knives and cheese knives! She was given a ridiculously small amount of money for the whole lot.

Lilli Ernsthaft told of the food ration cards marked with a capital 'J' that were introduced at the beginning of the war. Jews were not allowed any fish or meat. They were to be sold only 'rustic vegetables' like turnips and white cabbage and only at certain specified hours. She remembered as though it were yesterday how two SS officers knocked at the door one morning at number 3 and seized four transistor radios of the brands Blaupunkt, Loewe and Nordmende, a Kodak camera, an electric iron and a parabolic radiator. And then she had to sacrifice her moleskin and sealskin coats with their sable and blue fox collars! And the beautiful Mercedes, a gift from Heinrich, that was confiscated at the same time as her driver's licence!

A particularly traumatic episode was when Harry was ordered to work as a dustman just after completing his secondary schooling or *Abitur*. Dustman! – a horrible symbol of their cata-strophic fall. I could hear the disgust in Lilli's voice as she sensed her definitive ejection out of my street's cocoon of privilege. *Since at the time the dustbins were still carried on one's shoulder, he would go to the cellar every Sunday and practise lifting bins that were almost full. Once, when it was around noon and he was already exhausted, Harry stretched out near the bins and fell asleep. The moment he awoke he had just enough time to notice that a rat had walked over his stomach before scurrying away. The drivers of the dustcarts were probably not Nazis for the most part. And even though it was forbidden for them to have private conversations with the Jewish auxiliary workers, one of them said to him once, 'Don't worry, my boy, in a few years you'll be in charge again and we'll still be collecting rubbish.'*

She told of the deportation of the Jews in my street: *One day while my son was taking a bath, a knock came at the door and I was horrified to find two Gestapo agents who asked to see Harry Ernsthaft. Frozen with fear, I told them he was taking a bath but that I would go get him immediately. When Harry appeared before them in a bathrobe, they told him to dress quickly and follow them to the back courtyard where two elderly Jews were sitting on hastily packed suitcases. These two old people were too frail to carry their own things and the Gestapo was ordering Harry to be their porter. You can imagine what a state my husband and I were in, standing there, our insides in knots, afraid that they would simply seize the occasion to keep my son and not let him return. Trembling with fear, we sat down in our bedroom and waited. At ten in the evening Harry finally came back. He was clearly trau-matized, and in reply to our flurry of questions only gave terse, evasive answers in order to keep from making us even more nervous. Later we learned that absolutely horrible things had taken place there.*

A few days later, Heinrich and Lilli Ernsthaft went to call on their neighbours, the Grunds, who lived in a street parallel to their own. *We rang the bell. Herr Grund opened the door and we hear 'Gestapo!' My husband and I half ran to a room in the rear of the flat. To our horror, they had come in search of Herr Grund and his wife. You can see how absolutely awful that evening was for us. Frau Grund was a tall stunning blond, more Aryan looking than most Aryans. We received a final letter from them sent from Poland where Frau Grund was forced to work as a waitress serving German soldiers. They were both killed.*

This was the end of the grand life at number 3: *We stayed home more and more. My husband, who was seventy when the war started, steadily lost his morale and his physical vigour. He had been so agile and an incredible dancer, but now he shuffled hunched over and used a cane.* Harry's Bar Mitzvah – which Lilli Ernsthaft, so eager to assimilate, called his 'Einsegnung' (Confirmation), in keeping with the Protestant vocabulary – took place in the *temple* in Prinzregentenstrasse and was *the last celebration of any importance, with the rabbi and many other invited guests invited to our flat, before a few of our rooms were requisitioned to lodge Jewish families who were gathered there prior to being deported to Auschwitz.* The Ernsthaft's flat was turned into a mini-ghetto. An elderly man was placed in one of the front rooms, in another a couple, Mr and Mrs Winter, and their son Rudi occupied the vacant maid's quarters. Rudi was the same age as Harry and was training to be an optician. The three Ernsthafts all lived in a single bedroom. *You can imagine that it wasn't always easy to share the kitchen and the bathroom. But everyone was cooperative and we got along well. The coreligionists living in our flat were deported one by one. The trucks used to transport the Jews for deportation were a regular sight in our street.* The 'silent porter' in the entrance brings back to life the neighbours in Lilli Ernsthaft's building that she tried so hard to forget.

Lilli and Heinrich Ernsthaft escaped deportation. On 15

September 1942, at ten o'clock at night, they were taken, each with a suitcase, to the Jewish hospital in Iranische Strasse. This was an *Übersiedlung*, or forced move. The *transfer*, Lilli noted, *was not done by a private car, but by truck*. The Jewish hospital was a little island within the Nazi hurricane, *a concentration camp with a human face!*, Lilli joked. *Shortly before, Doktor Goebbels had published an order that said 250 sick and elderly Jews were to be given provisional refuge at the Jewish hospital. I always wondered why.* The Jewish hospital was the only Jewish establishment that survived the Nazi period, with its Jewish doctors, nurses and patients. The medical activities continued right through to the end. Some 800 survived within its walls. A sanctuary in the centre of the capital of the Third Reich. *A ruse*, said Lilli Ernsthaft, *to show the whole world how well the Nazis treated their Jews*. A collaborator of Adolf Eichmann, the organiser of 'the final solution', passed by regularly. He used his visits to go around with Doktor Lustig, the hospital director, and select those to be deported.

Lilli Ernsthaft became the secretary of the administrative director. The Ernsthafts lived in a miniscule bedroom on the ground floor: *A terrifying event took place each week – the visit by the Gestapo. Many of the residents had to line up in the courtyard and the hospital director, Doktor Lustig, accompanied by the Gestapo agents, would pass among them and point at those who were to be deported. That's probably why he was shot directly after the war by the Russians – for his actions as a collaborator. Still today, I don't know why my husband and I were never required to line up in the courtyard with the others. Was it pure chance or did we benefit from some kind of favouritism on the part of Dr Lustig that allowed us to be spared from this selection process?*

At the end of 1943, Elsbeth Doller, Lilli Ernsthaft's mother, came to say farewell to her daughter. Elsbeth Doller was given permission to have her teeth inspected at the Jewish hospital before her deportation to Theresienstadt. Lilli remembered her mother's last words, *But Lilli, you already have a few white hairs!*, and her smile and little wave of the hand as the truck took her away: *It was the last time I saw my mother.*

The presence of a few members of Berlin's high society there in the cellar of the hospital, *while swarms of bombs were falling on the city*, gave a little consolation to Lilli Ernsthaft. *The sick were confined to their beds in the cellar day and night. Among them, there were some personalities such as Theodor Wolff, the long-time editor in chief of the* Berliner Tageblatt, *and Ludwig Katznellenbogen, the former husband of the famous actress Tilla Durieux, a sparkling star in the Berlin theatre world. I was able to be of service to both of them by giving them food or simply by keeping them company.*

Harry spent two years, from March 1943 to April 1945, hidden in the cellar of his former governess Grete Rönnfeldt, in Neuenhagen near Berlin. Grete Rönnfeldt lived in her own house with her three daughters. Her husband Fritz was at the front. *Of course*, replied Grete Rönnfeldt when her former employer asked if she could hide her son. *But that a household with three young children would risk taking in a Jew when doing so was entirely against the law was hardly an ordinary course of action*, Lilli insisted.

Grete told the children that Harry was a friend of their father's, but no one was to know that he was living at the house, otherwise their parents would be killed and they themselves taken to an orphanage, and they wouldn't want that to happen, would they? Even the parents of Fritz Rönnfeldt, who lived in the house next door, were not to be told. Once, when she saw the shadow of a masculine form passing back and forth behind the window of her son's bedroom, the older Frau Rönnfeldt suspected that her daughter-in-law had a secret lover. Harry lived in the basement lit by a small cellar window. An armoire hid the door from view. Only at night did Harry venture into the yard. He gave piano lessons to the daughters, helped them with their homework, and recorded in his diary for all twelve months of 1944 – an odd double book-keeping – both the major offensives against Germany and the arias broadcast on the radio that he listened to sitting on a stool in the broom-closet while Grete did the cooking. For 11 June, he writes: *Attack of mosquito fighters. Rosenkavalier.* To be able to breath, he left the door open a crack. *Since when do you like opera, Grete?*, asked her aunt Trude, who appeared suddenly in the kitchen one Sunday morning. *Turn off that junk immediately!* One night, Harry and his mother met up at the opera. *To our horror,* Lilli recalled, *we noticed a few rows behind us two former classmates of Harry. It made us decide to leave at the intermission.*

When the Russians entered the Jewish hospital on 5 May 1945, they discovered in the air-raid shelters a hundred lost souls. The Russians could not believe that some Jews could still be alive. *Hitler kaput!* they yelled. *Niet, niet Juden!* Suddenly a Russian approached the bedside of Heinrich Ernsthaft. *We understood that the Russians were our liberators, but they first let loose the thrill they felt at being conquerors, which frankly meant behaving like vandals: they urinated on desks, they removed all the medicines from the medicine cabinets and threw them indiscriminately on the ground, and it's said there were also cases of rape. On the other hand, they organized outdoor kitchens in the courtyard and distributed treats to children. We were happy to have outlived the Third Reich; we felt we'd been freed from a terrible yoke. And the challenges that then awaited us, we would face them together with the rest of the population.*

4

A Needle in a Haystack

One hundred and six Jews in my street were deported. That is the number recorded in the *Berliner Gedenkbuch*, a memorial archive put out by the Free University of Berlin in 1995. One hundred and six in such a short street. Perhaps even more. Some had only lived there a short time. To make the pick-up easier on the day of the deportation, whole families from other neighbourhoods were parked in Jewish homes in the street. But most of them had lived there for many years. Often several families in the same building. They accounted for several pages of listings in the telephone directory.

When I head home, walking the length of the street starting from the U-Bahn stop, I study the facades and try and give concrete shape to the incommensurable brutality of this number. I imagine faces for each name listed, compose little scenarios: the merchants Albert and Salomon Schidlowitz leave number 2 in the morning, their faces stern, their gait energetic. Another businessman, Cäsar Cohn, with his emperor's first name and eagle eyes, looks out at the street from his balcony at number 11. I guess at their personality traits: was the widow at number 2, Emma Stillschweig, whose name means 'the silent one', perhaps in fact an unstoppable chatterbox? Was Sidonie Pfeffermann at number 17 as unembarrassed and forthright as her peppery name suggests? Isidor Apfel ('Apple') at number 6 lived four doors down from her soulmate Doris Saft ('Juice') at number 10. Isidor Lazarus and Felix Bing lived on the same floor at number 19. I imagine their morning greeting at the lift: *Guten Morgen, Herr Lazarus! Guten Morgen, Herr Bing!* The merchant Arthur Deutsch at number 7 and the singing soloist Fanny Opfer ('Victim') at number 17 made an ominous pair of names. And yet whenever I tried to imagine their lives, I always came back to the same question: What had become of them?

Was it possible that some of the Jews who lived in my street in the 1930s were sufficiently clairvoyant, rich and lucky enough to have escaped in time and were still alive? Finding the survivors from such a small street would be like looking for a needle in a haystack the size of the planet. I took a stab at it though, just to have a clean conscience and so as not to regret backing out of the challenge from lack of nerve. I plainly stated the goal of my research, *Wer wohnte in meiner Strasse?* ('Who lived in my street?'), in *Aktuell*, the bi-annual publication of the Berlin Senate that was sent out to the last Jews of Berlin living around the world. Not many remain, it would seem, judging from the mere 7,758 subscribers. Each year, the number goes down by a few dozen. Most of them live in the United States and Israel. *Aktuell* allows them to maintain a link with the Berlin of their childhood. *We report to you what's happening in your birth country*, declares the journal's publisher. This is not without its absurd side since, stripped of their German nationality, the vast majority of them only returned once or twice for brief visits after the end of the war. Cynically one could say they returned as 'tourists' of a sort, since they had rebuilt their lives elsewhere. Not for a moment did they think of returning to live in Berlin. Too many things had happened there.

My classified ad appeared on the second-to-last page in a salmon-coloured text box. I can't say I had any great hopes, and quickly forgot about this experiment that basically I expected would fail ...

Until one afternoon, returning home, I found the booming voice of Miriam Blumenreich on my answering machine. *Hello, hello. This is Miriam Blumenreich calling from Kiryat Bialik in Israel! I was born on the 3rd of September, 1931, at number 3. Call me back!* Miriam Blumenreich was not the only respondent. Thirteen people answered my ad. From New York, Berkeley, Boca Raton, Lexington, Haïfa and Randwick, Australia – living former residents of my street reached out to say 'We are here' in bumpy hand-written letters composed in old-fashioned German, emails in English, or with quavering barely audible voices on my answering machine.

There was the tiny envelope that came from Marion Weiner in New York. Inside, on blue paper, she had written this sentence of terrifying bluntness: *We other 'survivors' are not all in such great shape.* Taped at the top of the page was a crown of forget-me-nots. Inge Letkowitz exclaimed, as though she had still not got used to the idea, *I survived!* Henry P. Beerman called me from Lexington. He told me he was a friend of Harry Ernsthaft at number 3 from the days when they were both *jung und hübsch* ('young and handsome'). He was going to turn eighty-five in a few days and was humbly taking stock of his life. *All things considered, it was a full life. I can't complain.* In an email written in English, Walter J. Waller of Boca Raton, Florida confided to me that *Your ad in* Aktuell *was like a voice rising out of a distant past.*

My whole childhood I played in your street with Harry and our mutual friend John Meyer. John Myer had died two years earlier at Palm Beach. *'Alas, I am still around'*, concluded Walter J. Waller.

I could hear Hannah Kroner-Segal in New York laughing in her email: I am the needle in your haystack! She came across my ad one evening totally by accident as she was casually sorting through a pile of old newspapers. Had her glance fallen just a little bit differently, she would have missed it. Klaus-Peter Wagner from Rockville apologized for his erratic hand-writing: *I have Parkinson's and should not really be writing letters any more. Besides, I am eighty-seven and a half years old and I am astonished I can write at all, especially in German. With my sincerest salutations and those of my wife, Yvonne, as well. P.S. I hope to have news from you soon.* Some months later, he sent me a second letter in which he recounted the life of his uncle Louis and his aunt Anny who lived in my street before the war: *I am almost certain it was somewhere around number 20 roughly.* The letter was eight hand-written pages. Klaus-Peter Wagner had paused for a few days between each paragraph and changed pens several times. He told me what had happened to Louis and Anny Wagner: *They had a beautiful shop of fancy toiletry items (one of their specialties was powder makeup cases with a soft cotton applicator all designed by my aunt). In November 1938, they were forced to close their shop. They managed to escape to London by plane in November 1938. Their departure from Tempelhof was an important event that had the effect of saving my life, because my uncle found someone who was willing to act as my guardian; it was his former salesman in London, and that allowed my parents to send me to London thanks to a child transfer arrangement, known as 'Kinder Transport', on 22 August 1939, in other words ten days before the war started.* The parents and sister of Klaus-Peter Wagner were not able to get out of Germany in time, and *ended up being deported and assassinated.* His aunt Anny committed suicide one night in London, and his uncle Louis never got over it.

Wolfgang Simon, who had become a clarinettist and conductor, and whose father, a haberdasher, was sent to Auschwitz, sent me an aerogram from Randwick, Australia. He had lived at number 6 and gave this description of my street: *There were one or two stores, notably a hairdresser at the last address before the square though I forget its name. At the corner of the main street, there was a small café that was also a polling station. At the time of the last free elections at the Reichstag – at least in Berlin – I remember that I was holding the railing on the balcony when a truck filled with soldiers of the Reichswehr went down the street brandishing an enormous black, red and gold flag. They were all chanting together, 'From the Baltic to Switzerland we see the swastika flag waving.' I was only nine but I remember that like it was yesterday. However, in my street the Nazis could not count on having much success. There were only a few swastika flags here and there. I knew plenty of Germans who hated that party as much as we did, and no one ever did anything to us personally. Some Berliners donated butter, coffee and milk to my parents during the war and helped them as much as they were able. I will never forget that.*

Jochanan Beer wrote to me from Haïfa. He had lived with his grandparents Martha and Gustav Beer at number 19 *in that wonderfully tidy street that curved slightly to the left with its buildings that stood as straight as soldiers.* After their grandson left for Palestine, Martha and Gustav Beer were expelled. Their flat would be made available to 'Germans of the Aryan race' who had become homeless after a bombardment. They, on the other hand, were deported to Theresienstadt. Their son, Fritz, managed to escape when the Gestapo came looking for his parents. He moved to New York and lived to be almost 105. One night he stumbled and hit his head on the way to the toilet. Jochanan Beer included with his letter a tiny photo of number 19 that was taken on his first trip back to Berlin right after the war: *Everything seemed foreign to me. I felt nothing. I took a picture of the building and then went to the hairdressers on the square. My grandparents had entrusted their jewellery to the owner. I went up to him in my English uniform and spoke in a gruff voice thinking that he was going to say 'No one deposited anything with me.' But in fact he proved to be perfectly honest. Perhaps he was afraid. What became of the gold and silverware no one knows. For me, the chapter of my life in this street is closed. What was built later upsets my memories of what existed before. Theresienstadt, that's the end punctuation of the chapter of our street.* And Jochanan Beer concluded: *My wife and I lead a modest and healthy life; we take our medicines like we're supposed to in order to preserve our mental and physical reserves as best as possible. We are grateful for every day that we are able to enjoy in peace in the company of our large family.*

Erica Gorin from Forest Hills asked me, *What would you like to know? My English is better than my German. Kind regards.* The thin letters of her script seemed to barely touch the paper. She signed herself Erica Lang and Erika Lange, writing one name above the other – the immigration name on top and below the name of her Berlin childhood. Her second letter, written on a computer, was in English. She told me she had lived in my street for three years, from 1933 to 1936, at number 21, together with her father Hermann, the owner of a wholesale yarn business, her mother Emmy and her younger brother Hans-Ludwig, nicknamed Hänschen: *The house where we lived was like all the other houses on the street. I think we lived on the second floor. That street had nothing special about it. I'm not able to remember specific details, the shops that were there, etc. One day I was sitting with my brother in the square on a bench reserved for Jews, and some kids came by and threw stones at us. I don't know what was worse: the physical pain or the humiliation.* Hermann Lange, the son of a cantor, went to the synagogue early in the morning with his hat on. Looking proud, he strode along the pavement with a sure-footed gait. *Walk with your head up and be proud to be Jewish,* he called out to his Jewish neighbours. And when he practised playing the shofar in the living room, his wife would worry: *Please, Hermann, stop this instant. The police are going to come.*

Then, without a pause, Erica Gorin told one by one the essential fragments of her other life, her American life. She had been married twice, twenty-five years the first time, twenty-seven the second. One of her three daughters, Amy, had died of cancer. *When a child dies, it's as though part of you dies too!* She shared with me the worst heartache of her life. I was touched by her humility: *Besides, I tried, I think, to be a good mother and wife.* The keyboard had gone haywire and had decided to type in boldface: *I don't know why the type is so heavy now, the computer and I do not always understand each other.* She made some remarks about the weather, *quite unusual for the season.* It had snowed a few days earlier and several neighbours were without power, but not her. *Thank God!* She added by hand in a postscript: *I could write in German but it would be less natural. I feel more comfortable in English.* English was less painful. It didn't bring back any terrorizing memories nor any nostalgia for times gone by. The day she set foot on American soil in 1940, she stopped speaking German, including with her mother and her first husband who was from Frankfurt. *His parents were killed in a concentration camp. We both had such hatred for Germany that we spoke English with our German accents. There was nothing extraordinary about it, we fell into it quite naturally. It was only when we didn't want our children to understand us that we would switch into German*. Erica Gorin also sent me the verses that she wrote at number 21 in her bedroom and kept hidden under the mattress:

> How long will you remain
> A foreigner in this country?
> Here you are not recognized
> But bound to infamy –
> O Israel, return to Yerushalayim
> There where the Temple was built
> In Your country.

I wanted to become eine Schriftstellerin ('a writer'). Erica Gorin suddenly shared this childhood dream in German. She also told me that every night before going to sleep, she comforted herself by repeating out loud the old German lullaby *Der Mond ist aufgegangen*:

> While everything sleeps
> Protect us and watch
> Over us and our friends.

My street had suddenly spread out over the entire globe. It was becoming re-inhabited before my eyes. These exiles told me about the rise of anti-Semitism and the *little pogroms* – their name for the pushing and jeering at high school in the court-yard of the Hohenzollern-Gymnasium. On the pediment to the school appeared the motto *Litteris, Virtuti, Patriae* ('For letters, courage and country'). They remembered Professor Krüger who was an SA-Sturmführer, *but fair*, and Gertrud Stratmann, the *very strict* owner of the Kaiser-Barbarossa pharmacy at number

1 on the square. A member of the NSDAP (the Nazi party) since June 1931, membership number 541 154, Gertrud Stratmann explains in 1936, in a letter I discovered recently addressed to the tax collection agency, the reasons for her rapidly declining sales: *During the last years one cannot help notice the clear departure of the mostly Mosaic population from our neighbourhood and its clear effect in diminishing our business.* She goes on to request from the authorities the suspension of enforced stewardship: *It is hardly in the interest of the National-Socialist vision of the world to impose drastic measures unilaterally whose effect is to penalize those who, because of their National-Socialist positions, have not only defended these beliefs, but have even made sacrifices in favour of them, proving thereby their National-Socialist convictions. Heil Hitler!* My exiled neighbours had gotten wind of the misery visited on Julius Gottschalk, the owner of number 11, a Jew, who, as the director of municipal services observes in a communiqué of 30 October 1935, *had declined to renovate the cylindrical tower at the end of the street. This end building's outer appearance does not do honour to the urban land-scape! The rough plaster has become detached in places thus allowing the bare walls underneath to appear in a disgraceful fashion. Moreover, one can rightly fear that pedestrians are at great risk of large pieces of rendering stone falling down on their heads. Finally, it bears men-tioning that the repairs done to the roof of this building are extremely roughshod. We are certainly not working in concert with the campaign in favour of Germany on the occasion of the Olympic Games when we tolerate with no reaction that Jewish owners are content to carry out minimal improvements on their own properties with the sole intention of being in conformity with street regulations and without any concern for the general physiognomy of the city. Heil Hitler!*

In their letters they mocked the absurdity of the Third Reich's racial laws. Jews no longer had the right to own pets or walk in groups. They told of how blind the Jewish families in the street were, convinced that Hitler would be no more than a *Spuk*, a passing phantom, and that in any case no one would harm an old man who had been awarded the Iron Cross at Verdun. They all told of the singular discovery they suddenly made; namely, that 'the Jews' were not the caricatures that appeared in *Stürmer* – figures with hooked noses, thick lips and sly eyes. 'The Jews' that the Nazis were persecuting were them, the upstanding bourgeois inhabitants of this street. Them, all covered with degrees, titles and knowledge. Them, the influential. Them, the participants in the industrial, financial and cultural expansion of the Empire. Them, the perfectly assimilated.

All spoke of the noose that tightened steadily and of fleeing often at the very last minute. And of the uprooted feeling in a new world of skyscrapers or deserts with no money, work, or social standing. Their fathers became ordinary manual workers, building superintendents, elevator operators in New York towers, taxi or bus drivers, or fruit and vegetable sellers in Jerusalem. In the evening, their fathers were an erudite bourgeois class hunched like schoolboys learning lists of new vocabulary. But the *Herr Doktor Professors* would never lose their accent and continued to build sentences the German way with the verb at the end – forever incapable of throwing off the scaffolding of their native tongue. In their new worlds, they continued to kiss the hands of ladies and tip their hats to acquaintances. They never took off their suit coat and never left the house without a tie, or without a bouquet of flowers or gourmet treat for the lady of the house when they were invited out.

Those who wrote to me were forever astonished at the transformation of their mothers. These capricious bourgeois ladies had grown up at KaDeWe between the lingerie department and the sweets counter. Women who had killed time playing bridge and reproaching their maids went to work on assembly lines in Queens, wore the same dress for years, milked cows or picked apples on a kibbutz in the new state of Israel.

They told me stories of their flight and terror, of death and loss. *Sehnsucht* and *Wehmut*, German words that are so beautiful and also so difficult to translate, took form under my eyes.

But with an eager joy they also all recounted their happy childhoods in the big comfortable flats of my street. For an instant they forgot about what had come next and returned to their light-hearted early years. They told stories. They had finally found a sympathetic ear willing to listen to the life story that often their own children wanted to know nothing about. Lis Eres, ninety-two, the daughter of the pharmacist in Potsdamer Strasse, begged me to accept her old accounts and photo albums. Her three sons, raised on a kibbutz, urged her to throw out all those odds and ends. And in any case they would get rid of it all after her death.

They were the children of the bookish bourgeoisie, the *Bildungsbürgertum*, a word I had trouble pronouncing when I first arrived in Germany, it was so heavy and severe. Their upward path seemed so clearly set out before them. There was no room for the unforeseeable in this world that was perfectly ordered and turned toward succeeding and rising in society. The sons would follow their fathers and become doctors or lawyers. Every morning near the square, girls would pass under the helmeted Athena who watched from between two Corinthian columns at the entrance to the high school institute for superior studies for young women. There they would learn to play Schubert sonatas and to pluck geese, and would eventually marry a good catch and set about producing some hardy heirs.

All of that under the approving eye of Goethe and Schiller looking down from the shelves of their bookcases in fine leather editions. It was a world that no one imagined would one day disappear forever. *When we're gone, there will be nothing left,* said Miriam Blumenreich over the phone. I had no time to lose.

5

Günther Jauch at the Jeckes'

There was an early childbirth at number 3 on 3 September 1931. Two months premature. Marianne Gerda Fiegel – Miriam Blumenreich's name the day she was born – tumbled out from between her mother's legs in the bedroom of the ground floor flat two floors below Lilli and Heinrich Ernsthaft's apartment. There had not been time to contact the Jewish obstetrician. Someone ran to get the Catholic midwife at number 20. Four, five violent contractions and a little gooey amphibious ball erupted onto the white sheets of its parents' bed. All five pounds, eight ounces were quickly wrapped in a cotton blanket.

Marianne Gerda had just forced her way out of that confining pocket where she no longer knew how to contain her impressive energy. She had elbowed her way past her twin brother who was floating at her side in this aquatic paradise. She wanted to come out into the world first. Rolf Günter Simon made a fainthearted appearance a few minutes later. He was a frail new-born who couldn't stand for long the blinding light and died three days later. Marianne Gerda spent four months in the neonatal intensive care unit of the Jewish hospital in the Iranische Strasse, fed each day with her mother's milk, and only discovered my street afterwards, looking up from her perambulator pushed by a nursery maid in a white bonnet.

Eighty years later, Miriam Blumenreich waits for me on the pavement in front of her house in Kiryat Bialik, not far from the oil refineries north of Haïfa. The garland of white morning glory seems to have been printed on her dark blue dress to illustrate her bucolic name: Mrs Flower Kingdom. Just greeting her by name sets off thoughts of luxurious gardens, magnificent bouquets, infinite expanses of prairies dotted with colour at the beginning of summer. Leaning on a cane, Miriam Blumenreich clearly has trouble standing unaided. She half apologizes. *I weighed ten stone. Then they prescribed hormones for me and overnight I swelled up like dough full of yeast – bigger and bigger.* Miriam Blumenreich mimed her metamorphosis, throwing out her chest, her arms indicating a larger and larger circle around her hips, and she pretended to burst, but instead burst out laughing. *I can hardly walk any more. Even Professor Hoffmann has been unable to do anything. He said to me, 'We're going to have trouble curing that, Madame Blumenreich. The best thing would be to never look at yourself in the mirror again!'* She's not allowed to do housework any more either. *If you really want to end up in a wheelchair, go ahead and mop the floor!* With the last reparations payments that her Wolfgang had received for his forced labour, Miriam Blumenreich bought herself a small electric cart. She calls it her three-wheeled Rolls Royce. She zips around everywhere in the neighbourhood behind the wheel of this silent little vehicle.

It took only a few voluble minutes on the pavement for Miriam Blumenreich to tell me all that. She cradled me in her large flabby arm and pushed me toward the house bordered with cypresses and bougainvillea that her father, Doktor Doktor Fiegel, a lawyer and notary in Berlin, moved into on

17 November 1936 with his whole family. *Everyone died here at home!* she said jubilantly – her husband Wolfgang, her maternal grandmother Else Schiftan, her paternal grandmother Tolde, her mother Klara and her father Herbert, who had ordered from his deathbed in a hospital in Berlin (he had gone back to work there in the 1950s) that his body be sent back to Israel, his *Heimat.* Miriam Blumenreich is as proud as a shepherdess who has managed to place her little flock beyond the reach of wolves. They did not die in the camps. They did not die nervous and disoriented during their escape. They died in bed surrounded by their loved ones. They are all buried at the Kiryat Bialik cemetery right near their house.

Miriam Blumenreich nods at the stairs that lead up to the first floor. Her older sister Alissa lives up there. After their daughters married, the Fiegels divided their house in two, horizontally. The lower half was Miriam's, the upper half Alissa's. Miriam Blumenreich guides me toward a low table in the dimly lit living room. The shutters are closed on account of the heat. She adjusts the fan, pulls the curtains, prepares fruit, biscuits, tea, and searches between the cushions of the couch looking for her mobile phone. And while she's becoming impatient – *A house isn't cake batter, nothing can get lost! It's what my mother always said* – I unpack the little souvenir items that she asked me to bring her from Berlin. Twelve packets of *Käsekuchen Mix* to make cheesecake and twelve packets of *Sahnesteif* to stiffen whipped cream. I was very nervous at baggage check-in at the Tegel airport. Would the customs officers buy my story about an old Berlin neighbour nostalgic for the baking powder and other cooking ingredients of her childhood? Or would they think it was a clever way to transport cocaine? *Dr. Oetker* is Miriam Blumenreich's Marcel Proust. The cheesecake covered with stiff whipped cream icing – it's her whole past life that she places on the table for her *Kaffeekränzchen*, the get-togethers she hosts with coffee and desserts to play bridge with German friends from Prague on Fridays and Saturdays, *because those days there are fewer shows on television because of the Shabbat.* Miriam Blumenreich's bridge club members are ninety, ninety-one and ninety-six. *One has an intestinal obstruction, another is deaf. But they play really well. And most of all – they only speak German.*

Number 3 in my street was the flat of her grandparents, Simon Schiftan, a fabric salesman, and his wife Else. They moved there in 1905 in the very same month as Heinrich Ernsthaft. The Schiftans and the Ernsthafts were on friendly terms. Their daughter Klara, Miriam Blumenreich's mother, was a school-mistress for young children in the street. Her *kindergarten* was located on the ground floor of her parents' building. How slender and beautiful Fräulein Schiftan appears in a photo. She gently looks after the children lined up by height along the wall. Each has a hand on the shoulder of the next one, faces turned toward the camera. Everyone was sad when Fräulein Schiftan married Doktor Doktor Herbert Rudolf Chaim Fiegel in 1929. She was going to have children of her own. She would stop working. The wedding picture of the civil service was taken on the steps of the Schöneberg city hall. Fräulein Schiftan in her fur coat, coquettish bibi hat and white stockings stands arm in arm with Doktor Doktor Fiegel, who is wearing his long black over-coat and top hat. The married couple is accompanied on either side by their witnesses. On the left is Walter, Klara's brother; to the right is Arnold, Herbert's brother and practically his twin. Same ears, same little moustache, same round glasses. Walter and Arnold were both doctors. The young couple would move in with the bride's parents at number 3. *If you want me to tell you about my patients,* said Herbert Fiegel to his wife, *become my chief assistant.* Frau Fiegel stopped taking care of the street's children.

Miriam Blumenreich wants things to be perfectly clear from the start: We were not just anybody in your Berlin street! My father was *Dr. jur. Dr. rer. pol.* Got that? Doctor two times over – in political science and in law! The double detonation made me jump and I realized the rage behind that outburst. My visit is Miriam Blumenreich's chance to restore to her father the place he deserved at the very top of the street's honourable social hierarchy. Before his life took another turn. Before a Jewish lawyer was assassinated in the street in 1933.

Back home that evening, Herbert Fiegel declared: *It's over. That's enough. We're leaving Germany!* Herbert Fiegel was not a Zionist but he chose Palestine. His wife preferred America. In her view, only New York or Chicago could measure up to Berlin. *Palestine, Palestine,* Simon Schiftan used to mockingly lament, *Palestine is nothing but a dot on the map!* This grand bourgeois gentleman who had lost his entire fortune during the high inflation years would never have gone off to such a holy and far away country – after all, he was in the habit of taking a taxi to the synagogue, and taking care to be dropped off at the corner so as to arrive on foot, like any good practising Jew would on the Sabbath. Simon Schiftan died in 1931, a few months before the birth of Marianne Gerda. He would not know his granddaughter or the Nazi era. *He is at Weissensee* (the Jewish cemetery in Berlin), said Miriam Blumenreich, as though her grandfather had suddenly got it into his head to move to a neighbourhood that he found more to his liking.

On 17 June 1934, the Fiegel family embarked at Trieste on the ship *Polonia*. The destination was Haïfa. The grandmothers,

Oma Else and Oma Tilde, followed some months later. *Sand, sand, nothing but sand!*, cried Miriam Blumenreich while making desperate circles with her hands as though she were fighting to not be swallowed up by it. She was two years and eight months old when she arrived in Palestine. For her this new country was one gigantic sandbox. For her parents it was a desert light years away from the lush green streets of Schöneberg. Herbert Fiegel wanted a garden around his house. A garden! In the middle of sand and rocks! But he is stubborn. At Kiryat Bialik, he grows tomatoes and cucumbers and cultivates orange and lemon trees, and even roses. They remind him of the small green area at the front of the building at number 3 and of the easy life back then. The Dr. jur. Dr. rer. pol. Fiegel refused for quite some time before yielding and taking off his suit coat and loosening his tie while hoeing his flower beds under a blazing sun.

He knew he would not be able to continue his profession. He didn't speak a word of Hebrew and was not familiar with the system of Ottoman law practised in Palestine – *much more complicated than German law*. Plus, his diplomas were worthless. His suit and tie were the last bulwark against all this adversity. In 1937, when Herbert Fiegel was hospitalized for septicaemia, his wife went on a secret errand to see an antique dealer in Haïfa, Cohn & Lubarski. To pay the hospital bills, she sold everything she had managed to save from her Berlin household – silverware, crystal glassware, everything. She even swapped her diamond engagement ring for some money and a worthless pearl ring.

Klara Fiegel, who was very good with her hands, set about new tasks such as repairing oil-powered kitchen ranges. They are smelly objects. Miriam Blumenreich's mother worked *from sunrise until her soul left her body*. A doctor found tropical worms in Klara Fiegel's intestine. The family lacked everything. Oma Else would spread mustard on her bread because butter was too expensive. When the town's electric company sent someone out one day to check that the meter was not defective – because the electric bills showed consumption below one kilowatt – the Fiegel's explained that they only lit the twenty-five-watt ceiling bulb when they needed to find their way at night. To save money, they would go to bed as soon as it was dark. The Berlin flat with its seven rooms was only a crazy memory. *The four of us lived in this one room. In that room my mother opened a lending library stocked with the books we had brought from Berlin. It wasn't until 1958 that we could take over a space in a shopping mall and my mother set up her library there and we also sold newspapers. Everyone worked there – my father, my mother, and us the children. One of the rooms here that's a storage space for me now was rented by a certain Frau Pollack. No one else in Kiryat Bialik was willing to take her in. We had to start from scratch.* When she felt nostalgic about her comfy girlhood in the Berlin flat of her parents, Klara Fiegel would think of her aunt who was assassinated. Her aunt's husband had made his fortune in the years after 1871 and did not emigrate in time. He didn't want to leave his money. *No, no,* Klara Fiegel repeats to herself, *you shouldn't cling to money!*

In 1936, Kiryat Bialik was not yet a true city. It was more a construction site under oppressive heat with dirt roads, dust, stray cats, thistles and a few temporary shelters where immigrants lived, surrounded by their suitcases and their *Heimweh*, a homesickness that choked them. Kiryat Bialik was built by the parents of Miriam Blumenreich and other immigrant German Jews on land donated to them by the Jewish National Fund. Doctors, jurists and engineers lived in this enclave with their misery, their uprooted and transplanted condition, the heat, plus Hebrew – *a language worse than Chinese!* Herbert Fiegel was the only adult in the family to learn it. Klara Fiegel was seventy when she enrolled in her first Hebrew class for immigrants. Oma Else didn't even try. She continued to speak only in German. The old lady built herself a miniature Berlin in Kiryat Bialik with a circle of friends who were all Berliners like her.

They're called 'the Jeckes' – the stiff German Jews always buttoned up in their suits, or *'jaquettes'*. Herbert Fiegel left Germany because he didn't want his daughters to be called 'dirty Jews'. *Yet in Palestine they find themselves suddenly called Jeckes. There was such hatred against Germans here. My parents were told, 'Go back to Hitler where you came from!' Arabs shouted 'Nazis! Nazis!' at us. They had no idea what a German Jew was. We were shamed as Germans. But Jeckes were so different. Jeckes were cultivated. The philharmonic orchestra was founded by Jeckes. There was no culture here before. Take my husband, Wolfgang Blumenreich, a real Jecke from Berlin. He never would get on a bus before me, and he would never step off without offering me his hand. Where had he learned that? At Auschwitz? It was just part of him. And later people set about teasing us. We're a little slow to loosen up. We're stiff, correct, pedantic, and not big laughers. The mentality of the Poles and Russians was totally different. Germans were as straight as a plumb-line. Eastern Jews got worked up over everything.* Regularly, Miriam Blumenreich tallies up the last remaining Jeckes in Kiryat Bialik. Maybe twenty. New arrivals come from the former Soviet Union or Argentina. *Bialik has not been what it was for a long time*, she says.

Dr Dr Fiegel refused to allow olives at the table. Olives were too oriental for these Berliners who continued to eat their *schnitzel* (breaded cutlets) and kale for lunch even during heatwaves. They looked at everything foreign as a permanent threat. The open-air markets were a dizzying experience. All those spices, all those strange vegetables – courgettes, aubergines, figs, grenadines, chick peas, chillies, dried herbs, pepper corns of different colours and fresh Mediterranean fish that were practically still moving. All those colours. All the strong smells. So much exuberance. What a contrast with the orderly monotone of cabbage, potatoes, carrots, parsley, onions and dill from Frau Martens, the greengrocer at number 5 back in their Berlin street. Still today, Miriam Blumenreich will only eat German-style food. She can't digest olive oil. In the evening, she eats black bread with quark and cumin – like in Berlin.

Oma Else never agreed to changing her name. What a joke! Trade in Else for Deborah or Shlomi! *Nein, nein!* Out of the question! Klara became Esther. Marianne became Miriam. And she feels like both – Marianne and Miriam. She's adjusted to her double identity. Her mother tongue is German. Her homeland is Israel. *It's a constant pulling in two directions. As you can see, I speak German well. It's anchored as deep as can be inside me. But I was never taught to write in German. I taught myself, later.* Miriam Blumenreich places the verb at the beginning of her sentences, like in Hebrew. It makes for rather awkward German, as though her sentences were losing their balance and about to fall. *I am Jewish with all my being. My country is here. My children were born here. My grandchildren too. We were German and lost our country. After the war, I would not have been able to live in Germany. I wish for Israel to continue to exist. The Palestinians are not just going to throw us in the sea. Jews have to live somewhere too and have their own country.*

Miriam Blumenreich asked her daughter Nava to come by with her children and say hello. Nava has no German first name, nor do her three children. She has three boys. Real Israelis. They speak only Hebrew. And English. Who would have thought that so many new branches could grow from the genealogical tree of a Jewish Berlin family? The fourth and fifth generations sat down on the couch. I could tell that Miriam Blumenreich had more or less forced them to come over. This forty-three-year-old woman and these three teenagers have no desire to delve into memories of a Berlin street where they've never once set foot. What a queer idea, they probably think staring at me, to travel all this way to pluck a few anecdotes about a street of no importance. When Miriam Blumenreich observes that her daughter has arrived fifteen minutes late, Nava makes fun of her Jecke mother: *She's a little retro, and a little set in her ways. When we agree that I'll pick her up at 6:30 p.m., she'll call me at 6:31 to ask 'Where are you?'* Sitting on the arm of an easy-chair in a miniskirt and high-heel sandals, ready to jump up and do whatever needs doing, Nava is clearly more interested in the chips in her nail polish than in our conversation. She's thumb typing on her smartphone but stops brusquely when her pop music ring-tone breaks our awkward silence. Miriam Blumenreich apologizes for her: *She's put some unbelievably annoying music on her mobile phone. A song in English.* Mother and daughter speak in English in front of me. When they're alone they speak Hebrew. Miriam Blumenreich regrets not having spoken German to her children. *It was a big mistake. I felt a sort of inhibition. Our mother tongue is German but my grandchildren study English, French and Arabic. There are still a lot of people today who cannot stand to hear German. Why? After all, the language has nothing to do with the Nazis, nor with Goethe or Schiller.* Everyone in the family has a German passport. It was Herbert Fiegel who looked into it and did all the paperwork for his daughters and their husbands. Today Nava and her three sons are also Germans. It's a precautionary measure.

In Israel it's better to have two passports. Miriam Blumenreich insists on underlining an important point: *I was not naturalized, I was reintegrated. In 1958.*

Miriam Blumenreich likes telling the story of the *totally extraordinary* way she met her future husband Wolfgang. Nava and her sons have heard it told hundreds of times. After the war, Klara Fiegel went to visit her brother Walter in America. Walter was a doctor in a small town near the Canadian border. Herbert and his daughter Miriam took a taxi to the airport in Tel Aviv to pick her up on her return. But the plane was twelve hours late. They started talking with the taxi driver, Wolfgang Blumenreich. Herbert and Wolfgang hit it off immediately – two Berliners who had found each other! Wolfgang started making more and more visits to Kiryat Bialik. He enjoyed himself in the company of this intact Berlin family that gently teased the *Ostjude* – a Jew from the East, born in Swinemünde. *You're the only Polack in the family!* said Herbert Fiegel the day Wolfgang came to ask for his daughter's hand. They were married by a Berlin rabbi – an old acquaintance of Klara Fiegel from the days when she was still Fräulein Schiftan, the kindergarten teacher. He did the whole thing without any fuss. *He organized a European-style wedding and later a nice bris ceremony for my son at the hospital. Only the men were present. Today everyone gets invited, it's a real circus.*

My husband was marked with the number 17600. 17600! Stupefaction. Silence. Miriam Blumenreich's words threw a grey veil over the room, the July afternoon became suddenly cloudy, darkness fell on the photos of Berlin life that were scattered about the table. Nava stiffened over at the end of the couch. *At our home, even the walls breathe the Holocaust*, she said suddenly. She forgot about her nails and her mobile phone.

Nava was three years old when her father fell sick. At forty-seven, Wolfgang Blumenreich collapsed. He was admitted to the psychiatric hospital in Jerusalem. Neurovegetative dystonia accompanied by panic attacks was the diagnosis. Miriam Blumenreich would go to visit him once a week. The psychologist would tell her each time: *He doesn't say anything. It's no use.* It sounded like a reproach. *He didn't speak,* confirms Nava in English. *Not a word. We weren't allowed to ask my father about the number on his arm. Growing up, I understood it was no use asking him questions, so I stopped.*

Wolfgang Blumenreich didn't talk about his parents, his brothers and sisters, or their life in Berlin. He talked even less about his flight to France on 3 July 1939 as part of a convoy of a group of children. His father no longer had the means to emigrate himself, but he saved his sons. Wolfgang Blumenreich was nine years old when he left Berlin. *He was too young to be uprooted like that! I feel so sad for him!* says Miriam Blumenreich. Her maternal instinct is wounded. Torn from his parents whom he would never see again, Wolfgang was hidden at a Jewish boarding school in Chabannes deep in the department of the Creuse. 'Wolfie' was the tallest and most athletic of all the children at Chabannes. On 26 August 1942, the *Vichy*, as Miriam called the French police, descend on the school at dawn and seize six children. Wolfie was held at Drancy and then deported to Auschwitz. He survived thirteen selections: the weak to the left, those who could still work to the right. He would hide in the latrines. It's all his daughter knows about her father's life.

Miriam Blumenreich had written down the names of the different concentration camps where her husband had been imprisoned. *I've reconstructed his route through eleven of them. Two others are impossible to find. He was at Dachau when he was freed. At age twenty my husband weighed only thirty-eight kilos.* Miriam Blumenreich holds tight to the columns of numbers to avoid collapsing as she retells the story of her husband's horrible journey. The exactitude of the numbers, their mathematical impartiality, act as reliable cairns that can be seen from afar in the obscure mists left by the long silence that Wolfgang chose never to break.

Nava has trouble controlling her anger when she thinks about how her father was treated in the Israeli hospitals. *They were never patient, never kind to my father. Crazy or not, people shouldn't be treated like that. These people went through the war twice. Germany tried to exterminate them and when they arrived in Israel their new country didn't know how to listen to them. Maybe today people are a little more tolerant with those who suffer from mental illness.*

During the whole Eichmann trial in 1961 it was like a state of emergency in the Blumenreich home. Newspapers disappeared. The radio stayed mute. Wolfgang Blumenreich didn't want to see or hear anything about it. He wanted to protect his children. For hours, the survivors from the camps testify. There's no stopping them. All of Israel has its ears glued to the radio. Streets are deserted. Wolfgang Blumenreich is at home, prostrate, closed inside his silence. He had sort of collapsed into himself, remembers his wife. And many years later when the American television series 'Holocaust' was shown on Israeli TV, Miriam Blumenreich and Nava would wait for her father to go to bed before turning on the set. Each evening, they sat huddled next to each other in the kitchen. They kept the sound down low and the door closed. They feared that any moment Wolfgang Blumenreich might burst into the room. Every ten minutes one of them would walk on tiptoe and put an ear to the bedroom door. All was calm. He was sleeping.

He wasn't able to talk about it. The pain was too strong. He said he didn't want to be taken back to that past. And then one day we were in Chabannes, and there, surrounded by his friends from that time, things started to come out little by little. In French. Nava couldn't believe it.

'*It's incredible this capacity to hide stuff, to repress certain things ...*'

'*Talking, always talking*', interrupted Miriam Blumenreich. '*The exhibitionism on TV. There's a car accident and instantly reporters are there asking you questions. One also has the right to not want to speak! How about leaving me my privacy! Why should any random stranger have the right to stare into the bottom of my pots and pans?*'

Wolfgang Blumenreich died five and a half years before I arrived. Fifty-four years of living together and Miriam Blumenreich still doesn't know much about her husband's dark years. *The Holocaust, is it something one can understand?* She pauses. *No!*

When Nava went to the Black Forest on vacation, she too couldn't stop thinking about Jews hidden in the woods. It was so cold. *You have to look to the future*, she says. *You can't hold the third generation responsible. The world changes. We live in the 'global village'*, adds her son Aviv. Only Miriam missed the train setting off toward that planetary community. *You can't get rid of the Holocaust*, she says. *It leaves its mark inside your bones.* The first time she returned to Berlin in 1958 she didn't feel very comfortable. When someone in the street ruffled the hair of her oldest daughter saying *Isn't she cute!* Miriam Blumenreich felt a shiver up her spine. Thirteen years earlier, she wondered, would the person have thought her so '*cute*'? *That's what I was thinking deep down without saying it. If my mother woke up today and saw the number of young Israelis flocking to Berlin, she wouldn't believe her eyes.* She's not afraid of the Germans. She's afraid of the Muslims and that they might conquer Europe. And she's afraid of the *'devout in black'* – the orthodox Jews – that they're blackmailing the Israeli government.

Miriam Blumenreich has spoken for ten hours straight without taking a break. Ten hours to retrace the route from number 3 in the street where she was born in Berlin all the way to Kiryat Bialik. Today her Germany is hardly any bigger than a television screen. Twice a week, Mondays and Fridays, she watches the German version of *Who Wants to Be a Millionaire? It's my passion. I never miss a show for any reason! In Israel, it comes on at 9:15 p.m. – it makes the evenings seem less long.* She knows lots of proverbs that the contestants have no clue about, *even though they've always lived in Germany. The other day there was this young blonde woman who was twenty but looked about fourteen. So charming and nice-looking. If all Germans were like that, I would have nothing to complain about.* At night, with the windows open to welcome the cool night air, the voice of Günther Jauch, the host of the show, carries into the street. The ultimate dream of Miriam Blumenreich: *To one day appear on the set of the show and stand alongside Günther Jauch.*

6

The Balcony Across the Street

For Irma and Leon Rothkugel

Dear Madame,

My name is John Ron, alias Hans-Hugo Rothkugel. Thus began the email I received from the youngest child of the lawyer and notary Dr Leon Rothkugel and his wife Irma, my neighbours across the street. *I am a retired French professor. I was born in October 1922 in your street where I lived until April 1934. Today I have trouble writing but I have a good memory and could perhaps provide a useful contribution to your fascinating book project. I would be very pleased to hear from you.*

A line of cactuses along the windowsill prevents one from seeing very far into their flat. A discreet couple lives there today. I had never paid attention to these neighbours whom I only knew as two shadows moving behind panes of glass. In a few months the chestnut trees will be so high and leafy that my view will be entirely blocked. A pale light illuminates the living room, which was formerly the study of Dr Leon Rothkugel, the author of *The Rothkugel Tarif Chart*, an indigestible legal text. The handsome rooms that looked out onto the street were his office. Irma and Leon Rothkugel, their three sons and two maids lived in somewhat tight quarters more privately situated at the back of the flat.

When I am sitting at my desk, I look directly across at the Rothkugels' balcony. This observation deck above our street is part of a crystal-clear memory. A memory that has not dimmed at all despite the many years that have passed. It is a summer Sunday morning. Little Hans-Hugo is sitting in full sunshine. The sky is a soft blue. The church bells down at the end of the street are ringing. In the flowerboxes there are nasturtiums and petunias. Irma is at the piano in the living room. It's the memory of an immense feeling of well-being. Time is frozen like in the castle of Sleeping Beauty, when the valets and scullery maids halt suddenly, their gestures suspended in mid-air, their mouths open in the middle of a sentence. A sequence in stone: a little boy sitting in the sun, legs crossed, happy, on a balcony overlooking the street.

Today, Hans-Hugo Rothkugel goes by the name John Ron – an English first name and a Hebrew surname. He lives in Berkeley, California. I called him after receiving his sign of life. The doors to my balcony are wide open in the summer night. I hear the impatient orders addressed to a dog by a neighbour, the rustle of the breeze in the branches above my head, and the low rumble of traffic going by. *It's a miracle that fate should have our paths cross like this!* We can't believe it and we're both moved. *Il faut vous avouer que le fait que vous soyez française me touche* ('I must confess that your being French moves me'), says John Ron in the mannered French of another age. *The French language is the one and only love of my life. This new late chapter comes as a total surprise.* He's afraid of disappointing me. *The harvest of memories that I have of my street is rather meagre. Besides, I only led the ordinary life of a French teacher at an American high school. I liked to wander about. I was not a good organized Prussian. Except when it came to saving my skin.* At eighty-eight, John Ron is a man in a hurry:

Get going! I hope I will be able to hold on until your arrival! You will have the privilege of meeting a cadaver that is still alive thanks to a strict regimen of all sorts of drugs.

Two weeks later, I am in Berkeley. For thirty years, John Ron has been living in a small residence for seniors near Martin Luther King Street – 'MLK' to the taxi drivers. He gave me detailed instructions on how to reach him: *Ring the bell. Wait for the 'murmur' of the door. It will open miraculously. Ping, my home care assistant, will come to meet you.* Ping, a short, bright-eyed Chinese woman who sprinkled her sentences with the most delightful polite phrases, was waiting for me in the foyer. Leaving the elevator, there was a long dark corridor with a rectangle of bright light at the end. The flat door was wide open. What would he look like? We had spoken so much on the phone that I felt like I knew John Ron without ever having seen him, not even in a photo. *Come in! Come in!* I recognized the voice of our nocturnal conversations. John Ron is sitting in his bed. His back is propped up against a little wall of cushions and a hot water bottle lies on his stomach. He is wearing black pyjamas, and glasses rest on the end of his nose. He raises his head and exclaims, *Ah, vous voilà donc!* ('Ah, here you are!') It was as if we had only parted the day before.

John Ron gestured to me to sit in his wheelchair that was pushed up next to the bed. We exchanged a few polite remarks. *Speak a little slower, the old guy can't run that fast!* We laugh and feel little embarrassment. After all, we're neighbours. Despite the gap of a few decades, there's a special bond between us. He calls me *my dear* and only speaks to me in French. My *monsieur* makes him stiffen. He proposes John and the formal *vous* ('you'). *Even though I've never felt comfortable as 'John'. But I have not been Hans-Hugo for a long time. Like for a lot of Jews, my life is a piece of theatre. I play at hide-and-seek with myself. I don't really have a proper name.* John is a sheriff's name, an apostle's name, but certainly not the name of a German Jew. John is easier to pronounce than the impossible Hans-Hugo with its double 'H' that has to be blurted out all at once without taking a breath. *John* lets him get around in life and cross borders without annoying anyone. And most of all, it's not as heavy to carry around as the *Hans-Hugo* chosen for their son by Dr Rothkugel and his wife. This two-part articulated lorry of a name was made to have at least the tractor of a *Doktor* out in front of it, or better yet the sparkling locomotive of a *Professor*.

It was the new Israeli army that, during the war of independence in 1948–9, gave the meteorologist-forecaster Hans-Hugo Rothkugel the rank of officer and a new family name. *Rothkugel didn't sound very Hebrew. And Jochanan Rothkugel was clunky. So I got rid of my slightly ridiculous German name.* John Ron sometimes wonders if before he dies he should take back his original name to save the memory of his family. He is the last Rothkugel. *But in America, Mister Rothkugel ... No, no, it just can't be taken seriously! Here I am John H. Ron, a perfect example of the American middle class.*

John decided he would no longer get out of bed. To his right on a bedside table is Baudelaire's *Les Fleurs du mal* in an edition published in Munich by Kurt Wolff in October 1922, the year of John Ron's birth, *with that Fraktur font that grabs you by the throat. When the need arises, the book is there. It gives me some reassurance.* To his left are syrups, drops and pills. He calls them with some affection his 'little miraculous bottles'. John puts out his arm without turning at the waist. He feels around and touches the shapes of the bottles that he recognizes with his fingertips. He swallows a mouthful of a whitish medicine meant to conquer *all the little obstacles that make life difficult.* He then folds his hands together on his chest and lets a verse of Tucholsky slide voluptuously over his lips:

Wer viel von dieser Welt gesehen hat
der lächelt und legt die Hände auf den Bauch und schweigt.

The one who has seen much of this world
Smiles, lays his hands on his stomach, and remains silent.

From his bed, John contemplates the regular unfolding of each day. His hours are a bit odd, he says. He has trouble sleeping at night. He takes a sleeping pill at dawn and dozes until the end of the morning. Ping arrives at 2 p.m. and prepares tea with milk and bread cut into little triangles. He calls her Ping. Just Ping. It sounds like the somewhat burlesque name of a Walt Disney heroine. *Ping* is much better than *Dear Mrs Ping ... Dear has an air of condescension,* his maternal grandmother Anna had taught him – Anna had been the morose wife of the millionaire merchant Benno Cohn. *My grandmother was not a part of the Jewish clique that exhibits its diamonds and mistreats its domestic servants. She was much too Prussian for that. Her style was based on discreet luxury, never showy, and an impassive face in all circumstances.* In the sumptuous flat at number 20 Hardenbergstrasse, near the *Zoologischer Garten* underground stop, the lady of the house knew how to address her servants.

Ping faces every challenge with zen-like calm. And the challenges are as numerous as the desires of her elderly patient. The hours have to go by with clockwork precision. The curtain must be pulled exactly right. Mallarmé precedes Maupassant on the third shelf of the bookcase. And watch out if tea should be served in the wrong cup. An exact ordering of objects and hours provides John with a comforting feeling of security. Whatever the task, Ping hops to it, *Yes, sure, Mister Ron*. She glides around the flat without a sound. Her small feet barely touch the carpet. She never stops smiling. Mister Ron needs this pacifying presence. He has never been so spoiled in all his life. *It's as though I were in the ideal marriage*, he says.

Ping serves us a cup of Earl Grey and a plate of madeleines. John exclaims, *The good Catholic takes the host when his last hour comes. Me, I'll eat a madeleine – the perfect thing for a French professor!* Then all of a sudden he excuses himself for being a heretic because he doesn't like the inexcusable long-windedness of Proust who has become so fashionable in America that someone has entitled his book *Proust is Good for You*. John Ron addresses himself to Ping in a most courteous, meticulous British English. There is no way he's going to trade in this slightly arrogant but so elegant accent for the gargling and mumbling of the Americans. He is convinced that *upper class* English lends him *a certain cachet*. John often uses the royal *We* with Ping: *We do have respectable napkins to honour our guest, don't we, Ping? We do want everything to go smoothly!* This *We* acts as the bridge of symbiosis between the old Berliner and this Chinese woman from Canton – two uprooted people in the melting pot of America.

The ad about my research project caused a big commotion in this life of uneventful routines. *Ping! Ping! Something has happened to me! Somebody is looking for me!* Arriving one morning, Ping found Mister Ron sitting up in bed in a state of intense agitation. Finally an event was occurring in the static life of her patient. He had not left his studio flat in six months.

For a long time, the old man in the navy blue blazer, tie and tweed cap – with his umbrella when there were showers – had no longer been seen under the white wood pavilion of the Strada café across from the university. Sitting at a small solitary table, he would just *be* there, immobile, watching for hours the life that flowed and swirled about him. He marvelled at how fast the world had changed. With his rigid air of a retired colonel of the Indian army and festoons of polite requests addressed to the waiting staff, John was certainly an anachronism amid all the students in shorts and flip-flops hunched over their laptops. He came from somewhere else – another continent and another era. From a world that had disappeared forever. *I am the last German Jew*, he would sometimes declare. *A curiosity. A rare specimen. At any rate, the last survivor of an exterminated tribe.* A human species that Americans classify under the label 'Holocaust survivor'. They are looked on with respect, even awe, but no one is really interested in them any longer. John Ron doesn't know how he washed ashore at Berkeley. *I feel like an ancient mariner who hardly remembers where the boat hailed from that threw him onto this shore*, he says.

He preferred the reliable company of Tucholsky and Christian Morgenstern to that of his contemporaries. He would go find these German authors every afternoon in the shady reading room of the John D. Library under the campanile. Looking down at his books with his large, rectangular-frame sunglasses on, he let himself bathe in all this opulence. The discovery of an old and rare illustrated edition filled him with overwhelming joy. He would caress the softness of a leather binding and hated cheap paperbacks and re-editions *that never have the same fine character as the originals*. Books were his armour against the sad reality of things. Germany awaited him there, in the cavern of the John D. – silent, immutable. The Germany before Hitler.

At our second meeting, John wishes to erect a framework around our interviews. *The honeymoon is over. What do you want from me?* The question is abrupt. It startles me, but I'm relieved he's asking it. During the last days back in Berlin before my flight I'd been starting to have some doubts. Did I have a right to stir up all these memories in such an old man? How would we contain the painful feelings that would necessarily come with them? John Ron lived secluded in his little studio flat as though he were relieved that his tumultuous life had finally taken on the tranquillity of a large frozen lake. My advertisement came like a powerful chainsaw – a dangerous one, perhaps. For some days, his past had been coming up from the depths. His parents, his aunts and uncles, his neighbours, his childhood friends … So many deaths haunt his sleepless nights. John Ron has returned to our street. He's now living in the 1930s.

It has been raining non-stop since dawn – straight continuous streams of warm water that make long striations against a fairly light-coloured sky. The students run about over the campus, several huddled together under the same umbrella. Tuesday is Ping's day off. We are alone in the room. The rain beats against the windowpanes and the surrounding hillsides. One can no longer see the bay in the distance. John finds the California rain monotonous. He waxes nostalgic about the dramatic Berlin skies when, after a day of intense heat, a sudden brutal thunderstorm might erupt.

He asks me – *Would you in the kindness of your heart …?* – to bring him an extra cushion. He feels it easier to confront the past from a sitting position. He's afraid that coming back to his street he will be forced to open long-locked doors to interior rooms whose contents will annihilate him. Dark and terrifying rooms. The past, he says, has accompanied him throughout his life like the low melody of a bass whose sound, deeper and deeper, amplifies as he gets older and older. When he was young, after the war, he had not realized the extent of the catastrophe. He wanted to live, no matter what. And forget.

He prescribes limits to the walk that I want him to take along our street. Especially the order to not slip and fall. *Your project casts a shadow on the shelter that I built for myself. But at this late hour in my life, I feel a certain obligation to my parents whom I knew so little about really. Your book is in a way the grave that they never got to have at the* Weissensee *cemetery. It's the last chance to preserve their name and their story. I believe they would have liked that.*

Hans-Hugo Rothkugel was born in 1922 in a bedroom that looks out on a back courtyard. The last child. His sister Ilse was born in 1914, his brother Paul in 1915. His mother, Irma Rothkugel, free of her corset, decided to give birth at home and breast-feed the child. When he returns from the courthouse, Dr Leon Rothkugel recites Schiller ballads above the crib. Bubi, as they call him, spends hours admiring the reflections of the red crystal wine glasses lined up on the sideboard in the dining room.

John has in his possession only one photo of the street: Hans-Hugo Rothkugel at age six. He's posing, his torso slightly inclined to one side. He's wearing gloves and a hat with a knitted pom-pom. Behind, one can make out a line of facades. A pavement. A man in a hat with his hands in his coat pockets. My street in 1929. The temperature in Berlin had plummeted to -25 C that day. A Siberian winter.

Hans-Hugo grew up in a street *inhabited by a solid petite bourgeoisie.* He remembers its odours. The smell of the iron in the shop of Filipponi, the master Italian tailor on the ground floor of the building on the corner. The smell of vanilla-flavoured sugar and fresh flour in the waffle shop – a marvellous place. The vapour of the starching machine of Frau Kubeth, the dry cleaner. The bars of soap in the Gebrüder Kohn general store on the corner. *And then on your side of the street there was a bakery and cake shop with adjoining tea room that smelled lovely in the early morning. Simple, nice people ... My mother knew how to speak to every class of people. She was* leutselig – *affable.* Leutselig ... *what a beautiful word.* John paused to admire the charm of this adjective before passing on to consider the monumental rotundity of his Jewish neighbour Frau De Levie at number 4. *What a wonderful resource of the language to designate a derrière! We owe it to Erich Kästner: 'She felt already half-seduced / And joyously shook her rotundity.'* And Frau Mertens! – the very Catholic proprietor of the greengrocer *on the ground floor on the opposite pavement from you, to the left of your balcony.* Frau Martens brought her young child to mass on Sunday morning. He adored her.

So my little Leon, how is it going? The enticing women at the terrace café on the square called out to Leon Rothkugel in their Berlin accents and kissed his shiny bald head with their large red mouths when he came with his wife on those long summer Berlin nights to have a cool beer. Hans-Hugo would not be sleeping. He would wait up in his bed for his parents' return.

When he speaks of his childhood, John slides into German. The porters in his building were for him the incarnation of the *impertinent, bold Berliner gifted with an agile sense of humour.* In the porter's lodge there lived the unmarried couple Frau Schenkel (whose name means 'thigh') and Herr Schultze. Officially Herr Schultze was Frau Schenkel's uncle. Frau Schenkel took poor care of herself. She was as fat as a grilled bratwurst sausage. Bubi

Rothkugel called her Frau Oberschenkel, 'Mrs Thunderthighs'. *He'll go far this boy, Madame Rothkugel!* Herr Schultze would declare to Irma as he ruffled Hans-Hugo's hair.

Once a week, aunt Luzy, the youngest of Leon Rothkugel's sisters, came for lunch. Aunt Luzy Rothkugel had never married. She had a dyed red fringe and lived two streets away. When anyone asked her age, she always replied thirty-nine. And she was persuaded that every man desired her. One evening during a dinner party at the Rothkugel's she paraded about repeating, *To me, married men are like tubes of concentrated milk!* Hans-Hugo meditated for some time on this sentence. Aunt Luzy lived frugally in a furnished flat, but she was proud.

To enter the Rothkugel's building one had to ring at the porter's lodge. Herr Schultze would look out through his little window and then open the door. And each time aunt Luzy passed by the porter's lodge without the least sign or greeting, Herr Schultze would say to Frau Schenkel, *Every day I'm required to open the door to that hussy!* He had learned good manners. It wasn't for nothing that he landed the job as caretaker of a respectable building. Aunt Luzy was deported in January 1942. John reverted to English to say: *It is only at this late stage of my life that I allow myself to make jokes about a woman who was deported straightaway to Auschwitz. She was conceited. That is not a mortal sin.*

Indeed, a mini-rebellion on the part of Herr Schultze, a social-democrat, would confer on our street the grand aura of a resistance heroine. It was at the beginning of the 1930s. Hitler had just come to power. Three young Nazis had passed by and put up a poster in the passageway of the entrance. Herr Schultze placed a large potted plant in front of the poster. This gesture was found funny and gained the approval of all the inhabitants of the building, who included plenty of non-Jews. The same young Nazis eventually passed by again and exclaimed, *Hey, what are you up to here? Why have you blocked the view of the poster?*, to which Herr Schultze replied in his Berlin accent, *You're going to have to get up early in the morning if you think you're going to lecture at me.*

You know very well that you're taking a risk. Move that plant pot immediately!

Is it my plant pot or yours? It's none of your business where I put my plant and I think it's just fine where it is.

Then the twerps went on their way.

These memories form a reliable chain. There is no guesswork. John remembers that the street numbers were fashioned from horseshoes. He remembers the sobriety of his building's facade, which had already *turned its back on the Wilhelminian exuberance. No putti, no atlantes. The balconies were protuberances with no artistic ambition.* I can see the Rothkugels in the flat across from mine. I see the street life along the pavements. The past blends with the present. His street and mine. What a contrast there is when I superimpose them. How dead my street appears today. John is suddenly nervous: *But surely, it was carefully rebuilt in the style of the period, wasn't it? No Soviet-style makeover I hope?*

Hans-Hugo Rothkugel grew up in a family where everything Jewish was stained with an obscure shame like a venereal disease. Leon Rothkugel was an eccentric bourgeois gentleman, the son of Albert Rothkugel, a director at the Bleichröder Bank, the largest private Jewish bank that financed the Franco-Prussian War of Chancellor Bismarck. This grandfather was a stern, thrifty Prussian with no sense of humour whatsoever. A smile never brightened his face. Every Sunday, he obliged his family to go out for a walk, marching in a tight line, as far as Savignyplatz. In foul weather they wore capes. On a public bench the Rothkugels would unshell their hard-boiled eggs.

Leon Rothkugel was completely different from his father. He liked light opera, women, mathematics and chess. *Some hobbies more respectable than others*, the son teases. Leon Rothkugel would spend his evenings trying to find the mathematical law that would prove the periodicity of prime numbers. Irma Rothkugel was horrified by the risqué songs that Leon would teach their son. *I saw Miss Helen take her bath. It was beautiful, O so beautiful.* It is four in the afternoon in Berkeley. In his bed, a very old man is half humming, half singing *I kiss your hand, my lady, and dream that it's your mouth … I'm so gallant, my lady* – and then exclaims, delighted at having rediscovered his Berlin accent – *Ah, ah, and you're the one I'd fall for!*

Leon Rothkugel was hardly conscious of being Jewish. *He even had a slight anti-Semitic side to him*, admits his son. Leon Rothkugel was contemptuous of *Ostjuden*, the poor Jews that came from their Polish and Ukrainian *shtetls* with their obscurantist traditions. When Polish cousins would come on a visit to Berlin, Leon Rothkugel treated them haughtily. Hans-Hugo was thirteen when his father took him to Grenadierstrasse. Light years from the *Bayerisches Viertel* that the Berliners called the 'Jewish Switzerland'. There, he first heard the Yiddish 'jargon' as his father called it. He remembers the smell of boiled cabbage and wet laundry. He remembers the men dressed in black with their wide-brimmed hats, their long ringlets, and their many children. The Rothkugels' street is light years from the cramped medieval streets around Alexanderplatz. Leon Rothkugel was a member of the *Jüdische Reformgemeinde*, an ultra-liberal congregation. Services took place on Sunday not Saturday. The men did not wear hats. They spoke of 'confirmation' not 'Bar Mitzvah', 'temple' not 'synagogue'. The *Reformgemeinde* book of prayers was almost entirely in German. They didn't follow dietary rules and ignored the Jewish holidays. One year, on the day of Yom Kippur, Irma Rothkugel set a pork roast with sauerkraut on the table, and Leon burst out laughing: *Irma, you're pushing it a little here – pork roast on the Day of Atonement?*

It was from the cobbler at number 26, a skeleton with big ears, that Hans-Hugo discovered anti-Semitism. His mother had sent him out to pick up a pair of re-soled shoes that ought to have been ready by then. *If you're not happy*, the insecure cobbler shot out at him, *you can high-tail it to Jerusalem directly!* Hans-Hugo had no idea what he'd done to merit this angry outburst. Ten years later he would emigrate to Jerusalem.

Hitler? When she had her friends over for tea, Irma Rothkugel would crow haughtily, *What, this Bohemian wants to teach me my place and what a German is? Why, he can't even speak our language properly!* Irma and Leon Rothkugel were not aware of the danger. *My parents felt so German. They never would have thought such a thing possible. My father had fought at the front during the First World War. A grenade had blown off the end of his right middle finger while he was holding it in the air above a trench to see which way the wind was blowing.*

Life in the flat across from mine was blown to bits in 1934. John calls it 'the crumbling'. It began one year after Hitler gained power, as though a catastrophe in world history had triggered another more private one. Leon and Irma Rothkugel get divorced. Leon Rothkugel has deep money problems. He's mired in a particularly difficult trial. Divorce is the only way to save what remains of Irma's dowry. Hans-Hugo loses the home of his carefree childhood. He moves with his mother into a smaller flat in Charlottenburg. Like all Jewish lawyers, Dr Leon Rothkugel was no longer allowed to practise his profession. Without an income, he limps along miserably. In 1936, he flees to Prague. Hans-Hugo would never see him again.

In 1934, Hans-Hugo Rothkugel no longer had the right to attend the Hohenzollern high school. His mother sent him to a boarding school for Jewish children, the *Landschulheim Herrlingen*, near Ulm. The school was run by the Zionist Hugo Rosenthal. Its mission was to give a Jewish education to children from assimilated families. Hans-Hugo was the only scholarship student at the school and also one of the brightest. He learns Hebrew and Jewish history and traditions. He reads ancient texts, becomes vegetarian and kosher, and sneaks off in the afternoon to eat cured pork sausage in the village. He learns to work the land and plays all kinds of sports – *like in the Hitler Youth. We were woken up at 6:25. You had to put on your coat and go run in the forest and after five kilometres we had to do gymnastics.* He did his Bar Mitzvah in 1935. His mother and his sister Ilse travelled from Berlin for that big day. *I was Jewishified in Herrlingen,* he says. *In that isolated place in the middle of nowhere the teachers could mould us like clay. I had to really work at it to adapt to that lifestyle. I wanted to go back home. But after four years, I was sorted out for good! I was well-prepared to emigrate to Palestine. Herrlingen may have saved my life.*

During the war the Jewish boarding school was closed down and *Haus Breitenfels* was turned over to Marshal Erwin Rommel. Today it houses a museum dedicated to the memory of 'the desert fox'. *A curious accident,* quips John. *To think that a great German marshal lived in a Jewish house! Even if the pest extermination services had to go through and spray and clean a bit before he arrived!*

After *Herrlingen*, Hans-Hugo returned to his mother's place in Berlin. He had only one idea by then: emigrating. Irma Rothkugel wanted to go to Australia. She was convinced, with her usual optimism, that she would make it despite having no money and no contacts in the country. *It was pure madness! You didn't need to be overly pessimistic to see that by the summer of 1938, shortly before Kristallnacht, there was no way things were not going to get worse. My mother was an example of that extraordinary level of blindness.* Ilse worked for the *Reichsvertretung der Deutschen Juden*, the Reich government council that represented the Jews via its director, the Rabbi Leo Baeck. She witnessed the bullying the Jews had to undergo. She had only one idea in her head: leave. Leave, no matter what. She emigrated to Palestine in early September 1938.

Hans-Hugo received a letter whose contents he still remembers by heart. The director of the music conservatory in Jerusalem, Emil Hauser, an internationally known violinist, was inviting him to audition. Hans-Hugo practised day and night. Mozart and Bach would save his life. Emil Hauser offered him a stipend of 4,000 reichsmarks to cover his tuition and living expenses for two years. It was aunt Luzy who took charge of the matter. She invited uncle Erich, the only one in the family who still had a little money, over for tea: *Erich, you will curse yourself for the rest of your life if you refuse to help the little fellow!* Uncle Erich did not hold out against *the repeated assaults of aunt Luzy*.

Irma Rothkugel did not accompany her son to the *Anhalter* station. John hurries to describe in a neutral, indifferent voice the goodbye scene. *Don't imagine there were tears and hugs. I was so tense. If I had let out the least sign of emotion, it would have weakened me and kept me from leaving. When I clacked shut the door to the flat, I was relieved – like someone who's escaping from a fire. I knew I was never going to see it again.*

Hans-Hugo Rothkugel was almost sixteen when he boarded the train in Berlin for Venice, where he would then go aboard a ship of the Lloyd Triestino line. He got out of Germany just in the nick of time. It was the last week of September 1938. John no longer remembers anything about the journey. For the first time his impressive memory comes up empty. He has only fleeting recollections of the ship *Galileo* that took him across the Mediterranean – one being the loudspeaker that blurted out at regular intervals, *Peace in our time!* Daladier, Chamberlain and Mussolini were then meeting with Hitler to sign *the Munich catastrophe*, as John calls the pact of 30 September 1938 that, far from assuring peace, would tip Europe into war. When he disembarked in the port of Haïfa, he was met by a distant cousin of his mother and was put up for a few days in the Mount Carmel area. He slept in a bathtub cushioned with blankets.

Six weeks later, on 9 November 1938, Jewish shops were vandalized and synagogues burned. Leon Rothkugel was living day to day in Prague selling office supplies. He was doing everything he could *to obtain an entry visa for any country*. In a last letter to Ilse in Palestine dated 13 December 1938, he describes with icy lucidity the *terrible details* he has heard: *in Komotau* [present-day Chomutov in the Czech Republic], *young people were forced with kickings and beatings to crawl on their knees to the border zone. In Saaz* [today Zatec], *an eighty-year-old lawyer was forced to go through an animal pen on his hands and knees with a rope tied to his leg and a sign that read 'Dirty Jew' around his neck.* Leon Rothkugel was caught in *a rat trap*: *So this is the situation. The Prague government is still democratic, but Slovakia has already turned very fascistic. We're very dependent here on the powerful neighbour and end up having to do what* – here, Leon Rothkugel draws a head: hair combed across the forehead, little moustache, big ears; he refuses to write the name, Hitler, of the one who is hounding them – *orders. In these conditions, all immigrants must leave Prague. This provokes a huge panic. One of the difficulties is that the whole world sympathizes with the poor Jews who are expelled from their countries, but no one wants to take them in. This is why I have to take my fate into my own hands, because I don't want to wait until it's too late. It reminds me of the saying, 'No one knows the hour of his death.'*

Ilse was one of the founders of the Hazorea Kibbutz in the Jordan Valley. She lived in a tent, ate spare meals in a wooden refectory, and turned and sowed, hoed and watered the fertile soil. These young idealistic German intellectuals worked bare-handed to remove stones and plant a forest on the slopes of Mount Carmel which bears a strange resemblance to the Black Forest. In the evening, the young people would sing around a camp fire. Ilse, tanned by the sun, a scarf in her hair, is committed 100 per cent to her new life. Still, her German culture sticks to her skin. *My whole mental makeup is shaped by German culture,* she confides to her brother. Hans-Hugo quickly understood that he was not made for that sort of life. For him the Zionist ideal is not an alternative to German identity. He didn't at all feel comfortable among the muscly pioneers who felt so invested in their single-minded vision of constructing a new country. He was too near-sighted and not physically strong enough for long hours of manual labour. Being rather clumsy, he hardly saw himself driving a tractor or milking a cow. Besides, he would not have been able to put up with *the military ethos mixed with a sort of primitive summer-camp atmosphere that dominated kibbutz living at that time.*

Hans-Hugo preferred living in Jerusalem. At least there he didn't feel quite so out of it. He lived within an exclusively German and Austrian enclave. There were the professors at the conservatory; the music scores salesman; Herr Popper, the owner of the bookstore where he worked who was from Hamburg, and his assistant Jakob; the Berlin doctor who sublet him a room; the minister Heinz Kappes from Stuttgart who laboured for peace between Jews and Arabs – *the most saintly man I've ever met. He gave private lessons on the Bhagavad-Gita and Meister Eckhart;* the tailor who made him curtains to measure; the owner of the Viennese pastry shop where the German immigrants would gather under the chandelier for a coffee and a slice of Sachertorte, a chocolate cake with apricot, a specialty of Vienna. *Jerusalem was a mix of a very old Ottoman style and the spanking new – from the Middle Ages to Bauhaus. I lived in a street that was more modern than our Berlin street. And as soon as you went through the Jaffa Gate, you entered the souk with its narrow streets covered with canvas awnings that completely shut out the sun. It was another world of exotic people, Kurds, porters and legless cripples.*

A few weeks later, his brother Paul arrived in Jerusalem with his little suitcase and his love of life and pretty girls, but with no high school diploma, no job and no money. *Paul was more extroverted than me and better looking.* Paul became, *for lack of anything better*, a local reporter on the newspaper *La Bourse Egyptienne*, and fell in love with a young pianist named Miriam. The two brothers shared a small Arab-style house in a Jerusalem suburb near a ravine or wadi that looked out to the hills of Judea. It had an austere beauty. No other habitations around. *I was very comfortably settled. There was a piano in one room, a sturdy desk, ceramic tiled floors, and a fine rug at the foot of my bed. The bathroom was primitive with no running water. In winter rain was collected in a reservoir. In 1940 we threw a little party to celebrate my eighteenth birthday. We decorated the small garden. We invited my boss. There were about ten of us under the stars.*

If it weren't for this packet of letters that John entrusted to me and that I pored through in the evening back at my hotel room in Berkeley, I would have forgotten that the young care-free adventurer John appeared to be had in fact been ripped from his family, his country and his language. In a letter dated 16 February 1941, Hans-Hugo confides in his sister: *I have no possibility of opening up to anyone about my situation and how I'm feeling. Meanwhile I'm already used to that void and know that I have to work it out alone inside myself. I also know I've already very much closed in on myself – more in fact than I would have ever wished. I can't count on Paul even though he's a nice person and has often been kind. There's no way he can be an example for me, in fact it should be more the other way around. You know, I really think what I'm missing is a father or guide. Before, such a situation appeared so attractive to me – to exercise total freedom and organise my life as I pleased, but to do that one should not be as young as I am.*

After the three children left, Irma Rothkugel went to live with her brother Rudolf Cohn and his wife in Vionvillestrasse in Berlin-Steglitz. It was a Bauhaus building, very modern for the time, on the edge of the park. Hans-Hugo and his cousin Lola had spent hours playing there. Irma Rothkugel got letters to her children through the Red Cross. She would sign, *Voll Sehnsuchtsliebe, Mutter* ('Full of yearning love, Mother'). The let-ters were limited to twenty-five words. Irma Rothkugel cheated by using 'sausage words' – compound words that packed many into one. *German is a very elastic language. French does not allow itself to be manipulated that way!*, John says approvingly. In early 1940, John received a photo of his mother on a boat excursion on the Havel. He was happy to see that this little summer pleasure was not denied her. In July 1941, Irma Rothkugel, her brother and sister-in-law were confined with other Jews to a flat in Knesebeckstrasse.

The only consolation for Irma Rothkugel was that her three children were safe and sound in Palestine. After their departure, to pass the time, and to cope with her sadness and fear, she began to write *short unpretentious poems*. John has kept them in an envelope on his bedside table at Berkeley.

Sometimes it seems unreal to me
The happiness of having saved from this mortal hate
The children, all three, now in safety
Far from this maddening bloody fate!

They are spared hunger's cold bite
They are not scraping by in fear and fright
Their faces are not those of hunted beasts
They can make meaning out of their days at least.

They can work with joy and song
Dream filled nights not anxiously long
Take pleasure in nature feeling fully free
And only note what they achieve and see.

Ah, this thought is without a price
Though I offer my life as sacrifice
But my fate does not matter! The children are saved!
Lord, I know not how to thank you.

John regrets having underestimated his mother. *It's better than the compositions of your weekend poet, don't you think? I feel guilty about not having seen in her anything but a housekeeper and mother who played the piano and took up little philanthropic causes – she who was so unprepared for all this horrible business. It was in a situation of extreme distress that she discovered the true extent of her mental faculties. She did not commit suicide like a lot of Jews. I feel a bit guilty for not having thought more about my parents at that time. It was the egotism of youth and the relief at having narrowly escaped the Nazis. So many things happened in my life. So long as the letters from my mother were being delivered by the Red Cross, my worry was not excessive.*

1942, the year he joined the meteorology service of the Royal Air Force, was the absolutely worst year in John's life. I sensed that John was approaching one of the inner chambers. In the spring of that year, Paul drowned accidentally. John spoke in a terse manner about this new tragedy. He did not describe the circumstances of the accident, the funeral, or his grief. Hans and Ilse decided not to tell their mother. *Here's what I think,* writes Hans to Ilse. *We have to find a plausible explanation that does not upset mother too much. I thought, for example, of saying, 'Paul travelling outside the country', or, if the censors authorise it, 'He enlisted in the army, unable to receive letters through the Red Cross. He's well and sends his love.' If you have a better idea, write to me fast, I beg you. The more time goes by, the more it's likely to raise mother's suspicions.*

Irma Rothkugel would outlive Paul by only a couple of months. She was deported on 14 December 1942. A few days before her departure, she wrote three words of farewell to her children: *I leave today.* She died five or six days after her arrival in Riga, just before Christmas. On 4 March 1943, uncle Rudolf and his wife said their goodbyes to their daughter Frieda-Lore

Noemi, John's beloved cousin who also lived on a kibbutz. They were deported to Auschwitz. *My Dear Lola! I thank you with all my heart for the letter of May from the Red Cross! We are following Irma today. Do not worry, even if you do not receive letters from us for a long time. You have always been our darling. May God watch over you! We place all trust in God that this is only an Auf Wiedersehen – Papa and Mama.*

To prove to you how much I hesitated to approach the past … John tells me that he got up in the middle of the night to open the envelope that Yad Vashem sent him four years ago and that he had never dared to touch. He didn't have the courage. The envelope contains the deportation dates of the members of his family. *I knew the year my mother was deported. But not my father. I learned yesterday that he survived for a little more than three years after the Nazis arrived in Prague in March 1939. He died on 9 May 1942 in Lodz. Eight days after my brother drowned. My mother was shot in Riga at the end of the same year, 1942.*

John pauses. *As I tell you all this, the pain is coming back. 'Pain is faithful', Colette used to say. My body reacts strongly. The shock of Paul's accidental death upset me much more than the death of my parents. The drowning of my brother was not part of the collective destiny. How to live on without him? At the end of 1942 I felt like I really had very little strength left.*

John put little crosses next to the names of his aunts and uncles on Yad Vashem's list. He tallies up the numbers: *Each of my parents had three siblings. On my father's side the four Rothkugels, Luzy, Otto, Karl and Leon, were all assassinated by the Nazis. A clean sweep. On my mother's side, only uncle Erich, the one who saved my life, managed to escape to Ecuador at the last minute. Aunt Edith, the most modern of them all, had undergone an Adlerian psychoanalysis and complained of her 'Miko', the abbreviation of 'Minderwertigkeitskomplex', an inferiority complex that was very fashionable at the time – she died of cancer in February 1933 at the moment Hitler came to power. My mother and uncle Rudolf were deported. That makes 75 per cent of my family assassinated by the Nazis.*

On 25 August 1946, Hans-Hugo wrote this letter to his sister Ilse: *It will surely take us years to understand (and perhaps we will never even be able to) the mad fate that was reserved for our people. A deep sadness has taken hold of me. All the unspoken challenges and losses that cast their shadows over my childhood and my youth culminate with mother's death. If earlier I tended to revolt against constant troubles, today I kneel before the tragedy of our situation, ours personally and that of all Jews. We are by all accounts the remainder, those that luck (or fate?) spared. But aren't our reserves already half spent, can we still experience the new era that's coming and contribute toward shaping it? May good old Hope in its pretty shade of green, so maligned and yet the sister of Faith, continue to accompany us all along our journey! I ask you to pardon me these effusions, but I had to speak to someone!*

What remains of the Rothkugel family? A few photos scattered in a desk drawer in Berkeley, California. Not even a photo album where the uncles and grandparents could meet up again protected by the stiff sturdy pages. There is uncle Rudolf, his wife Grete and cousin Lola hugging each other on the balcony at Vionvillestrasse a few days before Lola's emigration. The wholesale merchant Benno Cohn with his wife walking in Bad Kissingen in 1921 *at a time when a large part of his fortune had already gone up in smoke.* Grandma Anna, a Victorian beauty around 1880 before her wedding. Leon as a young man in his soldier's uniform, his right hand bandaged after his return from the front. He looks like a character out of Proust. *Women were quite attracted to him. Not wildly, but quite attracted.* Irma is seated on the arm of the chair next to her husband who has his arm around her waist. Paul in Hazorea, *third from the right in a heavy jumper.*

There is also a picture of Jochanan Ron, the 'eligible bachelor' in 1950 when he's working as the meteorologist-forecaster at the Lydda airport near Tel Aviv. This serious young man with glasses and greased down hair was dreaming of only one thing: *to discover Paris before it is destroyed by a third world war.* He obtained a scholarship to study meteorology at the Sorbonne for one year. *I was a bit of a reveller. To satisfy my appetite for life, Israel was not the right place. I wanted to dance all around the fatted calf!* Flight was perhaps the only way to escape the storm rumbling inside him, he said.

Jochanan Ron lived at the Style Hotel in rue Claude Bernard that was run by a certain Monsieur and Madame Petit. He had a tiny room with tepid running water and a marvellous bidet that he took for a spittoon. He learnt to eat oysters with Doktor Zacharias, a Berlin family doctor who had emigrated to France, and discovered high luxury at the 'Marquise de Sévigné' *chocolaterie* on Boulevard de la Madeleine. Germany in the 1950s was still a time of great austerity, *but in Paris you could eat to your heart's content.* In a letter to Ilse he shares his first impressions: *It is difficult to describe this feeling of velvety enthusiasm that accompanies like a bass note all of my impressions. It's on purpose that I say 'velvety' because just as with that which characterizes the light, the people and the houses in Europe, the thinking and the sensations too harmonise gradually around a distinctive tonal mode: a grey saturated in old culture, a grey that has nothing sad about it though, which is on the contrary particularly accomplished and rich in nuances, which now pulls at you with a murmur, and now calls to you from old walls in a twisted little medieval street, before again fully showing its splendid self in grandiose general views charged with a truly dramatic expressivity.*

Of this Paris year there remains his *Petit Larousse* dictionary on his bedside table, Malherbe, *Where would we be without Malherbe today!*, Verlaine, whom he recites at full volume, taking pleasure in weighing the words and experimenting with new phrasings and inventing others. Totally worked up, he sits up in bed: *It's magnificent, don't you think? Do you hear it? Do you hear the melody of the words?* He's especially joyful when he jumps from one language to another – from German to French to English to Hebrew. John says that like a bee he *takes the pollen from each language. I like German for all of its mental restrictions. And yet there are some things I can only say in German. It's a language that touches me, I can't deny it. German is a part of my being. That is the great tragedy between my mother language and me.* John does not like Goethe – *Their idol! I don't know if you've ever tried to read* Wilhelm Meister. *It's awful! So stilted! So unnatural! If I had the chance to bring to hell either the poems of Goethe or Morgenstern's 'Songs from the Gallows', I wouldn't hesitate for a second. I'm dying to recite for you one of Heine's poems. No other poet would have dared write 'My sweet, my fat infant …' Are you like me? Do you feel the indescribable charm of it? Before I fade, I cannot resist the pleasure of reciting to you from memory a little delicious piece from the first chapter of the* 'Berliner Bälle' *of Rideamus, who describes how happy everyone was in Berlin under the Kaiser*:

Anne-Marie, the oldest daughter
Is still today quite a dish
She has the carriage of an American white pine
And the most classic waist
Alas her virtue is much less certain
But only God knows where these rumours come from.

I was a child who lived on words. My father recited to me everything that was in the air then. It was a rather idiotic time, a little unhappy, and especially very carefree. There were not a lot of ways to have fun. Words occupied a greater place than they do now. Now that we have email, do rhymes still blossom? Would you like another John Ron concoction? And not waiting for an answer, he bursts out with more lines:

> You were pretty
> Now you are sad
> Don't you ever see yourself this way,
> Lover of Letters?

A minor work, I grant you. But I am so enchanted to read something that has nothing to do with the large problems of life and death.

At the end of his Paris year in 1951, John decides not to go back to Israel. He has an aunt in the Notting Hill area of London. In order to avoid appearing like the proverbial country bumpkin, he orders himself a custom-made suit in olive green 'chez Medelon', a men's store in the XVth arrondissement. He settles in London. John has quite the collection of passports. German at birth, Palestinian in 1938, Israeli, then British. *Today I am technically English with an American green card. But German? How could I be? I was stripped of my German nationality. I never thought of getting it back. In fact, I have misplaced my German passport, that historic document!*

Because he could no longer put up with *London's yellow fog and the crazy English love of draughts and unheated flats*, John left for Bermuda. Then, because he got fed up with *fancy cocktails, water skiing, cockroaches and overly eager New York divorcees*, he immigrated to the United States – the land of liberty, wide open spaces, and the best plumbing in the world. He was thirty-nine. He taught English, German and French at various high schools. In 1972 he was living in Denver and made a last attempt to return to live in Israel. He managed four months. *At that time Israel was totally euphoric. I saw military parades on Independence Day that marched right through the Arab neighbourhoods without the least concern for the sensitive feelings that were right on the surface. What arrogance. I saw that the ultra-orthodox minority, the 'men in black', were acquiring more and more power. Sure, the country was flourishing economically. It was surfing on the euphoric victory after what had been a short, decisive war. But I didn't like that bragging nationalism.* John returned to the United States.

The smell of barbecue wafts up from below. We can hear salsa music, laughter and bursts of conversation. Middle-class white America is celebrating. It's the Fourth of July. Independence Day. I've come to say goodbye to John. He tries to recall the last words of our conversation. *As I age, I understand my father better. The money and the career were not that important to him. Like him, I was an adventurer. At this final stage of my life, I realize that I don't feel at all like I have a Jewish identity. It's more a solidarity with a certain fate. It has nothing to do with religion. The only things that have remained are the Hebrew songs I learned at* Herrlingen. *But between a song and a vision of the world there's a great chasm.*

Down in the street, John's bare-chested neighbours in Bermuda shorts and baseball caps are sitting in beach chairs and eating candy floss. American flags are hanging in front of wooden houses with little gardens planted with roses. Cars are parked in the garages. In the distance, a light warm mist covers San Francisco bay. Upstairs, Ping prepares Mister Ron's tea with milk. They are the only ones who will not go see the fireworks that evening.

7

Hannah's Dress

For Susanne Wachsner

God knows how many clothes Hannah took to the Goodwill charity shop. She got rid of so many tight-fitting dresses and blouses in young colours that clashed with her advanced age, she thought to herself as she looked in the mirror one morning. All but one evening dress that she took out with great care from its protective brown paper – that dress was one she had never had the heart to give up. Even when, some years back, she had gone through her whole flat sorting stuff, throwing out sacks of old things, donating entire boxes of clothes, because she knew full well that there would be no room for a whole life's worth of possessions in the little studio flat of the Bristal, the assisted living retirement home in the North Hills suburb of New York that she was moving to. It was a long dress in black Chinese crêpe, whose size testified to the narrow waist she had had at age nineteen when she was chaperoned by her father and mother, wearing it for the first time at a dance on the *S.S. Rotterdam*, the packet ship that took the Kroner family to New York in 1939.

I had arrived from Berlin the day before. We arranged to meet – me, Hannah Kroner-Segal, then nearly ninety-two years old, and her daughter Evelyn – on the platform of the Mineola station on Long Island. The train had travelled through suburbs of the kind one sees in American movies – wide, deserted streets, rectangles of grass as green as Granny Smith apples, cars parked in driveways next to houses with light-coloured wooden porches. This same arrangement repeated itself at regular intervals mile after mile after mile. Now and then there was a golf course or a shopping mall to break up the rhythm of these residential suburbs. There were lots of temples and churches with all manner of imaginative names. Banners draped on their facades praised the Lord, never exactly the same one it seemed, in a way not unlike the exaggerated slogans one sees at car dealerships promoting a particularly wonderful brand of automobile. It was a hot sunny day – easily 30 degrees Celsius (90 degrees Fahrenheit). New Yorkers were at the beach or in parks in the shade. The little railway station at Mineola was deserted.

Hannah and Evelyn were looking intently at all the passengers getting off the train. They recognized me at once. *You see, the girls from Berlin find their way to the end of the world!* Evelyn jokes to her mother. The mother and her daughter have always spoken English to each other. They both waved their hands enthusiastically at me. Hannah was standing solidly in her sandals, back straight, her head held like a dancer. She wore make-up, bright red lipstick, her auburn hair was done up perfectly – she absolutely did not look her age. *One has to cooperate when nature has given one advantages. Dance kept me in shape,* she tells me when I compliment her. *To think that at ninety-two I can still manage to extend my leg!* she adds as we exchange kisses.

We then all got into Evelyn's car. Hannah still drives to go to shows or to do her grocery shopping. She says she'd be lost if she couldn't drive. The Bristal is an island cut off from everything, nestled amid a tangle of three-lane highways. *The Bristal is located in the middle of Long Island's Gold Coast. You're only a stone's throw from the main roads that are the New Hyde Park Road, Shelter Rock Road, the Northern State Parkway and the Long Island Expressway*, so says the prospectus for this residence that wants its elderly renters to believe they only need move in to be catapulted into the hustle and bustle of real living. Hannah's studio is situated at the end of a long corridor covered in a thick carpet that muffles the click of canes. The rents go down as one moves further away from the lift. Hannah walks lightly, almost dancing between the wheelchairs and walking frames, greeting people on her left and right. *When I arrived here, almost everyone was still walking on their own*, she says in German so that her neighbours don't understand. She certainly doesn't want to hurt their feelings. She finds them a bit depressing, all these old folks under her windows lined up in their lounge chairs at the edge of the pool in summer. Wading in warmish water and spending hours roasting in the sun hold little attraction for her. Hannah taught dance until last summer. Even now, once a week, she still gives dance classes at the Bristal. *We encourage those who can still move to do so. The shoulders, the hands, the fingers, the waist, the head. It's never too late to dance.* And then Hannah bends at the waist, without bending her knees, her back straight and without effort she picks up the bunch of keys that had just fallen from her hands.

In her studio flat, around the little table where we struggle with over-sized turkey sandwiches, time, all this past time, suddenly comes to a head. *The older I get*, says Hannah, *the more the past comes back to the surface with surprising clarity*. And the past is Susanne. Susanne Wachsner, Hannah's childhood friend. In fact, it was their mothers who decided everything. On the first day of school, Frau Kroner and Frau Wachsner greeted each other in the primary school's courtyard. The two women conferred for a long time, weighing the pros and cons – a bright-eyed child, well-brought up, white socks and nicely shined shoes, same social class and Jewish to boot – in other words, all the factors that mothers in the bourgeois families of my street were careful to sift through in evaluating the social circle of their daughters. Then, as a concluding formality more than as a real question, Hannah's mother asked Susanne's mother, *So would you like our daughters to be friends?*

Susanne lived at number 9 in my street, right at the corner of the square where today the 'park' starts next to the supermarket. The building was destroyed by bombs and was not replaced. It was a sombre, cheerless building to which Hannah was often invited for lunch, but where she never felt entirely comfortable. One day, taking advantage of the momentary absence of Susanne's father who had left the room to answer the telephone, she even scraped the spinach off her plate into the basin of a potted plant. Being partial to a Prussian upbringing, Fritz Wachsner would never have stood for a child not finishing what had been served. When Susanne's mother died, this cold, severe man, a top executive in the Berlin offices of Staedtler, the famous maker of drafting and drawing tools, hired a governess to take care of his two children, Bruno and Susanne. When, one by one, the father and governess died, and Bruno left for England no longer to be heard from, Susanne found herself alone and orphaned in the big empty flat at number 9.

She was fourteen years old at the time. Hannah's parents, who didn't live far away, just across from the imposing facade of the courthouse, decided to take her in. They had room. The maid's quarters at the end of the hall were free. When Jews no longer had the right to employ female Aryans under forty-five as domestic servants – as though every father in an upstanding Jewish household was by definition covertly licentious and intent on raping them – Hannah's parents had to let their dear Maria go. Hannah, a timid only child, could only benefit from the presence of this adopted sister. She was delighted that this newcomer would divert somewhat the excessive attentions of her mother. Elsa Kroner never let her daughter out of her sight. She would lean out the window when her daughter left for school, and when she came back in the afternoon she would keep watch for the first sign of her return. Her mother was always there, and it seemed as though for the entire day she never left her observation deck above the street.

Susanne became part of the family. One year, on Christmas Eve, she witnessed a curious scene: Hannah's grandfather barrelled in with the lid of a box of cigars under his arm. He planted himself in front of the six-foot-tall Christmas tree that was standing triumphantly in the middle of the dining room, heavily laden with balls and tinsel. Small gingerbreads were suspended higher up so that the dog couldn't reach them. It was a marvellous sight. But the grandfather intends to teach his granddaughter a little something about Judaism. He refuses to have all traditions thrown into the big melting pot of assimilation. *Your mother*, he says to his granddaughter, *has put up this big Christmas tree and you don't even know that you're Jewish. Come here, I'm going to show you what you have to do as a Jewish child.* Then, Hannah told me, *he took the wooden lid of the cigar box, took nine candles from his pocket and placed eight of them on the lid. But what's he doing there lighting candles at the wrong end? He takes the ninth candle and starts singing* Ma'oz Tsour Ye-chou-a-ti *in a terrible voice.* Chou *what? I didn't understand any of it. Then the grandfather said, 'You mustn't blow them out, you have to let them burn to the end.' I thought he was going to end up burning the house down. Then, he removed his hat and said with deep satisfaction, 'There, now you know you are Jewish.' So there I am between the cigar box lid with the lit candles planted on it and the booming voice of my grandpa. But I was well brought up so I said nothing. Hanukkah lasts eight days. It's better than the two days of Christmas. But inside I was saying to myself, 'I'm also keeping the two days of Christmas, thank you very much!'*

That's why, many years later when Evelyn got engaged just after Christmas to a young man from a very conservative Jewish family, Hannah had a feeling of déjà vu. When the future in-laws came over to get acquainted and have an aperitif, Hannah rushed to hide the Christmas tree behind a desk and threw a blanket over it. *After our daughter got married, my husband and I asked ourselves, 'What are we going to do now?' And so we decided to celebrate Christmas just the two of us in Atlantic City with no kids and no tree. It was a little absurd! For fifteen years we managed to avoid an encounter between Evelyn's father and father-in-law. But at the Bar Mitzvah of Evelyn's son Ray the two men found themselves seated next to one another. And the first thing my husband said to my daughter's father-in-law was, 'You know what? We have a Christmas tree!' Ever since, at Evelyn's we celebrate both Christmas and Hanukkah.*

Soon afterwards, Hannah and Susanne, as Jews, were not allowed to attend the local high school on the square. They were strongly advised to learn a trade, a practical one from which they could earn a living after they had emigrated to America. Hannah chose to train as a dancer with the Swiss choreographer Max Terpis, the former ballet director at the

Berlin State Opera, who attempted a synthesis between classical ballet and expressionist dance. He resigned in 1930, opened his own dance school near the Lietzensee, and agreed to accept Jewish pupils. Susanne took sewing lessons. *In my family, there were only two imaginable career paths*, jokes Hannah. *You either studied law or medicine. So you can imagine the reaction we got for choosing dance and sewing!*

When Hannah and her mother wanted to go for their usual afternoon tea at the Silberterrasse on the fifth floor of KaDeWe, there was a sign above the staircase blocking their way that said *Dogs and Jews Prohibited.* (I interrupted Hannah, 'The two put together like that?' I asked. 'Are you sure?' *'Very sure!!'* she said.) They turned around. Then Elsa Kroner went directly to the women's department and bought her daughter a very expensive tailored suit: *We're allowing ourselves one last indulgence!* she blurted out to the confused saleswoman. The same neighbours on their floor who, when Hannah was little, would offer them a chocolate Saint Nicholas placed discreetly on their doormat on the 6th of December, now belted out *Heil Hitler!* She'd see the husband in his uniform, the wife in her long blond plaits – the blond plaits that Hannah and Susanne dreamed of having. They used to make their own plaits with pieces of wool and thread and tie them behind their ears. They called that 'playing the little German girl'.

The situation then became unbearable. The Kroners decided to emigrate, and to take Susanne with them of course. A cousin who had moved to New York before the war sent an affidavit. Without this notarized promise of aid, no permission to emigrate to the United States could be granted. The next step was to get the papers from the American consulate. A long queue had formed in front of the consular offices. Hannah and her parents joined the line. Susanne was informed. She arrived fifteen min-utes later all out of breath. Ten people were waiting their turn in front of Susanne. An attendant cuts the group in two and tells the last five in line to go back home. Susanne would have to come back the next day. Elsa Kroner was nearly turned away also. When the American attendant discovers that she's suffer-ing from hypertension, he scrunches his eyebrows. Frau Kroner doesn't let herself be intimidated. *Sir, if you were a Jew in Nazi Germany, you'd have hypertension too!* The attendant finally stamps her passport.

That evening around the dining room table, it is decided that the Kroners will go first as scouts, and that Susanne will join them a few weeks later. The departure date is set: 15 November 1939, Eugene Kroner's sixty-fifth birthday. A few days before the departure, Hannah comes down with appendicitis. Uncle Karl, Elsa Kroner's brother, is a doctor. In a military hospital during the First World War, he had treated a young soldier named Adolf Hitler. *Whatever you do, don't operate!* orders uncle Karl. *They will never let her leave with a fresh suture!* So Hannah spent her last days in Berlin lying in bed with a tea towel filled with ice resting on her stomach. To pay for the crossing, the Kroners sell their furniture at a ridiculously low price. A line of curious buyers forms in the stairwell. A grand piano is sold for almost nothing. *Who cares about a grand piano so long as we save our skins!* cries Eugene Kroner through gritted teeth. He buys three one-way second-class tickets on the *S.S. Rotterdam* and makes a grim joke about the two initials of the ship that will transport him and his family to freedom.

A packet ship to cross the Atlantic! The captain's ball, a string of lights on the upper deck, dizzying turns around the dance floor in the arms of young men in tuxedos ... Hannah and Susanne imagined the transatlantic crossing like something out of a romantic novel. They well knew that such adolescent reveries were a grotesque joke. This trip was no luxury cruise, but a last ditch effort to get out alive. The war had been officially on for two and a half months. Hitler had declared that it would require the extermination of the 'Jewish race' from Europe. Hannah and Susanne nevertheless allowed themselves the right to dream in the evening, snuggled up against each other on the sofa in the living room. So that Hannah will look splendid on the dance floor, Susanne spends her evenings sewing an evening gown. She cuts the fabric, adds a salmon-coloured lining of cotton, adjusts the shoulder straps, and rounds out the décolleté just so. The whirring of the sewing machine can be heard at night in the maid's quarters of the Kroner flat. On the third morning, Susanne opens wide the door of her bedroom. The dress is laid out on the bed. *For when you're on board the ship to America!*

It was a beautiful dress! I wore it once on the ship. Later I wore it when I went out with my husband. Then when I got pregnant, it didn't fit any more. So Hannah put the dress and her memory of Susanne away in the back of an armoire. She had to try and forget if she was going to move forward in this new life. Only many years later did she dare take Susanne's dress back out and give it to her daughter, who, in turn, gave it to her American daughter-in-law Courtney. Since the year her husband died, Courtney has had a hard time feeling light-hearted and the dress has returned to the back of Hannah's armoire at the Bristal. While we were speaking of Susanne, Hannah stares at me and says, *Life is strange ... As though someone up there were deciding in our place*, she adds looking up at the ceiling. *There's only one person who can wear that dress and it's you. I would be so happy if you'd take it, if you brought it back there where it belongs in Susanne's street. Maybe you'll have a chance to wear it once and revive the memory that it holds? Please, have it.*

The dress has outlived the dressmaker, said Hannah when I emerged from the bathroom wearing the dress Susanne had made. I feel a little uneasy in this evening gown that's seventy-three years old. Hannah arranges the shoulder straps, and passes her hand over my waist to unwrinkle the fabric. It needs to be ironed and perhaps taken up a bit, otherwise it fits perfectly. I am there, standing before Hannah, arms dangling, back slumped forward, feeling embarrassed. *No, no, no!* Hannah exclaims. *It looks terrible like that!* Then she shows me how to straighten my back, place one foot a few inches in front of the other, hold my waist, and put my hand on my hip with a proud look in my eye as though I were a flamenco dancer. *This is how to wear an evening gown!* Hannah looks me over. Tears come into her eyes – the tears of an old lady that barely wet her hazel eyes. *An evening gown made with a lot of love in the fateful year 1939. And if there's a heaven where Susanne is now, well I'm sure she'd be very happy today to see that!* She brings her face very close to mine. She's speaking German now. Slowly and very distinctly, as though she could only express this moment in her own mother tongue. *And what I'm about to tell you now, never, as long as I live, will I forget it. I will never forget the last time I saw Susanne. Susanne and my childhood nurse insisted on accompanying us all the way to our boat in Rotterdam. We made the journey together by train, up to the Dutch border. There, my parents and I entered an immense hall. First we were subjected to a thorough search. We were required to totally undress. Some women had hidden diamonds in their vagina. My mother had refused to humiliate herself in that way. 'It's life that counts, not diamonds!' And when we left the hall, as we were moving away to cross the border, Susanne began to scream 'Mother! Mother!' very loud. So loud. I can still hear that scream. My mother tried to pull away and push her way through the crowd of passengers to re-join Susanne, but my father held her by the sleeve, 'If you go back, Elsa, you will be sent back to Germany and they'll never let you out again! We don't want to leave without you!' Then my mother returned to her place in the line. A few minutes later, the doors opened and we were in Dutch territory. The last image I have of Susanne is of her crying and being held like a small child in the arms of my nurse.* Eugene Kroner tried to comfort his wife and daughter. *It's just going to be a few months. Susanne will be with us soon.* As the packet ship left the port of Rotterdam, Hannah hung her dress in the closet of the tiny cabin they had been assigned.

Night had already fallen when the *S.S. Rotterdam* arrived in New York harbour. Passengers were no longer permitted to disembark after 6 p.m., so they spent one more black night on board without the slightest moon. Hannah and her father stood close to each other on the bridge, squeezed and scared like penned up animals. They could distinguish warehouses in Brooklyn amid dark shadows and the Statue of Liberty holding up its muscly arm toward the inky sky. Straight ahead was the tip of Manhattan where they could make out the contours of the skyscrapers and the headlights of cars moving about like distraught fireflies. For Hannah it was like a movie scene unfolding before her eyes. Eugene Kroner had no illusions. He knew what lay ahead in this new life. In 1936, he had been forced to give up the high-end women's apparel company he owned. *I've got ten marks in my pocket, when all my life I was always able to pay for whatever I wanted. Come Hannah, let's have our last dinner. Starting tomorrow I'm an old penniless man*, he said taking his daughter to the dining room of the ship. That evening the waiters in their white gloves served 'Tomato Soup, Boiled Flounder with Hollandaise Sauce, Roast Leg of Lamb with Gravy, Brussels Chicory in Cream, Steamed Rice and Boiled Potatoes, Lettuce Salad with French Dressing, Ice Cream, Vanilla Éclairs, Fruit and Coffee'. Hannah kept the menu with its date, 24 November 1939.

As soon as they were settled in a miniscule Manhattan flat, the Kroners set about doing what was needed to get a visa for Susanne. They also bought a double bed for Hannah and Susanne. Everything was ready for her arrival. The Kroners were having trouble getting their bearings in the New World. Eugene Kroner became a salesman for an office supplies company. He would buy various items inexpensively at Woolworth's and go door-to-door to the secretaries of art galleries along 57th Street and pocket his meagre gains. *He was proud to earn his first dollars*, Hannah remembers. Elsa Kroner found a job on a factory assembly line. At age fifty-five she was gluing soles on house slippers – for hours at a time, the same mindless movements. But she never showed her fatigue. *We're in America, we're alive, we have no right to complain.* Hannah shows me two photos of her parents. The first from 1922: Elsa and Eugene Kroner at the beach on the Baltic Sea. Elsa, her square-cut hair swept a bit by the sea breeze, is holding the little Hannah in her arms. Eugene, smiling jauntily through his little moustache, is wearing an old-fashioned shoulder-straps swimsuit that covers the rounded contours of a well-nourished body. The second from the 1950s: Elsa and Eugene Kroner at the base of the walkway near the Brooklyn Bridge. Elsa cracks a little nervous smile as she leans against her husband. Eugene has lost the extra pounds, his hair and his handsome self-assurance. In the two photos, Eugene

Kroner has placed his hand on his wife's shoulder. In 1922, the hand is proud and protecting. In 1950, it seems hesitant and a little weak. The old husband and wife are clutching on to each other in the New World.

For Hannah, America meant the abrupt end to her life as a pampered child. She presented herself at a recruitment agency for dancers. In the waiting room she immediately recognizes the girl sitting next to her. It was Marion Leiser, her neighbour from the building across the street from hers in Berlin. Hannah remembers a particular rainy afternoon. An only child, she had placed her forehead against the windowpane in the dining room looking out enviously at the high times of the party guests gathered to dance and eat birthday cake with the little girl in the flat across the street. Hannah spent many minutes, sad and immobile behind heavy curtains, spying on the light-hearted happy play going on over there. And here was Marion Leiser, the little birthday girl of that day, sitting opposite her in this Manhattan placement agency for aspiring dancers. After their interviews, the two Berliners went to have coffee and decided to team up. They became the Corley Sisters, combining one syllable from each of their names: Kroner-Leiser. They performed in cabarets with men at their feet and a bright future in front of them. *It was a great time!* says Hannah placing photos on the table. *Seventy dollars a week! Thirty-five apiece. Twenty-five dollars for my parents. I had ten dollars left over to do what I wanted. It was a small fortune!*

One day when she was touring in Massachusetts, Hannah received a letter from her mother: *Susanne has done something really stupid. She's fallen in love and got married. They met at the soup kitchen. His name is Günther Cohn. He's a Polish Jew. That means,* Elsa Kroner explains, *that Susanne goes from the German waiting list to the Polish waiting list, and the latter is interminably long.* Hannah puts down the letter realizing that her friend is lost. She will never join them. *Susanne was so alone in Berlin. She needed to be reassured. And when one falls in love, one isn't rational any more. We knew there was nothing more we could do.*

The bad news came a few months later like an inevitable malediction. Elsa Kroner received a letter from a Christian neighbour in Berlin. *They* came for Susanne at dawn. The friend writes that she jumped on the bus and followed the car that had taken Susanne as far as the station. She saw Susanne getting on a *special train*. Susanne died while Hannah was dancing in cabarets in Massachusetts. The two friends had just turned twenty-one.

Why did they have to wait until Kristallnacht to finally wake up? Really I have no idea, Evelyn says to herself as though she were stumped by the million-dollar question that a TV quiz show announcer had just asked and that she can't answer. Some years ago, Hannah attended an exhibit at a college in Queens where lists of names of the deported were displayed for people to consult. For each one there was the deportation date and destination and the death date. Hannah passes her finger down the list of names, page after page in alphabetical order, and is startled when she suddenly sees, under the letter 'C', Susanne Cohn, the married name of her friend Susanne. *All that in black and white in a little college in Queens! I ran out of there and drove around in my car aimlessly. I didn't know where I was any more. I couldn't believe that they had written everything down with that minute attention – so typically German – in case anyone wanted to double-check later: Who? What? Where?*

Evelyn talked about Susanne with a natural familiarity as though she had known her. Hannah must have spoken about Susanne with her daughter very often. Sometimes Evelyn even continued some of the stories that Hannah would begin telling. It was Evelyn, for example, who recalls how Susanne served as Hannah's chaperone. The Kroners took no chances with the virtue of their daughter. When Josef Schechter, her first boy-friend, a violinist, took Hannah out dancing, Susanne was hired by Elsa Kroner to follow them like a shadow. Evelyn has heard this story dozens of times. Dozens of times she has sighed with pity over the dirty work given to poor Susanne who's made to look on during the flirting between Hannah and Josef. When conditions started getting worse in Berlin, Frau Kroner decided that her daughter had to break off all relations with this boy who wanted to marry her and keep her from emigrating. After the war, Hannah learned that Josef Schechter was brought to Auschwitz by the Norwegian police. *Every time, grandma had the right intuition*, says Evelyn. *She always knew when it was time to choose between life and death.* She said it as though her grand-mother were right there in front of the armoire, self-assuredly choosing between two dresses.

In New York Hannah married a Berliner. Their two mothers played matchmakers. They met for an afternoon tea at Schrafft's on the corner of Broadway and 96th Street. When Gustav Segal strode in wrapped in his overcoat, it was as if Cary Grant himself were descending from the Hollywood Olympus. Gustav Segal was tall, athletic and charming – a 'sonny boy'. Hannah, at five-foot-six and with curly brown hair, was speechless. Gustav Segal arrived in New York in 1936. This son of a good Berlin family had had a weakness for tall, blonde Aryans. Too dan-gerous, judged her mother. It was then decided to send the swinging bachelor across the Atlantic. He was put in charge of conquering the American market for his father's company, which made neon signs whose lights danced and flickered outside movie theatres and Broadway shops. But the deals fell apart because the American unions were opposed to assembling a product 'Made in Germany'. Gustav Segal wasn't really such a great catch any longer. The two youngsters like each other well enough, but they need a little time to get acquainted. One doesn't choose a husband for life in a few minutes between a Hot Club Sandwich and a Peanut Sponge Cake. But the United States has just entered the war and unmarried men are being recruited first and fast. The mothers decide that there's no time to be overly picky. They need to get the two married as soon as possible.

We met for the very first time on the 11th of December. The marriage took place on the 31st of January. After only three dates, chuckles Hannah, sure that she'll get a laugh with her story of the expressway marriage. *Still, it lasted forty-nine years,* laughs Evelyn. Two months later, Hannah was pregnant. She worked at a nightclub at the time and would get home at 3 a.m. Gustav worked at a munitions factory and had to leave the house at 5 a.m. Two hours of time together at dawn was not much time to get acquainted. Hannah gave up dancing and Evelyn was born in 1945.

After the war Gustav Segal became an interior painter. He invented 'stippling', a technique to apply paint to the wall with pieces of wrinkled up newspaper. *It avoids stains and fingerprints, and it gives a look similar to wallpaper,* he would explain to his customers. And when customers would frown a bit with scepticism, Gustav Segal would pull out his full-proof argument: *It comes from Germany!* His customers had forgotten the war and its horrors. German artisans were reliable and the stamp technique became the rage all over Brooklyn.

Evelyn never thought that her parents were poor. Corned beef and potatoes on Tuesday, spaghetti on Wednesday. Hannah and Gustav became the sole caregivers of their mothers. And these two German grannies took care of Evelyn when Hannah went back to work. To her parents' dismay, Evelyn learnt to speak English with a German accent. *It drove me crazy*, says Hannah. *I wanted a regular American kid!* As a result, Evelyn doesn't speak German – only a few words and the names of some popular dishes. In her pantsuit and sneakers, she is definitely American.

Hannah founded her dance school in 1947. In Berlin, Max Terpis had already warned Hannah – with your body-type you're never going to be a principal dancer in tutu and pointe shoes. He therefore taught her how to teach dance. She began by giving lessons to Evelyn and three of her friends in the living room of their flat. A few years later she opened the Hannah Kroner School of Dance. Today in the dance studio the walls below the barres are still free of the traces of footprints thanks to Gustav Segal's stamp-paint method. On the wall behind the reception desk, a photo commemorates the sixty-fifth anniversary of the dance school. Hannah is presiding at the head of the table in this celebratory photo. Her face is at the centre of a flower of pink serviettes spread out like fans amid glasses of champagne, silver streamers and bouquets of white and pink carnations. Pink is the regulation colour of the tights and leotards of the pupils at the school. Hannah's smile is a little stiff in the photo, but one can see she's proud. *Dancing protected me and saved me.*

On the walls of the Hannah Kroner School of Dance are photos of illustrious former students. Hannah is proud of those who went on to make it on Broadway. The Kroners so enjoyed walking the length of that famous boulevard when they arrived in New York. Broadway is on another scale from the Kurfürstendamm. It took walking along it for hours to realise that they came from a country of Lilliputians. The grand German nation that had terrorized them suddenly seemed smaller and began to scare them less.

No one at the Hannah Kroner School of Dance knows its founder's origins. Advertising copy for the school indicates simply that Hannah learned to dance in Europe. After the war, Hannah and her husband saw no point in letting everyone know they were Jewish and German. There was plenty of resentment against Germans in the United States and there was anti-Semitism too. They sent their daughter to the neighbourhood Catholic school. How many times did Evelyn find herself in front of the closed doors of the school on the day of Corpus Christi or the Epiphany! How many times did she feel like a stranger!

To overcome their homesickness, the Segals tried reinventing Berlin in New York. With their Berlin friends Ruth and Heinz Warschauer, Irma and Leo Barschall, and Lothar and Else Lisser, they would get together to eat *Rouladen* (stuffed rolls of beef, veal or pork) and *Königsberger Klöpse* (meatballs with caper sauce). Hannah would prepare *Rote Grütze* (a summer berry soup) for dessert. They would tell jokes with punchlines that only Berliners knew how to deliver. The circle of friends expanded when, in order to try and contact survivors of his rowing club, the *Berliner Ruder-Club Oberspree*, Gustav Segal put an ad in the *Aufbau*, the New York German-Jewish newspaper that's sent around the world. Several team members from that time contacted him. They also brewed their own Berlin Weisse, the traditional Berlin beer. And of course they spoke German. The men had more trouble integrating than the women. Some hardly spoke any English. The Segals did their shopping in the stores on 86th Street, known by New Yorkers as the German Broadway. There you could find *Sauerbraten* (marinated roast beef), *Knackwurst* (beef and pork sausage), herring, black bread and smoked eel. Before going to the beach, Gustav Segal would also make a stop on 86th Street. He always bought lard and *Leberwurst* (liver sausage spread) to make sandwiches. At Christmas time there would always be a large plate with marzipan, gingerbreads and Bahlsen biscuits. Despite all this Hannah makes a complicated declaration: *I feel American, but I can't just cut myself off from my past. I was born a Berliner. I had a very happy childhood. When I think of Germany, I think of the good things in my life.*

Back in Berlin, I send Hannah a photo taken on my balcony above the street. I'm wearing her dress. A few days later I get an email from Hannah. *The memory of my friend is passed on. She deserves it. You look so wonderful on the balcony of the street where Susanne lived, and I feel very strongly that the dress ought to remain with you instead of ending up in some museum where more people could see it but without understanding its history. I am in a way relieved that the dress will stay in your street! Please, wear it, and Susanne will sleep in peace! And me too! Writing a book about a dress that survives intact through a journey around the world in sixty years seems to me like an excellent project! I will stop here for today, please excuse all my typos! My thoughts always go faster than my fingers can on the keyboard! Affectionately yours, Hannah.*

8

The Spitting Image of His Father!

Liselotte stands up straight in front of the bathroom mirror with a pair of scissors in her hand. One, then the other. She slices off her two blond plaits. Her hand firm. No trembling. She rolls them in crepe paper, puts them in a box, and writes the name and address of her father, Gustav Bickenbach, Engineering Corps Captain, Gadebuschstrasse 30, Swinemünde, The Baltic. She then takes her parcel to the post office. It's the young woman's first act after moving into number 3 on the square that cuts my street in two on 1 February 1935.

Liselotte Bickenbach is nineteen years old and it's her way of breaking away from the Prussian spirit that dominates the paternal home in Swinemünde (present-day Świnoujście in Poland). Elbows stuck to one's sides at the dining room table. Back straight and stiff and barely in contact with the back of the chair. Hair kept in place with long severe plaits. Gustav Bickenbach, a graduate of the Officer Candidate School in Metz, was posted to Swinemünde. He is in charge of this fortified town on the Baltic Sea. When, on 12 September 1910, Gustav Bickenbach married Dorothea Margarete Helene Lau, he posed on the steps in front of the church: uniform, white gloves, spike helmet, impudent moustache, heels locked, and the young woman at his arm. In their large white house next to the barracks, Prussian virtues are the law: punctuality, reliability, thriftiness, self-sacrifice – to which is added the strict discipline of the Reich's officer corps concerning political neutrality and the absolute obedience to hierarchy.

Berlin was also a way for Liselotte to escape from her mother. That austere woman had only one idea: find a suitable husband for her daughter, preferably an honourable and ambitious young officer. Liselotte was no longer interested in accompanying her mother on Sunday walks in Swinemünde. When she attended a tea party with dancing, her mother shadowed her everywhere. And because Dorothea Bickenbach refused to allow her daughter to attend the high school that was mostly filled with boys, Liselotte was forced to learn stenography, sewing and housekeeping.

Gustav Bickenbach was wary of big cities. After months of discussion and relentless pressure, he ends up yielding: *As you like, my daughter, but on condition that I find you a flat and a position!* It was arranged that Liselotte would board with acquaintances of her father. Gustav Bickenbach gave them strict instructions: she is to be back home by 10 p.m. and most importantly must not go out with young men. After a few weeks, Liselotte had had enough of getting back from dancing after midnight and having to tiptoe inside with her heels in her hand – so she decided to move. One night after work, she was walking in my street. Little signs saying *Room for rent* had begun to appear on several facades. The economic crisis meant hard times for many, and one tactic was to sublet a room to help pay the rent. Liselotte Bickenbach rings the bell at number 3 on the square. Frau Nehrenberg invites her to come up. The two women hit it off right away. A few days later, Liselotte moves into a little furnished room. Frau Nehrenberg, a penniless widow with an ample bosom, knows how to console all wounds. Liselotte quickly began calling her Mutti Nehrenberg – mother Nehrenberg – and that struck her as entirely natural. From her window, she could see the school on the other side of the square. Mutti Nehrenberg sublets three other rooms. In the evening the subletters would gather in the kitchen and share stories. It was the first flat-share arrangement in my street.

Liselotte was a secretary in the high command of the German army or *Wehrmacht*. She was later transferred to the headquarters of the navy. She worked for the director of the service charged with supervising the international merchant marine trade routes as part of the submarine warfare against the Allies. Liselotte would leave her place in the morning, her hair cut short and neat, her soft muslin dress cut close to her body, walk along the street with a comfortable sashay, and descend the steps to the U-Bahn. In this Berlin street far from the home of her parents, Liselotte discovered liberty and love.

One evening after getting back from a weekend in Swinemünde, a young man calls to her on the platform of the Stettiner Bahnhoff and invites her for a drink. Since he was tall, blond and polite, Liselotte accepts. Mutti Nehrenberg pretends not to notice the male callers of her subletter. The older woman, who lost her husband so young, is moved by the young lovers. Liselotte and Wilhelm Wagner cohabit freely for several months before marrying. The ceremony, attended by just a few people, took place on 19 September 1942 in the Schöneberg city hall. Liselotte did not tell her parents and simply informed them of the fact afterwards. A celebration took place in the country home of the Wagner family in eastern Prussia. Dorothea and Gustav Bickenbach, who had dreamed of a grand marriage for their daughter that would display to all their happiness and social success, were not invited. During the first months, the young couple lived in the room at Mutti Nehrenberg's flat. They later found a flat at Tempelhof. Petty officer Wilhelm Wagner is an aeronautical engineer and test pilot. His military base is the Luftwaffe's flight test centre at Rechlin, north of Berlin.

Liselotte's happiness collapsed on 17 September 1944, two days before her second wedding anniversary. During a test flight, petty officer Wagner's plane blew up in the grey late-afternoon sky. It was a regrettable accident, said the telegram from the base commander. Liselotte received a bag containing the few remaining personal effects of her husband. One of his leather boots is missing. The young widow returns to live with Mutti Nehrenberg who consoles her. She rediscovers the same décor that was the backdrop to her love story and the memories are still so fresh. Liselotte's fleeting happiness is frozen inside this little room in my street.

I only met Liselotte Bickenbach once, a few months before her death. It was in the common room of the retirement home located very near our street. It was as though she had retraced her steps after a long life. She had come to get ready to die a few hundred yards from the home of Mutti Nehrenberg in the adjoining neighbourhood. And it was perhaps really no accident at all. Liselotte Bickenbach, a tall thin bony woman, was sitting up straight in her wheelchair. Her eyes stared. She was recovering from a small stroke. It was just before Christmas. She was awaiting the visit of her son. She did not smile at me. She complained about not having a vase for the flowers I had brought her. *What am I going to do with them?* I had tried to ask her a few questions, hoping that the evocation of distant happiness in the street where we both lived a few decades apart would stimulate her memory and unthaw the atmosphere that was as chilly inside the room as outside in the street covered with snow. But Liselotte Bickenbach could only murmur in a broken voice: *Yes, it was a happy time. I don't want to speak of it. It makes me too sad.*

It was her son Joachim who told me the story of his mother. We met quite by accident in my neighbourhood bookshop. At the counter I was chatting with the bookseller about my plan to write the history of my street. I had just returned from a fruitless afternoon outing to the snacks and card-game parties for seniors at the two local parishes in my neighbourhood. Neither the Catholics nor the Protestants were able to provide me with the puzzle piece that was missing from my project: a non-Jew who had lived on my street in the 1930s. I was determined not to break the rule I'd set for myself, namely that my protagonists had to have lived in my street or on the square at the end of it. I refused the idea of substituting the testimony of someone who'd lived in an adjoining street. Joachim Bickenbach cleared his throat and interrupted our conversation: *Perhaps I can be of service. My mother lived before and during the war at number 3 on the square.* And without much pleading he began to tell me the story of his mother right there between the shelves of crime fiction and the self-help section promising 'Happiness in Ten Lessons'. I understood afterwards that the story of Liselotte Bickenbach was situated precisely at that location halfway between solving an enigma and searching for happiness. That evening, I pondered for a long time all the chance encounters and lucky coincidences that had allowed me to find the trail of my former neighbours who had not lived in my street for a long time but who had witnessed this or that part of its life. That the son of Liselotte Bickenbach from number 3 on the square had suddenly had the same urge as me – on the same day at the same time – to peruse the recently arrived books on display in the bookstore, was this not one more little miracle?

One can see my mother's memory literally shrivel up day by day. I'm truly afraid that I've arrived four years too late with all my questions, says Joachim Bickenbach. While the mother's memory was declining, the son's was filling up – as though their minds were somehow connected and the contents flowing, like through an hourglass, from one to the other. *Now I know more than my mother!* her son declared. It should be noted that Joachim Bickenbach had been recording family stories for a very long time. Whenever there was a house call, the little radar boy was seated at the end of the table. The child's ears were constantly on high alert in the middle of all the adults stirred up by tumultuous conversations. He never lost a crumb of what went on. He detected indiscretions, sniffed out scandals, and intercepted family secrets. After a time, the adults would forget about him and loosen their tongues about matters that the little one ought never to have heard. Uncle Rudolf had an accident in a taxi and died of a brain haemorrhage. Aunt Klärchen threw herself out of a window in 1943 – already an anxious, fragile person, she was unable to stand the bombardments. Aunt Paula ran a music shop and sold scores. Her business really began to pick up when the store became a supplier for the brass bands of various National Socialist organizations. At sixteen, Paula's son Otto still let himself be dressed by his mother. They slept together in her wedding bed. Before dying, Otto travelled to put his money safely away in Switzerland. *I'd rather make a donation to the zoo than give it to you!* he shouted to his family. And then there was little Fritz, Gustav's youngest brother, whose other brothers enrolled him in the NSDAP so that there would be at least one Nazi party member in the family. Fritz got a job at city hall right away. For years he happily plied the hallways pushing a cart filled with files. There is still a photo of Liselotte standing next to Fritz in his uniform. When one comes upon it in the family photo album, the page is turned quickly. *It was another time!* But since it's the only photo of his mother on a visit to her in-laws just after the wedding, her son has cut out uncle Fritz to leave only the young bride. If only there weren't that cursed armband with that swastika!

At the time, I didn't understand much, says Joachim Bickenbach. *But now everything comes back to me: the names, the order of events ... I have an excellent memory for all that was said. But now I would like to know the why and wherefore of everything that I heard.* In fact, he has already begun writing the history of his family. His chronicle is entitled, 'What I Learned from My Mother'. He's afraid that his own children will no longer have any points of orientation – that all these memories *will gradually become entirely meaningless and foreign to them.* He wanted to *record and retain* all these things so that his children *could touch them and appropriate them for themselves.*

After the death of Wilhelm Wagner, lots of things happened in quick succession. A few days before the German surrender and the end of the war, on 12 March 1945, Swinemünde was almost entirely destroyed in one hour by an American airstrike. 1,609 tons of bombs were dropped on the town, which was full of refugees fleeing the eastern territories as the Red Army advanced. The streets of Swinemünde were jam-packed with carts, animals, furniture and bundles of personal belongings. It was total carnage. Only the neighbourhood of individual houses along the beach, including the white house of the Bickenbach family, is spared. A miracle. On the 30th of April, the Führer commits suicide in his bunker and Berlin surrenders. On the 2nd of May, Russian soldiers raise their red flag over the Reichstag. On 5 May 1945, the Red Army invades Swinemünde. The town surrenders without a fight. All the fortifications under Gustav Bickenbach's command are handed over. On the 7th of May in Reims and the 8th in Berlin, Germany signs its unconditional surrender. At 3 p.m. in London thousands of little Union Jacks are waved in the royal blue sky as the silent crowd listens to Winston Churchill's speech broadcast by the BBC: 'Hostilities will end officially at one minute after midnight tonight ... We may allow ourselves a brief period of rejoicing.' In Paris, General de Gaulle declares, 'The war has been won. Germany is defeated and has signed its surrender, whereas rays of glory once again shine on our flag.' In Moscow a jubilant crowd dances in celebration of victory in this great patriotic war, while in New York they celebrate Victory in Europe Day.

At dawn on the 9th of May, alone in his office, Gustav Bickenbach listened to the radio announcing the German surrender. The officer stood up and climbed the hill behind his house. A few minutes later a shot rang out. Gustav Bickenbach had shot himself in the head with his pistol. For the second time his officer's pride had been trampled. In 1918 already he returned with his tail between his legs, shoulders hunched, overcome with shame. The Treaty of Versailles had been a terrible humiliation. He had such hopes: Germany would take its revenge, raise its head, restore its tarnished honour. And here now were the French generals back from London throwing their chests out again. And here were the Russians strolling about in the streets of Swinemünde as though they owned the whole town.

One takes responsibility for what one's done, even if they are unspeakable things! says the grandson Joachim Bickenbach, commenting on the very Prussian act of his grandfather. The suicide was immediately hidden *under a cloak of silence*, Joachim's term for the unsaid things in his family. To this day, the uncles and aunts and all the cousins are unaware of the circumstances of this death. The reputation of the family had to be preserved at all cost. Officially, Gustav Bickenbach *died in combat from an enemy bullet*. The silence also has a purely practical side. After the war, his wife Dorothea received a widow's war pension that she would not have been entitled to if it had been recorded that her husband had committed suicide. *Many years later, that death was still paying out Deutschmarks come rain or shine. My grandmother was no fool. When one cheats, it's better that no one know about it.*

During the last months of the war, Liselotte Bickenbach worked at the headquarters of the navy whose offices had been transferred to Flensburg. On 15 June 1945, she was awarded the *Kriegsverdienstmedaille*, the War Service Medal, an honour created in 1940 to recognize the distinguished service of civilians toward the war effort. It was a surreal ceremony – the vanquished German army decorating its zealous servants. The next day Liselotte packed up to join her mother in Swinemünde. For weeks, columns of refugees fled west staying just ahead of the advancing Russians. Liselotte moved up stream as best she could to the east. *Watch out for the Russians!* she was told by everyone along the way. When she arrives in Swinemünde, she discovers her family's home has been requisitioned by the Red Army. On the ground floor, a doctor who had fled from Schneidemühl in Pomerelia [the Gdansk area in northern Poland] was performing abortions one after another. So many women had been raped by Russian soldiers. With a large white apron around her waist, Dorothea Bickenbach is assisting the doctor. This officer's wife, formerly so delicate, is handling blood-soaked forceps. Liselotte is pregnant. A few months later, on 18 January 1946, the abortion doctor delivers Liselotte's baby – a boy! Joachim.

When the Potsdam Accords establish the Oder-Neisse line that will serve as Germany's new eastern border, Swinemünde becomes Świnoujście, Poland. The last remaining Germans are expelled. They leave the town in droves. Liselotte, her mother and little Joachim have ten minutes to pack their bags and leave their home. They are taken to the Stettin station where trains are waiting to transport them westward. They live for a few weeks in a refugee camp near Hamburg. Joachim's birth certificate is issued there. Liselotte would like to return to Berlin. But with no flat and no money? Mutti Nehrenberg's building is destroyed. There is a serious housing shortage in Berlin. The orders are to dispatch refugees all over Germany. The two women are sent to a small village in Westphalia. The host family is not welcoming. It has to give one-and-a-half rooms to them. Liselotte works as a seamstress from home. She sews capes for British soldiers stationed in the region. When she goes on a delivery, Joachim goes with her. Along the entire path through the meadows, he plants his walking stick in piles of cow manure.

In late 1949, Dorothea Bickenbach's sister-in-law makes contact: you will join us here in Hagen! We'll work out a way to feed you properly! We will repair the roof that was torn open by a firebomb and make you your own flat! The rest of the family is less enthusiastic. Gustav Bickenbach was the only one of his siblings to leave Hagen and no one ever really forgave him.

They want to come here, the snobs of Swinemünde! We were never quite up to their standards! But now that they're down on their luck ... These and other murmurings greeted Dorothea Bickenbach and her daughter when they arrived penniless in Hagen, the family seat.

In January 1950, Liselotte Bickenbach finds a job as executive secretary at the chamber of commerce and industry in Hagen. But her fate is soldered to the fate of her mother, whom she does not love. *I had to put up with the ordeal,* she tells her son. *Grandma would have died. Family is family.* For years this invasive grandmother lives in the little flat in Hagen with her daughter and grandson. What's more, Liselotte Bickenbach does not like Hagen. Her dream is to escape from this provincial hole. She finds her father's family *repulsive. It's Sodom and Gomorrah!* she blushes when learning that her grandfather had nine children by three different wives. Gustav was the oldest of the second *batch.* Liselotte Bickenbach lost everything: her husband, her father, her home town, and especially the freedom of the little room at Mutti Nehrenberg's. The important thing was to survive.

Joachim grew up in Hagen. A fatherless child like so many others. In the classroom when the schoolmaster takes attendance and asks the profession of the father, half the boys, including Joachim, jump up from their seats and say: *Dead!* Prominently displayed in a leather frame hanging from a hook on the wall across from the sofa is the portrait, in profile and well-cut civilian attire, of the handsome Luftwaffe test pilot. This father, whom the little boy never knew, never leaves his eyes. Father and son established over the years a virtual complicity. They are inseparable. *He's the spitting image of his father!* exclaim visitors when they observe little Joachim from the side. My husband fell at the front, explains Liselotte Bickenbach, as though the aviator had tripped over an errant root in the road and never stood up again. The clumsy fellow.

People no longer speak about the war. No one talks about Nazism any more, and not about politics at all. *Anything that has anything to do with politics is crap*, Liselotte Bickenbach teaches her son. Change of subject. We were so busy with just managing day to day, explains Joachim, that we didn't have time to let anything *bubble up to the surface*. Everyone was happy *to be able to shut up*. Liselotte Bickenbach didn't have a subscription to a single newspaper or magazine. For years she didn't vote. The first time she voted was in 1969 for the FDP and the Brandt-Scheel coalition. She approves of the 'Ostpolitik' of Willy Brandt: *What's lost is lost!* She wants to hear no more about Swinemünde! And above all never set foot there again!

At school, Joachim's history lessons stop at the First World War. Joachim would have to wait for Herr Marx – a destiny sealed in a name! – his history teacher at the *Gymnasium*, to discover National Socialism. *I was seventeen. I asked questions. But I didn't get many answers. My mother would say that she had had nothing to do with Nazis because she had worked for the army, among generals of the old Prussian forces. She is one of many who efficiently squashed the past into a tiny box and put it away. It's what allowed her to survive. Others came out broken into pieces. My mother followed the practical example of many others and was a little cog that worked. For her the case was closed. She did not want to be confronted with details. And yet she had seen details herself: trucks at night that carried off families of Jews, including those in the building where Mutti Nehrenberg lived. When she went about Berlin she wasn't blind. Sometimes she talked about things but in a way that suggested they were foreign to her. But that she didn't take an interest in any of it is something I don't believe for an instant! In her home in Hagen there were shelves full*

My street in 1915. When it was built in 1904, my street was still on the outskirts of Berlin proper in a purely residential neighbourhood. As the capital grows, it in effect comes to be a part of the enlarged city centre.

'Schmuckplatz'. My street is intersected by this 'jewellery square' – a purely decorative open area composed of large geometrical forms. This layout stands in sharp contrast to the cramped atmosphere of the older Berlin centre.

The parade of the Master Bakers of Schöneberg, 8 May 1911. My street has none of the pretensions of the large prestigious avenues. This is the only photo I ever found that shows it being host to a particular civic event. An extraordinary spectacle in a street ordinarily so calm.

The first occupants. Lilli Ernsthaft and her mother at the window
of their flat at number 3 in the 1920s. Lilli spent seventy-nine years at
this same address. She was the last survivor of the perfectly assimilated
Jewish-German bourgeoisie that moved into my street at the beginning
of the century.

Heinrich and Lilli Ernsthaft with their son Harry in 1925. A simple love story. They met at the home of friends and then later each morning at a tram stop of line number 62. Lilli was a stenographer-typist. Heinrich was a businessman. On their way to work they fell in love.

An invitation at the Kutschera's. On the left, Karl Kutschera and his children Gert and Karin; on the right, Heinrich and Lilli Ernsthaft. Lilli Ernsthaft enjoyed talking about her worldly social network in the years before Hitler came to power.

The survivors. Lilli Ernsthaft (right) and Josephine Kutschera (left) in the 1950s. The Kutscheras and their two children were deported to Theresienstadt in 1943, but only the parents would survive.

COMMANDEMENT EN CHEF FRANÇAIS EN ALLEMAGNE

Carte d'identité de Personnes Déplacées

Nom ___ Ernsthaft
née Doller

Prénoms ___ Lilli

Nationalité ___ Indéterminée

Adresse ___ Berlin, N.65,
Iranische Str.4

Cercle de ___

Né le ___ 31.3.1902

A ___ Berlin

Profession ___ néant

Situation de famille ___ mxxxíxxx
veuve

Taille 1,68   Nez droit

Visage ovale   Yeux bruns

Teint clair   Cheveu gris

Empreintes digitales

Pouce gauche	Pouce droit

N.120860

Date d'émission : 14.12.47.

Signature
du chef de section des Personnes Déplacées

Signature du titulaire :

imprimerie nationale - (Gr.) ....

The Displaced Persons identify card of Lilli Ernsthaft issued in 1947. Lilli and her husband escaped deportation. They spent the war years at the Berlin Jewish Hospital in the Iranische Strasse, the only Jewish institution to have survived the Nazi period. After the war, the Jewish Hospital was located in Berlin's French zone.

On the steps of Schöneberg City Hall: Herbert and Klara Fiegel, the parents of Miriam Blumenreich, accompanied by their witnesses on their wedding day in 1929. The young couple would move into the home of Klara's parents at number 3, the same building where Lilli and Heinrich Ernsthaft lived.

Klara was a kindergarten teacher. Her school was located on the ground floor of the building where her parents lived. The whole street was sad when she got married since she soon stopped working so as to have children of her own.

Miriam and her mother Klara shortly before their emigration to Palestine.

Miriam Blumenreich today at the front gate to her home in Kiryat Bialik, near Haifa. As soon as we met, Miriam Blumenreich wanted to make sure I knew that 'We weren't just anybody in our Berlin street! My father was a doctor twice over with degrees in political science and law!' She wanted to restore to her father the honour he once had before his life took a different turn.

Jochanan Beer on the boat taking him from Trieste to Haifa.
Jochanan lived with his grandparents at number 19 in my street. After
their grandson left for Palestine, Martha and Gustav Beer were expelled
from their flat, which was given over to 'Germans of the Aryan race',
and they were deported to Theresienstadt.

Hans-Hugo Rothkugel, today John Ron, on his first day at primary school. When he speaks about his childhood John slides into German. He remembers the smells of his street – the scent of the steam-iron at the dry cleaners of Frau Kubeth, or the scent of vanilla in the shop of the waffle-maker at the end of the street.

From left to right: The maternal grandmother of Hans-Hugo, his parents Leon and Irma Rothkugel, and his uncle Rudolf.
Leon Rothkugel is hardly conscious of being Jewish. He's the eccentric bourgeois son of Albert Rothkugel, an executive in one of the largest private Jewish banks that financed the Franco-Prussian war of Chancellor Bismarck.

Paul (third from the left), the brother of Hans-Hugo, with some of his kibbutz friends. In the spring of 1942, Paul drowns. Hans-Hugo never tells his mother about this accident. She had stayed in Berlin, taking solace in the belief that her children were safe and sound in Palestine. She only outlived her son by a few months and would die during her deportation in December 1942.

Hans-Hugo alias John Ron in 1950. This serious young man with his spectacles and neatly greased hair has only one dream – to discover Paris. He wins a scholarship to study meteorology for one year at the Sorbonne.

John Ron in Berkeley with Ping, his personal assistant. Latterly, Hans-Hugo Rothkugel went by the name of John Ron – an English first name and a Hebrew last name. He spent his last thirty years in a small council flat for the elderly in California.

Hannah Kroner and her parents at the beach on the Baltic Sea in 1922.

Hannah and her friend Susanne. In fact, it was their mothers who decided everything. After assuring themselves that the girls were both well brought up, from the same social milieu, and wore white socks and well-polished shoes, Frau Kroner and Frau Wachsner introduced themselves at the entrance to their children's school. 'Would you like our children to be friends?'

Hannah in New York in 1941.
When Hannah and Susanne
are no longer allowed to attend
school because they are Jewish,
they are advised to learn a trade
that will be useful for when they
emigrate to the United States.
Hannah chooses to become
a dancer and dance teacher.
Susanne takes sewing lessons.

**Hannah at her dance
school a few years ago.**
In 1947, Hannah opens the
Kroner School of Dance on
Long Island. There, no one
knows the founder's origins.
Hannah and her husband
never thought it necessary
to explain that they were
German Jews.

Liselotte Bickenbach at her office. At a young age, Liselotte tries to escape from her rigid and oppressive childhood home. In Berlin she lands a job as a secretary within the High Command of the German army.

A radiant Liselotte Bickenbach before the war on the beach at Swinemünde. And as a sad-eyed war-widow in the 1960s in Hagen. What happened between these two photos?

Assistant Captain Wilhelm Wagner. Liselotte's husband, an aeronautical engineer and test pilot, is stationed on an airbase north of Berlin. Liselotte's happy life is dashed on 17 September 1944, two days before her second wedding anniversary. On a test flight, Wilhelm Wagner is killed when his plane falls from the grey late afternoon sky and crashes to the ground.

Joachim Bickenbach and his mother Liselotte. Joachim is a child with no father, like many others. At school, when the teacher calls the roll and asks the profession of the father, half of the boys answer, 'Dead'.

My street after the war. Of the thirty blocks of flats on my street, only eight are lightly damaged and inhabitable.

A few days of family leave. Wilhelm and Annaliese Krüger move into number 19 in 1936. Wilhelm is a cutlery salesman. During the war, he's called up and sent to the Russian front.

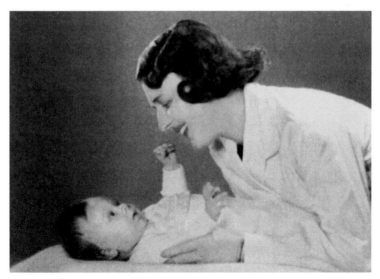

Annaliese and her daughter Ursula.

The Krüger's flat. Every night the air raids risk destroying the building. Annaliese has pictures taken of each room to at least have a memory of her furniture. The dining room (top) and the den (bottom) where one sees an ornate clock and to the left a plaster bust of Hitler. In another picture is the bathroom with its tub permanently filled with water – a precaution in case of fire.

Tangerine Dream in 1972 in Los Angeles. From left to right: Chris Franke, Peter Baumann and Edgar Froese.

David Bowie in Berlin in the summer of 1976. He lived in Berlin until 1978. The Thin White Duke wants to escape the limelight and get unhooked from cocaine. He no doubt found in my street the sanatorium atmosphere he was eagerly looking for.

Bärbel and Kurt Soller's wedding day in 1966. They arrived in a horse-drawn carriage in front of the little Protestant church of Schöneberg.

Bärbel Soller at her retirement party at KaDeWe. Frau Soller worked thirty-eight years at the large department store, Kaufhaus des Westens. On the eighth floor, she was in charge of the labelling and display of women's apparel.

The German economic miracle. Starting in the 1950s, Germany rebuilds and throws parties. The Soller's photo album makes the time appear to be one big surprise party.

A quiet street in a beautiful neighbourhood. My street, which had become more socially mixed after German reunification, is on the verge of returning to its high-class bourgeois origins. The real-estate boom is attracting developers who are building luxury flats. In a way, things have come full circle.

of books about the Third Reich, enormous tomes. She had read them all and underlined many things. Sometimes she even expressed anger in the margins: What's written there is false! She knew it! She'd seen it with her own eyes! In the evening in her armchair, Liselotte Bickenbach would read. When she went to bed, she would leave the hall light on and her bedroom door ajar. Since the war and Mutti Nehrenberg's basement, she cannot stand dark rooms. She never closes the curtains, so that the light can come in. The street must be visible.

Liselotte worked hard, from 8 a.m. to 6 p.m., and half the day on Saturdays as well. She would accompany her boss with her steno pad ready. Seated beside him in the back seat of the company car, the chauffeur in front, she would take dictation riding over all kinds of roads, potholes and swerving turns included. When the boss was through, the chauffeur would drop off Frau Bickenbach at the nearest station and she would catch the next available train to return to Hagen. As soon as she arrived, she would rush to her office and transcribe her notes on the typewriter. The next morning the boss would find his letters in impeccable order on his desk. Frau Bickenbach was devoted to her boss, who was, in a sense, the only man in her life. She never allowed herself to become infatuated. Never a flirt, never a man over for a dinner or a night. What's more, Dorothea Bickenbach is not above reminding her daughter – with a jerk of her chin in the direction of the portrait of Wilhelm Wagner – that her husband died for his country. A war widow must remain faithful unto death!

At meal times, Liselotte Bickenbach teaches proper manners to her son: *Above all, don't attract attention to yourself.* Alone in the kitchen, mother and son train in the evening: No flapping one's elbows like a bird, no dipping one's head toward the spoon, and no massacring the butter. And since it might come in handy, Joachim even learns how to dissect lobster and eat snails – on an entirely abstract level, that is, because those unaffordable luxuries were never served in Hagen. Instead there was sad *Abendbrot*. Also, there's training in parsimonious *Schiebewurst* eating – placing one's slice of sausage on the bread and pushing it with one's teeth so as to conserve it as a prize until the very end. Liselotte belonged to the war generation. She would never eat slices of sausage without black bread, and never would she eat fresh bread before the old loaf was entirely gone. In the evening, Liselotte Bickenbach would go down to the pantry and use a sturdy wooden stick to stir the laundry that was boiling in a large pot. There was no going on vacation. There were no treats. There was little time for dreaming between the precise daytime routines at work and the hours of ironing in the evening. Never did Liselotte Bickenbach consider abandoning everything – the ironing board, the shrewish mother, the moody boss, and the little provincial town where she doesn't feel at home. When the company Krupp offers her a job in Essen, she turns it down on account of her son who goes to school in Hagen. It's the rule: one makes sacrifices for the next generation. Her one and only and adorable son is her unique reason for living.

For three years Joachim keeps buried inside him the secret he discovered one day while taking his mother's tax declaration to the office in Hagen. The little man is twelve years old. Taking a peek in the envelope, he sees the date of his father's death. The pilot in the photo crashes in September 1944. Joachim is born in January 1946. In his bed, the boy counts and recounts the months. No, there is clearly no way he can be the son of the man in the picture frame that's now hanging above the brand new television set across from the sofa. It's mathematically impossible. But he doesn't dare ask any questions. He imagines the most horrible scenarios. Was his mother raped on the way from Flensburg to Swinemünde by a band of sweaty vodka-soaked Russian soldiers? He redoes the maths. May 1945 to January 1946 – that's exactly nine months. Joachim is terrorized. He is very afraid of learning the truth. On the eve of his Confirmation, Joachim is seated for the *Abendbrot* meal with his mother. Casually, Liselotte reveals the secret to her son. You know, there's something I still need to tell you ... The day she learned of Wilhelm's death, she took a vow never to remarry. But she wanted to have a child, no matter what. She chose a sperm donor from among the swarm of young men who flirted about her. A number of civil servants were stationed at Flensburg. Liselotte spends one night with a captain in the merchant marine. He was from Hamburg. His name was Albert. Albert is Joachim's second name. When the English dismiss the civilian personnel, Albert and Liselotte travel together as far as Schwerin where they spend a few weeks. Then they separate. When he learns that Liselotte is pregnant, Albert wants to marry her. She absolutely refuses.

This explanation gives Joachim an enormous sense of relief: *Something happened, you don't dare ask what, and suddenly the fog lifts!* Liselotte shows her son the only photo she has of his father: in Berlin on a balcony with flowers around a table set for tea, Liselotte, thin and elegant, her hair pulled back in an attractive chignon, is smiling at two young men in shirts and ties who stare back at her admiringly. The second from the right is Joachim's father. One can barely see his face. Liselotte tells her son that his father has been sending a food stipend since he was born. *That was my decision,* she decrees. *It's up to you to decide what you want to make of it.*

An illegitimate child is a horrible infamy in the prudish Germany of the Adenauer era. She could hear it already, the cutting gossip as she walked by: while her husband is dying for the fatherland, she lets herself fall into the arms of another man! Shameful! Dorothea Bickenbach knows the truth. She helped her daughter give birth in their house at Swinemünde. A stain for the entire family! Joachim remembers that there were many arguments about this between the mother and daughter. One day, in a rage, Dorothea screams at her in front of the petrified child: *In any case, I didn't even want you to be born!* Her husband's family forced Liselotte to take back her maiden name. It was out of the question to drag the Wagner name through the mud!

Liselotte Bickenbach constructed such a scaffolding of lies, she built so many teetering passageways, and dissimulated and falsified so many dates and events, that her son had the darnedest time reassembling the true facts. He has tried to steady the shaky edifice as best he can. He would like to give a solid foundation to his family chronicle. He would like answers to all the questions that run through his head even now: overcome with shame, did Liselotte turn down Albert's marriage proposal with the idea that no one would take notice of this suspicious birth amidst the chaos of the last months of the war? Was Albert already engaged somehow but out of a sense of duty offered to pay to support their child until he became an adult? Had Liselotte invented the story of a grand passion with no future in order to dissimulate her lust as a young woman? Did she somehow want to atone for her adultery by being a model widow? Today it's too late. The story of his mother will remain a mystery.

Two photos are more eloquent on the subject than all the scenarios imagined by Joachim. When one puts them side by side the transformation is almost terrifying. The first, on a beach in Swinemünde, a beautiful young woman in shorts and a tank top, suntanned, radiant, her hair pulled back by a polka-dotted scarf, shoulders and legs bare, her arms crossed over her legs bent at the knee. The second, Liselotte Bickenbach in the 1960s in Hagen. A black hairband holds her short wavy permed hair in place, a white collar covers her neck. She is looking up slightly, like those sad little virgins when the archangel Gabriel appears at the Annunciation. Her lips are pursed. In her eyes there is infinite bitterness. What has taken place between these two photos?

Many years later, Joachim attends a conference in Hamburg. During the break at noon he decides to walk about near the house of his father, Albert. An old man is standing on the balcony about sixty feet away. Joachim approaches along the pavement. Whatever you do, don't trip, don't speed up, don't attract attention, and don't stop. His hands in his pockets, he feigns indifference. *What an absurd situation. What was I going to say to him anyway? Guten Tag, I'm your son? I knew he was married and had children. Wasn't I just going to cause a lot of problems? What was I going to get out of it? He was a stranger to me. My conception was the only thing we had in common.* The whole thing lasted at most four minutes. Joachim turned at the corner and rejoined his colleagues.

As soon as he had graduated from high school, Joachim left home. He went to study mathematics and physics at the University of Marburg, a progressive school with a very left-leaning reputation. Joachim wanted to get away in more ways than one. In

Marburg he read the works of Wolfgang Abendroth, the classics of the German worker's movement, rubbed elbows with the KPD, the German communist party, let his hair grow long and wore a beard too. It was his revenge for the proper Prussian haircut his grandmother forced on him each time she took her grandson to the barber's in Hagen. *I've thought about it and don't see what any woman would find pleasing about that, but it's your business!* was his mother's verdict. Like for Liselotte when she arrived in Berlin, the Marburg emancipation began with a new hairstyle. Joachim wanted at all cost to escape from military service in the *Bundeswehr*. After completing an initial officer training course, he asked to be granted conscientious objector status. When he announced this to his mother, she congratulated him. *This Bundeswehr, after all, is not a real fighting force like the imperial army of your father! You're lucky not to have to join those sad ragamuffins! One can't take them seriously! They're too soft!*

Joachim Bickenbach remembers a certain afternoon from a few years ago. He had gone to visit his mother in Hagen. A wooden candy jar had been placed at the centre of the coffee table in front of the couch. Around it were porcelain cups and saucers for the coffee, the photo of Wagner the test pilot in the leather frame, a childhood portrait of Joachim, a candle, and a packet of Muratti cigarettes. Liselotte Bickenbach had carefully set out the props for her drama on the little table. In the jar was a little capsule lying on its pillow of absorbent cotton, a capsule filled with a brown liquid. Joachim had always lived with it – *it was part of our household, like a poodle or cat.* He knew the capsule was locked away in a little chest, and he also knew where his mother kept the key. It was the capsule of cyanide that an officer of the Navy High Command had given Liselotte in Flensburg in 1945. Liselotte wanted to return to Swinemünde across the entire east that was crawling with Russians. If a company of Russians should capture her, she would be ready. And that afternoon, as she poured out the burning hot coffee, the mother warned her son: *I keep it in case anything happens to you. I've lived through enough misfortune already!* She then stared at the little red capsule with a disquieting tenderness.

Liselotte Bickenbach and Mutti Nehrenberg kept in close contact throughout their lives. Liselotte came to say a last goodbye to her former landlady when she was on her deathbed in Berlin. But she never wanted to return to our street. Yet Joachim had proposed to take her there in the car one sunny day. Mutti Nehrenberg's building no longer exists. It was one of those classified as damaged between 51 and 100 per cent during the inspection conducted by the municipal services department for all of Berlin in 1947. In its place a new block of flats was constructed in the late fifties. But perhaps the fountain in the middle of the square, the high school for girls that was now a community college ... perhaps these would bring back pleasant memories, thought Joachim. Liselotte Bickenbach recoiled. *It was her strategy for coping with her unhappiness,* said her son. *One bold stroke crossing out the past.* One day she tells her son that she would like to be buried on the Golm, the hill in Swinemünde where the unidentified bodies of those killed in the bombardment of 1945 had been thrown into a mass grave. She wants to be buried there, *with all the others.* On that hill that she had climbed on horseback with her father. But Joachim informs her that the Golm has become a memorial space and that it's not possible. They decide on dispersing her ashes at sea.

Liselotte Bickenbach died quietly on 5 October 2011. Two days after the German national holiday. She was ninety-six and a half years old. Joachim and his children went for the first time together to Swinemünde. For my children, says Joachim, their grandmother is a figure wrapped in a dense fog. The Baltic was as smooth as a pond in a park that day. A thick mist hung in the sky above the boat. The urn with some flowers around it was placed on a little table near the bow. Once out at sea everyone gathered there. The two Polish sailors running the boat placed themselves on each side of the urn. No pomp. No speeches. No music. Suddenly the mist lifted. The captain took hold of the urn: *And now, Liselotte, we give you to the Baltic!* The urn sank immediately. Only the flowers stayed on the surface and the boat circled about them several times.

9

We Have to Save the Furniture!

It's midnight on New Year's Eve. From my balcony, I'm watching my street during the war. Firecrackers, lightning, thunder. Silver comets cross the night sky. Red and blue bouquets explode above the roofs. The sky is lit up as though it were daytime. There's an odour of sulphur. As my eyes follow the sparks of a Bengal light falling on the opposite pavement, I think to myself that this spectacle resembles what it must have looked like on my street during the airstrikes that almost completely destroyed it.

Around the dining room table in French homes, bomb shelters and night-time bombings are rarely mentioned when stories of the war are recounted. One hears about ration tickets, the black market, collaborators, people in the resistance, and – without fail – about some blond German officer with ice-blue eyes who barks inhuman orders. Unlike for the Germans, bombardments do not occupy as terrifying a place in the French collective memory for the simple reason that French cities were not systematically annihilated. Ports such as Brest, Toulon and Le Havre suffered damage, but Lyon hardly any, and Paris survived intact.

My encounter with Ursula Krüger is the result of a web of chance occurrences. At the end-of-year party at my younger son's school, I happened to mention my writing project to the school's former director, who happened to be in Berlin that day. That evening he mentioned it to his wife who, two days later during her Italian class in the adult-education night school programme of a local university, mentioned it to the woman sitting next to her during a break between conjugation exercises. Ursula Krüger turned to her and exclaimed breathlessly: *Oh! Oh!, but that's the street where I spent the first years of my life – at number 19!* And then the whole chain runs backwards: at home after class, the wife tells the former school director what she has learned from Ursula Krüger. The next morning he tells the whole story to his daughter who runs a chocolate shop in my neighbourhood. Two days later, I'm having a coffee and three macaroons at the little back table in the shop, where I'm a devoted regular. The owner approaches, stops in front of me, and relays her news as though she were tossing me a hot potato: *My father told me yesterday that an acquaintance of my mother used to live in your street, at number 19.* Then, as she was asked to do, she gives me a telephone number. I immediately call Ursula Krüger. That same week she comes for an espresso and three macaroons at my place – in other words about fifty feet from where she had lived with her parents for the first six years of her life. She talked about it as though it were yesterday.

It's a memory in her ear. Ursula is snuggled under a puffy eiderdown. She's covered her head to protect herself from the silence – because since the start of the bombing in her street, the silence now seems suspect. It usually only lasts a short time. A mere prelude. Ursula does not really sleep. She's on watch. She listens for sounds in the street that has no lamp-posts now. She hears people running faster and faster. Tap. Tap. Tap. On the pavement down below little agitated steps scratch the surface of the silence. Faster and faster. Now some nervous voices, some doors that bang shut. A moment later a siren starts whining. It invades the child's room, a corner room separated from her parents' room by a simple doorway cut in the wall. Ursula is scrunched up in her bed. She hears her heart beating in her chest. She hears the wooden slats of the blinds clack. Her mother rushes into her room: Get dressed! Quick! Faster, faster! Ursula had placed her clothes on a chair before going to bed to be ready to get dressed very fast. A skirt, a light wool sweater, her coat. She kept on her wool stockings and undershirt to sleep in. She hadn't worn a nightgown in a long time. You have ten, fifteen minutes at the most before the bombs arrive. Come on! Faster! The danger is getting closer. Ursula cups her two hands over her ears.

One after another, they descend the circular stairs into the cellar. Not forgetting the little suitcase prepared especially for these circumstances. It contains all the essentials: papers, money and a portrait of father in his uniform. He is far away, over there, at what the adults call the *Eastern Front* – a mass of grey on the map that Ursula is unable to make out precisely. She imagines the place where her father is fighting as a lunar landscape with no trees, no rivers and no hills. The *Eastern Front* doesn't really belong to planet Earth. The suitcase is always ready at the door. Ready to be grabbed. It stands right next to a bucket of sand that can serve to put out the beginnings of a fire. Michael, Ursula's little brother, has to be carried in someone's arms. Kira, a maid of sixteen originally from Sebastopol, carries a basket with some food and drinking water. Kira is a forced labourer. When she first arrived in the family a few years back, she refused to eat. She had been told that the Germans' food was poisoned.

Then there was the confined space of the black hole with its fetid odour. The person in charge would close the iron door to the cellar. On the ceiling a single bulb would light the walls whitewashed with lime. In semi-darkness the residents of number 19 would sit huddled together on benches wearing their winter coats. Each would have a designated spot. There were only women, children and the elderly. They were all torn from their sleep. The women knit, darn and converse in low voices. Someone murmurs an Ave Maria. All are waiting for the storm to pass. Above their heads the street is lit up by the explosions. There's the drone of the Lancaster bomber planes. Veeeee. Here they come! Cluster bombs, incendiary bombs, unexploded bombs, a flood of fire … Ursula recites by heart the rhyme of aerial warfare.

The air-raid-shelter captain would stand guard with his helmet and his *Feuerpatsche*, essentially a wet broom for putting out small fires. Ursula wondered what giant insect he was going to smother with that big swatter. She would watch the light bulb sway on its cord with each explosion above on the street. Her mother, Annaliese Krüger, has brought a foldable mattress down to the cellar. Ursula goes back to sleep. It's the miracle of childhood. Michael and Andreas cling to one another like two scared little foxes. Ursula curled up in a foetal position squeezes Kira's hand tightly.

These terrifying nights have left Ursula Krüger with a panicky fear of small and dark spaces. This is why she doesn't like going to movies, or firecrackers on New Year's Eve, or factory whistles.

Annaliese Krüger is sitting still and stiff on the corner of the mattress, as though this proud pose would help surmount the fear that wrenched her stomach. She is thinking about the incendiary bomb that a few days earlier fell into a corner of her bathroom without exploding. Coming up from the cellar, she discovered this big egg behind the door. She called the air-raid-shelter captain who with great dexterity and calm defused the bomb and removed it like someone taking a simple splinter out of the slightly reddened ball of one's foot. Annaliese Krüger congratulated him on his skill and slipped a coin into the pocket of his coat as though she were tipping an efficient delivery boy.

All around one could hear the low rumble of the sides of buildings collapsing onto the street. Walls vibrate. Some plaster falls from the ceiling. And then silence. A strange silence. The residents of number 19 try to guess which building has been damaged. Number 20 perhaps, or was it number 11 across the street? Oh God, let it not be ours! Annaliese Krüger is thinking about her furniture up there on the fourth floor with no elevator – so vulnerable. And what if an incendiary bomb were to lodge itself in the roof of number 19 and spread flames everywhere? What if the flames swirled from room to room and devoured everything in their path? The flat would be consumed like a handful of straw. Her parents' home in a nearby street had recently been destroyed in a bombardment. *When we got out of the shelter, we had nothing left,* they recounted. Annaliese Krüger is unable to halt these images that flash quickly, one after another, before her eyes. The cherry-wood dresser – a wedding present from her parents purchased from one of the most fashionable antique dealers on the Kurfürstendamm – in cinders. The elegant English sideboard that had pride of place in the dining room – also a ridiculous pile of charcoal. The clock encrusted with lapis-lazuli that marked the passing hours in the den – now a skeleton of blackened metal covered in soot, its two hands sticking up into space like a dead beetle on its back. Only three years earlier this same clock had kept the time in the Krüger's harmonious, orderly bourgeois household: mealtime, bath time and bedtime for the children, coffee with the neighbours, washing day, and house cleaning day in springtime. Annaliese Krüger can still see herself on her knees polishing the feet of the chairs in the dining room.

Seated on the mattress in the cellar, Annaliese Krüger sees an enormous inferno consume her carefree life as a young married woman. A life that had barely started. Wilhelm Krüger and Annaliese Steinmann met between 1934 and 1935 on New Year's Eve at the Haus Vaterland – the biggest palace playground in the world – on the Potsdamer Platz. There were streamers, paper hats, glasses of champagne and a firework display. Wilhelm invites Annaliese to dance. The young couple turns and turns on the dance floor of the Palmensaal. The parents of the young woman keep her under close watch. The marriage takes place on 4 June 1936. Annaliese's uncle, the vicar at the Catholic Saint Norbert Church across from the Schöneberg city hall, performs the service. A few weeks later, in mid-August, the young couple is posing in front of the crowded grandstands at the Olympic Games. A special photo album is devoted to the Berlin Olympics of 1936. There is Annaliese and Wilhelm Krüger looking radiant under the colonnades of the stadium. *We managed to get to the walkway!* Wilhelm has annotated with a flourish of his pen. One can see them exiting side by side after the female gymnastics competition: *Fighting to conquer!* is written next to the photo. In another, one can see Annaliese in the packed grandstand: *The best seat! The prize of a hard-fought battle!* She's standing among other spectators who are doing the Hitler salute: *For us it's the most emotional moment when the German flag rises up the flagpole to mark the first victory.* And there's another photo of the closing ceremonies: *All the victorious nations present themselves at the closing parade!*

The young couple moved into number 19 in my street. Wilhelm is a sales representative with Zwilling-J.H. Henckels, the blade, knife and scissors company in Solingen. His office is a few tram stops away from Friedrichstrasse.

Ursula is born on 30 May 1937. Annaliese Krüger gives birth at the Virchow Hospital in Wedding, in the obstetrics ward of Professor Stickel, a doctor famous for his modern methods and strict hygienic standards. Sheets are changed every day. What a funny idea, Annaliese's friends chuckle – going off to have one's baby in Wedding when one lives in such a bourgeois street! Ursula owes her name to the popular tune by Marita Gründgens, *Ich wünsch mir eine kleine Ursula, hellblond mit blauem Augenpaar* ('I'm wishing for a little Ursula, blond with blue eyes') that her mother used to sing to herself all day during her pregnancy.

My street is the backdrop for the family photo albums. August 1941: on the balcony, Annaliese Krüger picks up little Michael with a big enthusiastic gesture. One can make out the roofs of the neighbouring buildings – the stucco on the facades, the trees, the cloudy sky. In 1942, on the same balcony, Ursula and Michael are turning the pages of an illustrated magazine. Michael is sitting on his father's knees. The photo is badly framed. One sees only the right half of Wilhelm Krüger's face, a single eye and a bit of his tie. In 1943, their last child, Andreas, has just been born. Grouped around the baby are his mother wearing a bright necklace and Michael and Ursula. Annaliese Krüger had this portrait colorized at a special photography shop – a gift for Wilhelm Krüger who was far away in Russia.

Bleib übrig! ('Stay alive!') the survivors at number 19 wish each other wryly when the air raid is over and they return above ground. Life for the residents in my street hangs by a thread. Who knows what the next day will bring. And especially the next night. This time the little enamel-tiled brick walls of the gardens in front of the flat building, walls the children used to like to use as balance beams, were blown to bits. Annaliese Krüger can't understand why the British are so determined to bombard so often such a tranquil little street that never harmed a soul. On the radio, a nasally voice speaks out indignantly again this latest terrorist attack against the capital of the Reich. Those who have lost their roofs and everything else in the bombardments pass in single-file along the pavement. They might carry a still-life painting saved from the flames, pieces of charred furniture, a mad canary flapping in its cage, or whatever else remained of their lives that had been still intact the day before. Before abandoning the pile of rubble that used to be their home, they would attach somewhere visible a little piece of paper for their relatives and friends, letting them know who survived and where they could be located. All day long, bodies, sometimes badly burned, would be dragged from the ruins and lined up on the pavement to be taken away. An ardent party member whose residence was damaged is assigned a room in the flat of the elderly couple on the first floor at number 19. The new lodger sits from morning to night at her sewing machine working away. She's making BDM uniforms for the female branch of the Hitler Youth (*Bund Deutscher Mädel*) and has completed whole boxes of them. With the remaining scraps of fabric, she pieces together neckties.

Once again number 19 narrowly escaped destruction. But the bombers would return. When the radio announces squadrons in the airspace over Hannover-Brunswick, the residents in my street know what that means: we'll soon be next. Everything could still be destroyed. So Annaliese Krüger can think of only one thing to do: We have to save the furniture! And if she can't manage to evacuate every piece in time, she's determined to at least keep a memory of them. Annaliese Krüger hires a photographer. She gets everything ready before the agreed meeting time. She straightens, dusts and smooths. She wants to show her home as wholesome and whole as possible. The photographer goes from room to room setting up his tripod.

He makes twelve black-and-white portraits. Annaliese loves old furniture. Every piece she owns, she chose one by one. In the smoking-room, on opposite sides of a shelf, there is a clock and a plaster bust of Hitler, a present from her uncle the vicar. In the parents' bedroom is the white varnished bed with gold trim, and yellow and blue curtains. On the bed is a comfortable blanket of beige wool. In a chest down in the cellar Annaliese has already stored the silk bedspread decorated with light blue Japanese flowers. In the nursery is the changing table and some toys. A pennant with a swastika is hanging like a sort of mobile above the crib. In the bathroom, the tub is filled with water – a precautionary measure in case of fire. A missing windowpane in the kitchen has been covered with a piece of cardboard. Along the entire street you can count on the fingers of one hand the number of windows still intact. Even the little maid's room squeezed between the kitchen and the bathroom is immortalized in black and white.

1943 is the year Annaliese Krüger left my street forever. Her husband is far away. Letters from the front are few and far between. The bombardments become ever more intense. At the end of the summer, the women and children of my street are forced to leave Berlin. Signs ordering the evacuation are posted on the advertising column on the square. A child pictured on these posters shouts out to the passer-by, *Mother, take me far away from here! The terrifying air raids continue!* Annaliese Krüger, her three children and two maids will take refuge in Zehdenick near Oranienburg, where her in-laws' large farm is located. A few days later all her furniture arrives from Berlin. Transported on flat barges, it glides slowly along the canals of the Havel, crossing fields and brushing against hazelnut tree branches in forest glades. The villagers applaud this surreal procession of fancy goods as it passes under the bridge at the entrance to Zehdenick.

The arrangement of the Berlin flat is recreated room by room. The children actually have a marvellous time for a while. No cellar, no sirens, and their hunger is less severe. Annaliese launches into cultivating a small vegetable garden. Local farmers have acquired three pianos and have crystal glasses in their kitchen cupboards. Berliners come out to trade furniture for a ration of butter or ham. People are ready to sell anything in exchange for something to eat.

On Ursula's first day at school, the radio operator Wilhelm Krüger has been granted leave. Her teacher who returned from the front with a mangled hand and one eye missing frightens Ursula. In Zehdenick the adults do not talk about the war in front of the children. The war is only murmured about – a sort of background noise. Hidden behind a door left partly ajar, Ursula eavesdrops on conversations. Annaliese Krüger and Kira whisper. Ursula slides along the corridors, listens at doors, holds her breath. One day, she even breaks a pane of glass with her fist. The adults had closed and locked the door to talk without interruptions. *I wanted to know the secret,* she says to her mother while holding up her bloody hand.

During the night of 22–3 November 1943, our street was carpet-bombed. Some neighbours say that the street was not the intended target and that the Royal Air Force had actually meant to bomb the streets near the zoo. Once they had completed their mission the Lancasters made a U-turn and flew off. But they had not emptied all their cargo. The bombs in the hold weigh a lot and the planes need to be lightened in order to save on fuel and be able to reach the coast at Norfolk. The pilots were therefore ordered to drop their bombs wherever before leaving Berlin airspace. And this time, as chance would have it, they were dropped right on my street. There is a more cynical version of the incident, as told to me by a shopkeeper in the street: *It's the Jews who did it on purpose, out of vengeance. They wanted to bomb the neighbourhood because they knew that bigwigs in the Nazi party were assigned lodgings in their flats.* When I pointed out to him that the Jews in our street had been deported to Auschwitz or else had emigrated to the other side of the world, and therefore it was unlikely that they would return piloting English bombers, he gave me a knowing look and added: *Yes, but you know these Jews, they have their network around the world,* upon which I left his shop dumbstruck.

A 'carpet of bombs' – this metaphor derived from the lexicon of good housekeeping lends an air of innocence to the violence that laid waste to my street. The hundreds of bombs dropped by the RAF that night destroyed it almost completely. In Zehdenick, Annaliese Krüger and her children rush into the yard to observe the eerie halo of intense light in the distance over Berlin. Ursula senses correctly that this reddish sky means more bad news. Had the bombs destroyed number 19? The next day Annaliese Krüger takes the train to Berlin to see for herself. The ground is still smoking. Half the street is destroyed. But number 19 is still standing. On the square at number 1, the building that forms the corner of my street, the Kaiser-Barbarossa pharmacy is completely destroyed. Since 1906 it had occupied the ground floor of a sumptuous building constructed by Robert Zetzsche. On 16 October 1944, Ludwig Guercke, the owner of the pharmacy, writes to the prefect of the Berlin police: *The terrorist attack of 22 November 1943 totally destroyed the Kaiser-Barbarossa pharmacy that I administer. Important documents burned during that attack.* He requests duplicates of his lease agreement and his inventory, *so as to restore my records. Heil Hitler!* On 19 July 1945, Ludwig Guercke chooses words with fewer ideological connotations when he writes again to the prefect: *The Kaiser-Barbarossa pharmacy that I run was totally destroyed on 23 November 1943 by an aerial bombardment.*

Günther Wolowski, an engineer who lives at number 25, makes a sketch of the destruction. He marks a large star in red pencil on the damaged or destroyed buildings. Number 25 is missing its right side. Numbers 26, 3, 5 and 6 survived. He notes down the missing walls, the placement of water and gas lines. Günther Wolowski draws the air-raid shelters, the stairs leading to the cellars, and the fire escape stairs. This sketch, now conserved like a relic by the current residents at number 25, resembles a delicate little pencil drawing by Paul Klee.

I do not know how many civilians were killed by the air raids in my street, or even if a count was established. The 1939 census states that 306 people lived in my street – a very high number for such a short street. How many of them survived the war years?

As the Russians approach there is a new exodus. At the end of January 1945, Annaliese Krüger, her children, and a large bundle of their stuff get on the last train out. They take refuge in her family's house in Erfurt. The house has classical columns and was formerly a summer residence for Ursuline nuns. It is now packed with refugees from the Ruhr area. One family per room. The Krüger's get two rooms. The parents on the first floor, the children in the attic. This time the furniture stays in Zehdenick. Kira too – to guard the furniture. She sends parcels to Erfurt with clothes and other small items. Until the very last days of the war, the German postal service operates normally. Wearing Annaliese Krüger's bridal gown, Kira marries Ivan, the head farmhand. To this day, Ursula Krüger does not know what became of her. Did the Russian combat troops kill her? She had been so afraid of her countrymen. Or did she return to Sebastopol?

When Annaliese Krüger returns to Zehdenick in 1947 to retrieve her furniture, Kira is not there. Nor is the furniture. The villagers had helped themselves piece by piece. Annaliese Krüger goes door to door and presents her twelve photos to prove that the furniture belongs to her. The mahogany dining room table with its extending leaves had been hacked to bits. She was only able to rescue the chairs. She found her tablecloths embroidered with her initials in a neighbour's cedar chest. The house linens had been used as toilet paper. The Murano glass chandeliers were all broken. Annaliese Krüger pretended not to see the books from her library on the shelves in the mayor's office – she's relying on his help. At least this city official is interested in books, she thinks to herself in a burst of philanthropic generosity. The mayor is effusively apologetic about the misbehaviour of those he administrates. *A single sack of hay per month, that's all they deserve!* he says deploringly – all the while standing righteously erect in front of the Krüger's book collection. The rescued furniture is transported to Erfurt.

In 1945, the Americans are the first to occupy Erfurt. They open up the German army's warehouses and distribute leather shoelaces, biscuits and the stocks of emergency rations intended for tank and air units.

Then the Russians arrive. One room in the house is seized to lodge a Soviet officer from Georgia. He speaks French and offers gifts to the ladies. But one day he announces: *Combat units are arriving! It's going to become more uncomfortable!* On 3 March 1946, Annaliese and Wilhelm Krüger are dancing in celebration of Carnival on the first floor when a Russian officer arrives and orders them to move out: *You have forty-eight hours to empty your house! It is being requisitioned as the communications headquarters of this command!* The Krügers are allowed to take what they can carry in their arms. All Ursula's school friends come to lend a hand.

When Annaliese Krüger returns to Berlin for the first time, she goes straight to my street to recover a few things she had left in the flat. Number 19 is still there. But the roof has collapsed and the upper stories are damaged. A portion of the facade has also crumbled. *The building is a teetering ruin that seriously risks further deterioration and makes rebuilding highly problematic. Even if no immediate danger to the public can be identified, the complete demolition of this ruin seems necessary, perhaps even before the end of the summer.* So reads the official report of the urban planning service of the city of Berlin filed on 21 June 1949. A wooden board placed diagonally across the stairwell blocks access to the upper floors. They might collapse. Ignoring the risk, Annaliese steps over the board and goes up to inspect what remains of her flat. A few years later, the authorities use dynamite to demolish the building. Legend has it that someone fired a few shots from one of its windows. A resistant to the last? A madman who refused to accept the capitulation of the Third Reich? It is said that the Russians had the building blown up in a spirit of revenge. The real story is much less extravagant but not without a certain zest. On 19 April 1953, a certain Dr Heinemann, who probably lived in a building very near to number 19, complains as follows in a registered letter to the Berlin roadworks department in charge of removing debris: *By means of this letter, I wish to inform you of the necessity for your service to turn its attention to an urgent situation that absolutely needs to be remedied. The premises of building number 19, located directly across from the training institute for female primary school teachers, must be emptied without fail. Besides the fact that gusts of wind in recent days have once again caused pieces of the building to detach themselves and fall, passers-by are routinely walking into the ruins to make use of it as an improvised outhouse, and this without the least regard for the young female students across the street who are perfectly aware of what's going on. Also across from number 19 is the park of the children's hospital, whose young patients are entitled to breathe fresh and not foul air. I therefore request, for reasons of both public sanitation and morals, that this corner building be completely demolished and the ground cleared of all debris – a request which if not carried out I will be obliged to pursue through higher authorities. Dr Heinemann.*

On 19 May 1953, the sanitation services of the Schöneberg district write as follows to the roadworks and public works department: *The ruins in the building lot mentioned above are largely a public responsibility and in their present state constitute a risk to public health and hygiene. We kindly request that you act to remedy the situation by either removing all remaining debris or, at the very least, by walling off the entire lot including blocking all cellar doors and windows. Moreover, we request that this work commence promptly so as to be completed before the first hot days of the summer season.*

On 29 October 1953, Philipp Halter, a specialist in explosion-aided demolitions, bridge abutments, industrial flooring, chimneys, underwater demolitions, farm-related explosives and cinema pyrotechnics, and formerly director of a company in the Berlin metropolitan area specializing in complex demolitions and work with compressed air, writes the following to the urban planning commission of Berlin-Schöneberg: *Mission, completion of the demolition work and clearing of the building lot at number 19. I inform you with this letter that the work of demolition and clearing at number 19 has been completed.*

In 1951, the Krüger family is finally authorized to move back into their house in Erfurt. Wilhelm Krüger has trouble finding work. He is arrested three times for espionage. Annaliese Krüger visits all the prisons of Erfurt in search of her husband. He's nothing but skin and bones. He's never been the member of a political party, neither the NSDAP nor the SED. Only when he ends up joining the Ost-CDU does he manage to get a job as an accountant for the cooperative supermarket Konsum. On 20 November 1953, at dawn, Wilhelm Krüger is walking to the station to take a train to his office. A Culemeyer articulated lorry belonging to the Reichsbahn (the East German rail company) pulls suddenly out of a side street. There is fog. There are no streetlights at the intersection. The driver was partying all night and is totally drunk. The lorry ploughs into Wilhelm killing him instantly. He's fifty-one years old. The driver flees but he's eventually identified. For five years, Annaliese Krüger battles in court. Accompanied by her daughter, she appears before the supreme court of the German Democratic Republic in Berlin. Thank goodness we have a house and furniture, Ursula says to herself, as she looks out the window at the streets of Berlin. Annaliese Krüger wins her case.

In July 1961, Ursula's godmother buys plane tickets, Berlin to Hanover, for Ursula and her brother Andreas. They are German and have never seen the Rhine! On 13 August Ursula is staying in a youth hostel in Heidelberg when she learns that a wall is being erected in Berlin. Ursula and Michael cannot return home. In a refugee camp in Marienfelde they are questioned by the Allies. They decide to study medicine in Bonn.

On 30 May 1963, Ursula's birthday, her mother joins her children in West Berlin under the auspices of a family reunification programme. From a café on the Moritzplatz, Ursula and her brothers observe the sentry-box at the border. All is calm. The square is empty. Suddenly the gate opens and Annaliese Krüger appears, escorted by an East German *Volkspolizist* carrying her two suitcases. She is holding the leashes of her two dogs, Peter and Putsi.

A few days later, two removal vans, thirty-feet long, eight-feet wide, and seven-feet high, transport the Krüger household furnishings to West Berlin. Annaliese Krüger had to manoeuvre through a thousand bureaucratic obstacles to finally get her furniture delivered. She had to fill out a form, in quadruplicate, for each book, indicating the author and date of publication. She was required to have every painting evaluated by the director of the Erfurt museum. The young Workers' and Peasants' State must not allow anyone to make off with valuable works of art. *It was brilliant brinksmanship that she pulled off to get everything out!* Ursula exclaims in admiration. Annaliese had become a *Powerfrau* who knew how to impose her will. Ursula is fond of using this word borrowed from the lexicon of the feminist movement.

Number 19 in my street no longer exists. But a flat needs to be found. Annaliese Krüger, as a victim of war damage, has a right to housing benefits in Berlin. She is assigned a flat in a housing complex built in the fifties. Squeeze her furniture into a matchbox with low ceilings and tiny rooms? Out of the question! In Lichterfelde-West she finds a big flat in a building that dates from the same 1900-era as her former number 19. The flat was used as storage for the Hotel Walther, an establishment with a mediocre reputation, nicknamed 'Ami-Puff' – the 'brothel for American soldiers'. Annaliese Krüger is sixty-one years old and declares: *I'm not moving any more.* Her Titan vitality is exhausted. When I first entered the flat in Lichterfelde-West, Ursula had been living there for fifty years. I had the odd feeling of landing smack in the middle of an exact replica of number 19 in my street – as though a magician had snapped his fingers and turned the twelve black-and-white photos I'd seen into living colour. Ursula Krüger had recreated, room by room, the exact décor of her childhood. The furniture had survived the bombs, the repeated expulsions, the pilfering villagers, the sequestering in the DDR, the administrative trickery, and the wear of time. Pieces had been mistreated by movers and knocked about by the stopping and starting of freight cars. *Things resist aging better. When you buy a good chair, it will last you at least thirty years. Everything then was built carefully and didn't fall to pieces like today's stuff,* says Ursula, who considers IKEA a prime example of the decline of civilization. She is proud to have bought only three pieces of furniture new: a sofa-bed, a cot and a bookshelf.

The reconstitution is almost perfect. The clock is in the same place on the bookshelf, give or take a centimetre. The furniture is arranged the same. Ursula Krüger fears that the least modification of its positioning would cause the fragile memories to fade. The succession of rooms at the front resemble a crowded antique shop overflowing with items. There is stuff everywhere in somewhat random juxtaposition. In a drawer is her brother's sweater from when he was five, her parents' marriage papers, a packet of letters bound by a tired elastic band, and a charm bracelet with the Eiffel Tower and Arc de Triomphe on it that her soldier father had brought back from Paris. Inside the glass case in the living room there is a large collection of porcelain figures: shepherds, chimney sweeps, dancers, hummingbirds, periwinkles. The bust of a muscly Venus can be glimpsed behind an island of houseplants. The prize for top oddity goes to the silver clips, each engraved with a number, that party guests would slip on the lip of their cocktail glass to identify their drink and avoid the germs and lipstick of other guests. The whole place would bring on a panic attack in a specialist of feng shui. Every centimetre of wall is covered with paintings – including one behind the coat rack in the hall. Next to the piano is a portrait of Mariechen, a schizophrenic cousin assassinated by the Nazis. Even grandma Sidonie, with her seven children and mean eyes, stares out at you from the wall.

Recently Ursula Krüger has again been having sleepless nights. Again she's on watch. She listens to the silence. Who will want to take over all this after her death? The younger generation no longer wants this bulky furniture or these plates with gold trim that can't go in the dishwasher or the microwave. Ursula Krüger has thought about donating some pieces to the museum of decorative arts. But who knows if the curators will even want them? Will she dare sell off to an antique dealer the furniture her mother spent her life rescuing? Impossible. She would feel as though, post-mortem, she were planting a large dagger between her mother's shoulder blades. So Ursula Krüger turns over in bed. She listens to the sounds of the street. *It's enough to drive you crazy*, she says. *You keep everything but you never find peace.*

10

The Roof of the World

To hear my neighbours tell it, the rubble piled up in my street after the war was as tall as Mount Everest. They describe ridges and canyons, summits and valleys – a breath-taking Himalayan landscape that emerged out of an asphalt plain at the intersection of two Berlin neighbourhoods.

I went to climb the Insulaner – that's the Berliners' name for the artificial mount composed of 1.5 million cubic metres of debris piled up on an immense open piece of land. Before the war it was an open-air dump surrounded by clay quarries, an anti-aircraft unit, and workers' garden allotments, but immediately after it became the place where all the rubble was collected, including the remains of the ruined buildings in my street. My visit was on a February afternoon marked by the last mix of snow and rain of a wet winter. I only came upon a circular mound rising amidst a knot of three-lane roads and flanked by small garden plots and a cemetery. On the surface of a flat city, the least little rise above the surrounding lowlands appears as something gigantic. But one must not be fooled by appearances. The Insulaner stands 250 feet above sea level, but it is not the result of tectonic plate movements or glacial events, even though its trompe l'oeil effect would suggest it. This protuberance is too sudden to be authentic. It's a foreign body resting on a smooth surface that extends all around as far as the eye can see. Birches, pines and mulberry trees were planted hastily at the end of the forties – a green screen to mask the memory of the *Luftkrieg* and the countless bombardments. The trees have grown so high now that one must wait for the leaves to fall in autumn in order to see the square tower of the Schöneberg town hall with its flag floating in the wind, and to guess at the line of my street somewhere in the compact mass of buildings. From the summit of the Insulaner, the city appears way off in the distance, and between the two lies an immense valley enveloped in mist.

In 1945, the women of my street, wearing aprons and kerchiefs, formed human chains to remove the rubble piece by piece and place it on small open wagon cars pulled by a steam locomotive along tracks that run through Schöneberg and on to the Insulaner. At the time it was still known as *Mont Klamott* – Mount Bric-à-Brac. For hours, the women would chip and scrape the old mortar off the bricks so that they could be reused at other construction sites to build new buildings. In the administrative lexicon they were called 'auxiliary construction workers'. Berliners, being both less abstract and more tender, called them *Trümmerfrauen*, 'women of the ruins'. Husbandless, courageous, muscly with calloused hands and strong backs and arms, these women never complained, showed no signs of weakness, and never asked questions. The *Trümmerfrauen* were mothers who did the painful grunt work of year zero and took on mythical significance in the foundation of post-war Germany. They spent twelve years, through the dictatorship and war, in single-minded concentration on their job, with no waste of time and even a certain joyful enthusiasm, clearing and cleaning. Fairly quickly after the war ends my street is as bare as a steppe. Everything is smooth. Everything has been removed. My street seems to have forgotten all.

The stones that witnessed my street's violent history are buried under 500,000 cubic feet of humus and clay. 2,500 kilos of lupin seed, clover and sweet peas are sown to stabilize the ground and prevent the past from returning to the surface with the first torrential rains. Bushes and trees further solidify the amnesia. For five years, the neighbourhood gardeners design and shape with their hands a man-made mountain. *The ruins and rubble of the Second World War formed a hill whose contours blend harmoniously with the moraines of the surrounding Berlin countryside,* says a report by the local city planners dated 8 August 1951. *The plantings were conceived to form not a garden but a nature park made of wooded and grassy areas. A track for sledding equivalent to four football fields in length will allow young Berliners to enjoy this winter activity easily and safely.*

The Insulaner, I soon realized, is not a sordid public dump or wart that one seeks to hide under the silky skin of the city. The residents of my street are proud of it. The Insulaner is the result of their hard work, built with the stone and tile of their buildings. It's their answer to the hard knocks of outrageous fortune that were visited on them. That the Insulaner was for many years the highest mountain in Berlin fills them with a kind of childlike and, one must add, blind pride. On 25 June 1950, the *Tagesspiegel* proclaims in a burst of lyricism that *If each neighbourhood erects its own mound of ruins, Berlin will soon be able to advertise itself in tourist guides as 'the city of the twelve hills', and build its own funicular. Not that long before, people were complaining about the anticipated 'waste heaps'. Hygienists spoke of 'nests of vermin' and feared chronic illnesses provoked by 'rubble dust'.* But this newspaper describes *chains of hills,* and *trucks out of breath negotiating hairpin turns up a track to the summit. At the very top there is an invigorating breeze. On a clear day, there are stunning views. Perched over the roofs of Berlin, one can see as far as the Havel. The Tempelhof airport appears so close and next to the city centre, the towers and domes shine in the June sun. With binoculars one can even see the electrical towers at Nauen.*

I recognize here the gift the Berliners have for overcoming adversity and singing the song of themselves without the least hesitation. Like Buddhist monks they turn misfortune into merriment. Their city is reduced to a pile of rocks? They will reconstruct Rome on the Spree – and add five additional hills to clearly mark its superiority vis-à-vis the legendary *Civis.* Air raids have flattened hundreds of streets? Thanks to the thoroughness of the Royal Air Force, one can now climb to the roof of the world and gaze far, far away into infinity. In a drawing celebrating the tenth anniversary of the Insular, two gentlemen in hats standing atop a verdant mound look out into the distance and say to each other, *See how the splendid grass grows gently over the Second World War!*

In 1951, a contest was organized in neighbourhood schools to come up with a name for the mound of rubble. The list of suggestions sent in by the school children reveals the strong symbolic significance that this mountain of ruins possesses: *Mount Debris, Mount Stone, Mount Rubble, Mount Ruins, Thousand Rock Mountain, Mount Strong Arms, Mount Reconstruction.* Then there are those with not much imagination who propose *Mount Bellevue* and *Berlin Mountain*; those who conjure up bucolic possibilities:

Flower Mountain, Mount Green Breast, Sparrow Paradise; and others who think of tender diminutives: *The Little Berliner, The Bump of Schöneberg*. Some get carried away with whimsical ideas of grandeur: *The Summit of Schöneberg, The Berlin Zugspitze, The Alp of Ruins, The Schöneberg Alps, The Berliner Peak*. The class that proposed *Schöneberg Olympus* was, I think, under the spell of a serious hallucination. It's sad to admit, but I have to say that those who favoured *The Schöneberg Crumb* had a more realistic vision of the geology of their city. I'm struck by the number of selections that denote suffering or penitence: *Mount Misery, Pain Mountain, Mount Suffering, Mount Forget, Awful Memories Mountain,* and *Mount Warning* – which I can see including an index finger pointing toward the sky.

On inauguration day, 11 August 1951, the Tonkünstler Orchestra of Berlin welcomes dignitaries to the sounds of Richard Strauss's *Solemn Entry*. Dr Ella Barowsky, the Schöneberg mayor, baptizes the pile of ruins *Insulaner*. The president of the chamber of deputies, Dr Otto Suhr, makes an ardent speech. This mount is a symbol of the perseverance of Berliners who have managed to move mountains. The governor-bürgermeister of Berlin, Professor Reuter, unveils a commemorative stone that bears the following epitaph: *The Insulaner, erected between 1946 and 1951 from the rubble of the Second World War, despite shortages and blockades.* Then a brass band bursts into '*It was in Schöneberg in the Month of May*', a song composed by Walter Kollo who lived at number 26 in my street. I am sure that this was a gesture of particular homage to our street in thankful recognition of its substantial contribution – the Insulaner owes at least a few metres of its height to the rubble that it donated. *At the end of the ceremony, the two guardians of the municipal parks and gardens service went on their appointed rounds for the first time. They call themselves the good genies of the hill and one of them was a former magician,* notes *Die neue Zeitung,* thus promising to transform the pile of ruins into a 'Magic Mountain'.

Sixty-two years later, on that February afternoon, one has to admit that the Insulaner has lost much of any magic it might have had. With the passage of time, this Mount Everest has even shrunk some, a bit like a cheese soufflé when your dinner guests arrive late – if Berliners will pardon me this unflattering comparison. As I walked along, I left the asphalt path that climbs to the observatory perched atop this very typical Berlin park, with its overflowing rubbish bins, its dog poo marinating in plastic bags, broken benches, graffiti, lovers, suspicious wanderers and solitary joggers. I advanced over the dead leaves and last patches of snow, between birches and thorn bushes, through places where the ground is soft and one's heels sink in deep. At times, I thought I felt under my feet the edge of a roof tile, at others I narrowly missed tripping over pieces of brick. Had they come back to the surface after a day of heavy rain? I was walking over the ruins of my street buried here under moss. A few metres beneath my feet were the remains of the dreams of the property developers Max Moniac and Richard Barth. Their bricks, their roof tiles, their mortar, the tiles of their entryways, the ceramic tiles in their bathrooms and the terrazzo in their kitchens all compressed under my heels. There, in the bowels of that mountain, lay the caryatids and cherubs of the facades. I could hear them moaning.

A report from October 1947 prepared by the Schöneberg neighbourhood association gives an inventory of the damage. Of the thirty buildings that lined my street, only eight are classified as 0–15 per cent *light damage* and therefore, *inhabitable*; three are

16–50 per cent *medium damage*, and therefore, *perhaps restorable*; nineteen are 51–100% *heavily damaged* or *beyond repair* and given the verdict, *demolition recommended*. But it was only when I visited the Historical Archives of Tempelhof and Schöneberg and opened for the first time the folder containing a few photos of my street after the war that I truly grasped the scale of the disaster. These photos are unbelievably shocking. It is no longer a street – more like the alien landscape of another planet, with mounds of debris and the tippy skeletons of a few buildings. Crests of bricks mount to the sky. Two window frames are all that remains of number 28. Against all odds, the chimney of number 27 somehow survives intact and casts its spindly shadow on the remains of the flattened building. Some images show a vertical cross-section of a building with no facade, and one can see a bit of wall with flowery wallpaper, a stovepipe, a broken sink or a ceramic-tiled fireplace – all reminders of a domestic ordinariness that was annihilated in a matter of seconds. On the facades are traces of bullets and fire. Dark grey stucco detaches from the wall of number 2 giving the impression of open wounds. Assorted pieces of metal lie on the pavement in front of numbers 21 and 22. The advertising column is still standing in front of number 30, which is now gone. A few tufts of grass and scraggly bushes have grown over the ruins. How many cadavers are still buried under there? In the middle of this scree field there's the odd silhouette here and there. A man wearing a suit and hat rides by on his bicycle. A woman enters a still-standing ruin with a crate. I have difficulty recognizing these fragments of blown-up buildings as much as I am trying to reassemble them piece by piece to put my street together again.

The *stehende Ruine*, or 'still standing ruin', as these skeletons of buildings are called, is not an inert pile but a large living body which, in its own way, contributes to the daily life of my street. Sometimes it spits back up something genuinely useful, a real nugget – a fork or a nearly undamaged cup, for example. Gerd Böttcher, the director of the demolition and clearing firm in charge of cleaning the street, reminds his employees of the company's policy: *Every recovered object must be returned to its owner, and if the owner cannot be identified, it is to be declared a found object and handed over to the proper police authority.* If the workers come across unexploded bombs or other arms, they are instructed to cease operations immediately, establish a security zone around the area in question, and contact the nearest police station.

The ruins of numbers 8/10 and 22 were not closed off. Until the early 1960s, the area was used as an open dump for kitchen garbage and a shortcut to get from my street to the adjacent one so that clearly beaten paths traversed these lots, according to an internal memo of the Schöneberg municipal service. Like tightrope walkers, children would play on beams suspended above the rubble below. Sometimes as high as the fourth floor and with no stairs underneath! They would also make campfires in the cellars and fly their kites in the empty lots. A neighbour told me of the find he once made with a band of buddies in the particularly spacious cellar at number 10: an enormous stash of old pornographic magazines. Large-breasted naked women in black and brown – a palace of erotic treasure amidst a pile of ruins!

All of these anarchic goings on in the ruin next door to Katherina Tschiersch, who lived in the garden flat at number 6A, offer a mission to enliven the morose life of this retired divorcee. She decides to send complaint after complaint to the police. She fills pages and pages of lined school notebook paper with her crabbed little handwriting. For years she would denounce to the police the kids playing football on the vacant lot under her balcony. I can just see her, a mean little old grey woman spying on everything happening in the street from behind her semi-transparent tulle curtains. And the sadistic thrill when she would see a ball fly by. A police report gives an idea of the atmosphere during those austere times. *Frau Tschiersch is partially paralyzed from maladies affecting her spinal cord, hips and legs such that she is confined to her flat most of the time. Due to her condition, Frau T. is particularly sensitive to any and all noises, especially since she herself rarely has the benefit of outside visitors. The distance between her balcony and the ruined building lot is about seventy-five to one hundred feet. On orders from the chief officer for the neighbourhood, the street has been patrolled on a regular basis and this has allowed officers to put a halt to football games there. It's true that recently young children and teenagers have on two occasions used a small spongy ball to conduct football matches on the vacant lot in question. The names of those caught playing have been taken down and the individuals holding parental authority over them have been summoned to the police station where they have been reminded of their responsibilities.* Some days later comes a new complaint from Frau Tschiersch: children are roller-skating. After long proceedings, Frau Günther, the neighbour across the hall from Frau Tschiersch, *proposes calling the police station* each time that the residents wish *to complain about something upsetting their tranquillity.* These improvised playgrounds end up being closed off.

My street at that time resembles an old-fashioned Meccano set ready to fall over with the next gust of wind. Schöneberg's municipal services department is on a constant state of alert. On 31 May 1949, the architect W. Rerenkothen offers this report on conditions at number 6: *A ruin of bones, no roof, risk of collapse due to humidity. On the first floor, which is still standing, the renter*

Herr Hermann is living in unimaginable conditions! The occupant must leave the premises. At the end of the year, the residents of the building receive a registered letter from the municipal services department: *Regrettably, we are hereby forced to prohibit you from occupying or renting your flat (whether as principal residence or for commercial or professional activities).*

Cracks appear in the walls. Portions of facade fall to the pavement. Several houses have no roof. Balconies and chimneys risk collapsing. Exposed beams covered with smaller rubble may rot and give way. Remains piled up in damp back courtyards allow mould and rot to develop. Owners attempt to rebuild and repair, but they lack the proper construction materials. Everywhere roofs are improvised with salvaged materials and holes are closed with whatever works. The archives of the municipal services department describe the trials and tribulations at number 6, where there now stands a pale yellow four-storey apartment building. An important firewall has a thirty-foot-long crack. On 12 May 1954, the owner Frau Frieda Kottke receives demolition notice #182/54. Demolition of the building is hired out to the company of one Ulrich Sperling. In August, Ulrich Sperling informs the Schöneberg municipal services that a fatal incident has occurred at the site: *An accident has taken place today around eight o'clock. Employee Paul Schlag fell when a third-floor balcony gave way. He was seriously injured and died shortly afterwards from his wounds.* Police officers immediately conducted an investigation at the site, interviewing all witnesses and having pictures taken. The next day, the police report identifies the victim as Paul Arthur Schlag, born 20 May 1908 in Leipzig – German; Catholic; electrician; divorced.

Several months later, on 13 January 1955, Walter Schäfer, a wholesale textile merchant who lived at number 25, complains to urban services about the interminable salvage operation going on at the partially ruined building across from his own: *The goal of the current operation seems to be nothing but the careful extraction of large stone blocks intended for resale. The rest has been left as is, and I invite you to verify for yourselves the shameful state of the site at present. The wind lifts the lighter particles of rubble and the dust penetrates into my flat even with the windows shut. I believe it is unacceptable to treat a ruined building lot as a quarry, carrying off everything that might have some resale value, and then when there's nothing left to take, leaving behind a field of waste that's worse than in 1945 after a bombardment. It is well known that a worker died at this site. Indeed, one can consider it good fortune that the collapse of ceilings and overburdened cellar arches did not cause other deaths.*

This is exactly how Frau Rath pictured the apocalypse when she was little during her catechism classes. *Our beautiful street was literally flattened. I couldn't stop crying. What a sight! Ruins, nothing but ruins! All the way to the corner, everything was gone. Everything was ravaged, reduced to ashes. Number 25 was still standing, but one whole side was destroyed.* Frau Rath was ninety-six years old when I went to see her at her retirement home located just a short distance from our street. It was her former neighbours from across the hall at number 25 who put me in touch with her. Frau Rath knows all the stories of our street. She moved into number 25 during the war and only left her flat recently. My neighbours had run into her at the market. She was in good form. Take advantage of it, they told me. *At ninety-six, you're the witness of an entire century. But sometimes the mind gives out and then overnight – poof! – there are no memories left.* I was well aware that I had to hurry. Sylvia, a medical secretary living at number 26, confirmed that this was a unique opportunity: *Frau Rath! She is so sweet! And believe me, they're not all like that at her age. Frau Rath still has all her marbles and I'm sure she'll be very pleased to have a visitor. It's exactly what all of our older patients lack – someone to take an interest in them and their lives.* I trust Sylvia. She's been a reliable beater in my hunt for the old ladies of my street. Always smiling, always poised and in good humour – Sylvia is the living example of the maxims written on the 'Calendar of the Good Life' hanging on the wall behind her in the reception area of her medical office. Every time I leave Sylvia's office my life all makes sense again. Ok, this time I've got it all figured out! *Chalk up your mistakes and failures in the long column of Experience! Have the courage to take a chance! Happiness and satisfaction can only be found inside yourself! Look for open doors instead of focusing on those that are closed! Every misfortune contains something good, it's up to you to discover it!* Her simple do-it-yourself list is an effective remedy for metaphysical dizziness.

I am sure that Sylvia knows all the best kept secrets of my street. Too bad she's as silent as the grave. I often go and see her. She puts her index finger to her mouth and consults the index cards of her patients arranged in alphabetical order in a wooden box: *Hmmm, let's see, who have we here? Ah no, this lady is really too far gone! Oops, this one died last month,* and she quickly pulls out the expired card. Sylvia collects hardy natural specimens like others collect stamps. She tosses about unbelievable ages like confetti: ninety-five years old! Ninety-seven! Centenarians are her trophies. She has a handful under her care. Sylvia never betrays her duty of confidentiality to her old patients. She contacts them and asks with all due precaution THE QUESTION. I hear how she raises her voice on the telephone: *Yes, a French woman who lives in Berlin. She wants to know how it was* back then. *Yes,* BACK THEN, HOW IT WAS. If they agree, she gives me their telephone number. Frau Rath accepts right away and we make an appointment.

*

I wait a long while in front of her door with my bouquet. The florist advised me to choose bright colours. *At that age, I wouldn't choose light pink or white. She probably doesn't see much any more!* A large woman opens the door. Born in 1913, it's her skin – barely wrinkled at all – that first strikes me. I compliment her. *A little body oil and soap and water. Never creams, nothing else!* She proudly explains how she's never turned to make-up, rouge, eyeshadow or any other artifices that would in her eyes, I suspect, betray a fragile virtue. Her only coquettish indulgence is a pair of delicate gold hoop earrings and slight mauve touches in her hair that can be seen under a light hairnet. *I had magnificent thick auburn hair. Hair and feet have to be just right.* And then she apologizes, explaining that her leg has been swollen for the past few days and thus she's not wearing stockings or socks and has her feet inside plastic clogs decorated with big purple flowers. These garish shoes make her walk a bit like Minnie Mouse. *I never thought I'd live to be so old. Imagine, two wars! Inflation! Mass unemployment! And this sombre post-war period. We think that there's no way out, and yet we get out of it one way or another!* Today, Frau Rath is no longer afraid. She wears a security charm on a small necklace – an alarm system for seniors.

The flat at number 25 was assigned to Frau Rath in 1943. The building where she lived in an adjacent street had just been bombed. Frau Rath and her two children were homeless. They had to be housed somewhere as soon as possible. *We were sitting there between two smoking ruins, and they gave us this flat. It had just become available. We hardly dared enter the building, everything was in marble. There was a grand mirror above a fireplace in the entryway. It was taken down after the war. There was red velvet carpeting in the hallways. They were all rich there. They even had a concierge!* To borrow a phrase from the world of air travel, one could say that Frau Rath had been bumped up to first class.

She had barely put down her suitcases when she and her children were evacuated to the countryside. When the war was over, she returned to Berlin. But she didn't recognize her neighbours. *Those who had lived there before were no longer there. There were refugees in most of the flats, people from elsewhere, often several families in the same flat.* Frau Rath wonders if she's the only survivor in her street. *We started by blocking all the holes in the windows with cardboard. We sanded and refinished the singed parts of our furniture in the bedrooms. Ah, it's really unbelievable. But we had to get through that, and in the end we did. We were relieved to finally be at home.*

At home. Frau Rath is a little uneasy about having chosen that word and she corrects herself saying, *At home, well, you know what I mean.* When she went into the kitchen for the first time, the dinner table had not even been cleared. Frau Rath describes how breadcrumbs were still on the tablecloth, cold coffee in the bottom of bowls, and the chairs had clearly been pushed back in a hurry. Everything indicated a sudden departure. Engraved on a copper plate on the door to the flat was the only name she found: May. It's the only information she has. A simple name – no faces, no history. The Mays left no address and took none of their belongings with them.

I didn't know them. One day, the Mays weren't there any more! Like rabbits in magic shows. Poof! Gone! An entire family swallowed up by a top hat. Indeed, few people in my street stopped to wonder about these amazing disappearing acts. They weren't there any more, they were gone, *weg* – as though that clipped little word explained all and allowed no further questions. All of a sudden there was silence in the second-floor flat. One no longer heard any of those noises that come with living in close proximity in an apartment building: the parquet creaking on the floor above, someone's repeated coughing in the night, the almost imperceptible low buzz of a sewing machine, toilets flushing and taps being turned on and off. Yes, repeated Frau Rath, *they were simply not there any more! They were Jewish. So one could suppose that* … Everyone gets to imagine for themselves what's behind the ellipsis in that interrupted sentence.

In the Berlin Memorial Book, one learns that the flat Frau Rath moved into was formerly occupied by two women, Helene May and her daughter Charlotte. Helene May, born in 1864, in Gembitz, Posen, was part of the 54th *Altertransport*, Transportation of Seniors, on 1 September 1942, to Theresienstadt. Place of death: Minsk. Charlotte May, born 1896 in Breslau, was part of the 29th transport that left Berlin some months later on 19 February 1943. She died at Auschwitz. I went to consult the declarations of ownership of the two women in the central archives building in Brandenburg, near Potsdam. At the end of an endless series of suburbs, on a wooded hill far away from my street, I hoped to learn a little more about their identity and perhaps their lives. On the table at the spot reserved for me in the reading room was a single, soft, very thin grey-blue folder labelled Helene May, born Lewin, widow, no profession, Jew, resident at number 25 since 1 April 1937. Just before her deportation, the old woman must have completed, under the auspices of the 'Department for the Recuperation of Patrimony' of the financial services department of Berlin-Brandenburg, a form listing all of her possessions (assets and liabilities) in Germany and abroad: cash, bank account balances, stock portfolios, contents of safety-deposit boxes, property, insurance policies, salary, commissions, pensions, rents, security deposits, legacies and inheritances, usufruct, licence revenue, patents, author rights, brands, protected drawings or models, debts and tax records, any unpaid electricity and gas bills, furnishings and clothes (a complete list including the value of each item) – from the ceiling light to the bedspreads, from his dinner jacket and pyjamas to her stockings and ski boots. Even the amount in kilos of the apples and coal in the cellar had to be declared.

Helene May had crossed out all the categories with a long line in fountain pen ink. Was it a line of rage, fatigue or resignation? Most likely terror. Helene May has nothing left. This is the last document written in her hand, 24 August 1942, a few days before her deportation. But in the dossier, one never finds that word – only euphemisms. Helene May was *evacuated, expelled* or *emigrated*. The trembling signature at the bottom of the form – a bit indistinct because the paper didn't absorb the ink well – is the last sign of life and the last official act of Helene May. Afterward, she is only a number: *Berlin A 500 573*.

I feel I'm committing an indiscretion as I read, seventy-one years later, this questionnaire of an incredibly maniacal precision that reduces this woman, who was once my neighbour at number 25, to a wisp of information frozen within their mad bureaucracy. A whole life in sixteen pages. That's why I'm relieved when the director of the archives informs me that the dossier on Charlotte May has traces of mildew and cannot be consulted. *It has been placed in a sealed box and sent to a workshop for restoration. It could take months*, a jovial shelver replies when I ask him about it near the coffee machine where I've gone to settle my nerves. He describes a type of black mould that can devour your respiratory tract and turn your lungs into porous sponges. We laugh. It's the nervous, totally inappropriate and uncontrollable laughter that can happen when one is trying to bear up under the sadness of a funeral. *The dossier must have been badly stored during the war in a damp basement. For years one doesn't see the mould, and suddenly it appears when the conditions are favourable.* I do not have permission to consult the dossier and I have the uncanny feeling that Charlotte May is protecting herself. She does not want hungry eyes poring over this obscene act of naked display. So she has hidden herself behind a veil of mildew. She's keeping quiet. It's just as well, I think, relieved.

The only information I get from Helene May's folder is that Herr Rath purchased the Mays' furniture on 20 April 1943 ... *very likely for less than its true value, a real bargain,* the archive director says to me. Frau Rath, on the other hand, has the impression of having lost out by getting the Mays' fancy but old furniture. *At our place, everything was new!* Just before losing everything in the air raids, the Raths had entirely renovated their flat from top to bottom.

Frau Rath resents the *portiers,* the concierges in our street who, she says, behaved badly after the departure of the Jews. *They helped themselves to everything,* she says. *They had sets of all the keys. As soon as the trucks hauling off the Jews had gone down the street and turned the corner, they immediately went into the empty flats. They would take what they wanted before the places were officially registered and padlocked – rugs, fur coats, fine lingerie. All that was left were empty armoires. They were too heavy to move, otherwise they would have taken them too. It was booty they'd never imagined and everything got resold. Later, they would pretend it was the Gestapo's doing. No, it was the portiers. They had a nice little setup. After the war, they had Persian rugs piled one on top of another in their lodges. And us, we were living in ruined rabbit hutches up there!* After the war, the woman who ran the newsagents wore a mink coat, *stolen during*

Kristallnacht from a store window, people whisper as she goes by. The *portiers'* wives wear astrakhan fur and otter. The coats still have the musky fragrance of the previous owner. The legal folders of the dozens of suits filed in the 1950s by the descendants of Jewish residents evoke countless items that are *missing* . . . just like their owners.

In the 1950s my street is sad, hunched over and silent. It's a depressing, grey, mute time. So many things have been lost forever. So many people have died. My street looks like a slum and is filled with disturbing figures. Some are missing a leg, others are missing a bit of chin or an eye, says Frau Rath. They were called the *Kriegsversehrten*, the disabled veterans. Their wooden crutches tap regularly along the pavements. Their stumps are wrapped in gauze as though mummified. They are as rickety as the surrounding buildings. Seeing them, one has a better idea of what went on at the *Eastern Front* otherwise referred to so abstractly. For a long time, little papers with the name and sometimes the photo of a missing soldier were posted on the ruined buildings of my street. *Who knows Wilhelm Strutz?, I am looking for my brother!* People don't talk about the weather when they meet a neighbour on the pavement – they tally their dead. Frau Rath's favourite brother *remained* at Stalingrad. She says *remained* as though he had chosen not to go back home. There aren't many men in the street. Frau Rath clucks as she calculates that *the proportion was about one man for three women. These gentlemen had plenty to choose from. And you can bet they took advantage of the situation!*

My street deployed enormous energy to recreate a semblance of normality. *Necessity is the mother of invention*, repeats Frau Rath. *After the war, everything revolved around finding ways to obtain what was necessary for daily living: clothes, building materials and especially food. In Berlin-West there were ration tickets for eggs, powdered milk, dried potato flakes, a pad of butter and a handful of carrots. The supply of provisions was really low. One had to be very organized. We made new clothes out of old ones and the results were not bad in fact. Out of the Wehrmacht capes, we made winter coats. We'd turn curtains into trousers and steel helmets into cooking pots. And we'd make cakes with potato flakes and dried oats. There was only fake coffee. At the time, there was not a scrap of paper left lying on the pavement. We used everything. Our generation experienced many hardships. When I think back on all that we lived through!*

Durch and *aus*, prefixes which express the idea of tests that one endures and survives thanks to grit and perseverance, occur frequently in post-war German. *Durchgemacht, durchgehalten, durchgekommen, durchgefroren … Ausgebombt, ausgehungert …* These verbs, which evoke the daily struggle against adversity, privation, hunger and cold, are the shared idiom in street conversations in those days. In conversations about complaints, abnegation or pains. The Kaiser-Barbarossa pharmacy, whose original location on the square was completely destroyed, was able to reopen at number 26. On 22 January 1952, the pharmacist, Ludwig Guercke, sends a whining missive to the tax collection services: *This request for payment strikes me as exceptionally harsh given the fact that, as someone who lost everything in the air raids, I have had no revenue from the pharmacy; and what's more on 28 April 1945 I was a victim for the second time with the total destruction of my flat. I would also like to mention the pain sustained from the loss of my son at the front. The pharmacy as it exists at its current location is in the middle of a wasteland, and due to the low level of revenue it brings in, it is impossible for me to meet all my obligations. The tax service is aware of this situation, and yet insists on dunning me for the sums owed.*

The arrival of the Russians is an episode that gets retold tirelessly over and over. Miserable and famished, they made their way through the ruins and into the cellars where they found little huddled masses of terrified people who had been there for three days. Someone told me that a neighbour had hung a red flag at the entrance to her cellar. She had cut out the swastika from her Nazi flag and sewed the pieces together. The Bolshevik is even worse than he appears in Nazi propaganda. Russians cut down trees, hog the water pump at number 3, and rape women. *They appropriated everything that came into their hands,* says Frau Rath. *When I see Russians in uniform on the television news, I always feel a bit uneasy.*

In the summer of 1945 the first American tanks appear at the corner of my street. The *Friends*, as they're called, get enough to eat, wear new uniforms, and keep their boots shined. They bring with them white bread that can be obtained with ration tickets. My street falls within the American sector. In the ranking of the occupation forces, the Russians are at the bottom, the French are mediocre, and the British often sadistic. One is sure to be treated correctly by 'the Friends'. They have an officers' club near the post office in the Hauptstrasse. That's where all the young women go to dance the boogie-woogie with the handsome *sergeants* of the U.S. army. *Don't get the wrong idea!,* insists Frau Rath, who doesn't want to be taken for one of those girls falling for American soldiers. *I was married. I had to take care of my household. I couldn't go off dancing!* The *Friends* are responsible for quite a bit of corruption in her eyes. *In our city, before the war, everything was just as it should be. We went to school in our school uniforms and wore our Sunday best at the end of the week. Today, everyone's wearing jeans all the time. We copied that from the*

Americans. Germans imitate everything, and yet Germany's a country of high culture!

When one listens closely to the tone of Frau Rath's voice, you can hear a hint of pride, even a tremolo of pleasure, linked to the fact that they made it through all that. Frau Rath enjoys remembering those years of austerity. She and her husband started with nothing. They had worked like dogs. *Today, they ought to take inspiration from us! When one thinks back at the speed with which we rebuilt everything!* Frau Rath can't get over it. *Were we good builders, or what! Everything was destroyed, and by the middle of the 1950s Germany was again at the top of the world economy. Today we're in a better situation than all the others. And we did it all in only a half-generation.*

From the window of her room at the retirement home, Frau Rath can see the Christmas market down below in the square. All the useless stuff, the ridiculous gadgets and piles of candy and sweets. All this abundance. She belongs to the generation that finished what was on the plate, reused leftovers and remnants, and smoothed out gift wrapping to use it again the following Christmas. *Today we overdo everything. My God! Something new is always being proposed all the time. People are selling the most incredible things. Yes, children today live in a fairy-tale land. Doing without, as a motor, is missing from our society. Privation changes everything. Needing something brings cleverness and ingenuity. In the past, people were more flexible and had more dexterity. Today we feel cramped.*

11

And to Think They Lost the War

It's like when a new slide appears in the projector. Clack, clack. The high Wilhelminian buildings with their ornamental mouldings disappear. Then there's the blinding blank white screen. And then comes the new slide: plain Lego-like structures, four stories high, simple flat roofs, nothing fancy. At the end of the 1950s my street's appearance changes dramatically. Out go the extravagant developers of 1904 and in comes the sober regional government of Berlin-West with its *Aufbau-Programm* for building subsidized housing.

The post-war urban planners are in a hurry. The most urgent cases need immediate attention and all these homeless people wandering the streets need to be rehoused – those whose homes were bombarded and refugees who have arrived from lost territories to the east. The word *EILT!* (*Urgent!*) appears stamped in blue ink on the correspondence of the regional directorate for housing programmes and the urban services department of Schöneberg. *Urgent!* No more time to continue patching up and jerry-rigging the tired old buildings that are cracking more each day. They have to be blown up. The photographers Scholz and Westphal immortalized each ruin before demolition. It was important to document the deplorable condition of each building in order to fend off possible future complaints from a former owner who had not yet been heard from but who could reappear one day. On the back of each photo is the demolition date. Number 2, dynamited 21.4.1949. Number 8, dynamited 28.3.1949. Number 11, dynamited 6.7.1949. Number 20/21, dynamited 27/28.7.1949. Number 27, dynamited 20.4.1949. Number 30, building in ruins, dynamited 13.4.1949. The ruined remains of numbers 9, 11 and 19–22 are not blown up until the early 1960s. After the dynamite there are so many holes to fill. *Urgent!* No time to think about beauty or spend hours poring over blueprints from avant-garde architects or invent a new street. *Urgent!* Things have to be done fast, simply, efficiently and especially in a public-minded way. *Licht, Luft, Sonne* (light, air, sun) are the watchwords of the day. Finished – those perpetually shady back courtyards, the narrow opening of the street, and the buildings pressed up one against another. There needs to be space. In front of the new buildings will be a wide band of grass surrounded by a fence. When you place the pre-war map over the post-war map, you can clearly see that the path of the street has deviated a bit. The new street is crooked.

The flats in the new buildings are light, well heated, and their small rooms have low ceilings. No more old doors that creak as you open them. No more draughty windows. No more outsized rooms that are impossible to furnish and heat. No more temperamental stoves with their damp heat and offensive smells – only adjustable radiators and central heating. To move into a new building is a sign of being on the way up socially. Above the front door is the brass plaque of the *Aufbau-Programm*: the Berlin bear in profile with its paws up and tongue out.

Of the few old buildings that were still standing then,

practically all had mouldings that were flaking off and sometimes falling on the pavement. No owner had the money to restore the sophisticated ornaments on the facades. And in any case, those kinds of mouldings had been out of fashion for some time. Too pompous! Too ostentatious! Too ugly! – so said the critics pioneering the new architecture. I can only imagine how upset the stucco artists and artisans who did all that fine work at the beginning of the century would be if they could hear this storm of criticism. And how disappointed Georg Haberland would be if he could see the passion of his life denigrated in this way. Piece by piece, during the reconstruction years, the damaged mouldings are destroyed. And in fact, the new residents in my street become weary of the daily reminders of a past that's fading away before their eyes. These vestiges are a pitiful sight that clashes with the triumphant economic miracle they are working so hard to advance. They have no desire to bear the burden of all these bits and pieces of an imperial past. They want all to be clean and clear. So the ornaments and fanciful touches return to dust little by little and disappear. Smooth stucco of a drab grey colour that leaves no trace is applied to the facades. My street loses a little bit of its soul.

I have often wondered, when looking at these facades stripped of all ornament, why the Germans in the post-war era showed so little affection for the rare old stones that had survived the bombings. This methodical destruction of all mouldings did not happen in France. And even in Alsace, where Wilhelminian blocks of flats were built during the Reichsland period, there was no such mutilation. Yet after the Second World War, the Alsatians would have had every reason to want to cover over the traces of their German past that weighed so heavily on their torn identity. In 1945, they wanted to have nothing to do with their neighbour, now fallen into disgrace, on the other side of the Rhine. That's why my Berlin street seemed immediately so familiar to me. It looked like a cut-out from the décor of my childhood in Strasbourg. It was almost identical to the street where I'd lived in a top-floor mansard flat as a student in the German neighbourhood behind the Place de la République (formerly Kaiserplatz). The layout of the flats, the stairwells, the little terrace in the kitchens and the stucco of the facades were all the same. It's just that in Strasbourg my street was intact and displayed a peaceful beauty that no one dared to disturb, whereas in Berlin my street was broken and barely recognizable.

It's easy for a foreigner to mistake the age of these naked facades that resemble plucked chickens. When Hannah Kroner-Segal's daughter Evelyn came to see me in Berlin some weeks after our meeting in New York, she thought the 1904 buildings were from the 1950s. I had to take her past the front door and show her the entryway and stairwell before she was able to make a link between the exterior and the interior, imagine the facade as it was back then, and begin to form a picture of her mother's living situation before her emigration to America. In the name of what doctrinaire principles were the buildings of my street deprived of their memories? One is entitled to ask what destroyed them the most: the many bombs unleashed by the RAF or the unimaginative post-war urban planners who rushed headlong to either dynamite or to scrape, polyfilla and stucco over the last vestiges of its imperial past?

My street presses on with the rebuilding at a frenzied pace and with a triumphant air. For the second time in less than a century, steam shovels, backhoes and cement mixers transform my street into an immense building site. Cranes are erected that touch the sky. Workmen are on the job from dawn to dusk, and sometimes at night with the aid of powerful bright lights. They work in rain, snow, and even on Saturdays. They seem to never stop hammering, excavating, digging, extracting. The noise is constant. People roll up their sleeves and set to it – sweating, aching, slaving away. In a darkly comical way, my street has landed back where it started. On the surface, there looks to be the same effervescence in the fifties and sixties as there was in 1904. But my street has lost that carefree eagerness it had at the start of the century, that naive joy at the thought of building an eternal future. Now there's a relentless animal desire to fix what's broken, cover over the horror it has survived, and smother the fear.

In fact, my street is hardly a chic address any more. The grand luxury of the pre-war haute bourgeoisie is over. The directories from the sixties and seventies show a clear social makeover. Gone are the professors and lawyers, the wealthy retirees and high-ranking military personnel. My street is taken over by artisans, retailers, ordinary employees and petty civil servants. In these registries one finds a railway conductor, a seamstress, a house painter, a lathe operator, a machine assembly worker, a car body specialist, several electricians and construction workers, a waitress, a cloakroom attendant, a cook, a restaurant owner, three bakers, a pastry chef, a butcher, several accountants and office workers, a hairdresser, an embroiderer, a dressmaker, two truck drivers, a constable, a police chief, two postal workers – one retired, two window washers, a rug merchant and a retired manager. Then there are a few rare birds such as the composer who goes by the name Voicu Petru, a ballet master, an actor specializing in secondary roles, and a concert pianist. They live in the new housing blocks or in the old subdivided flats.

At the urban planning office, requests for building permits flood in. The shoe repairman Johannes Jawerts sends in a request for permission to hang up an advertising sign. It is to be a clear, nose-shaped panel with a text in red letters bordered with black on a white background that says: *Rapid Resoling – Express Shoes*.

At number 5, the retail business of H. Müggelberg – a seller of fruits and vegetables, gourmet foods, milk and spirits – requests permission to place a red sign with the Coca-Cola logo on it in front of the shop (and includes two photos). The letter has been typed on carbon paper in a shaky style with spelling mistakes. In the same building Richard John requests permission to install two glass panels with an ivory border 70 x 180 cm in size on which are written *Bärenbier – The Beer that puts you in a good mood!*

Marta Schreiner requests permission to attach an automatic cigarette distributor to the side of her tobacconist's shop at number 26.

These requesters all include a little black-and-white photo of the front of their establishment. One sees a bare wall, a narrow window, and a little glass-panelled door. And the corny publicity signs that were known as *Reklame*: *Express Service. Heels repaired in five minutes! Shoes lengthened and widened*, advertises the shoemaker. *Gourmet Foods – Milk* is written between two Coca-Cola logos in front of H. Müggelberg's shop. The owner has announced in white paint on the window the sale price for potatoes and the arrival of new fruits. As the years pass and the requests accumulate, the store fronts multiply and the items on offer diversify: tubes of concentrated milk, pineapples in syrup, assorted vegetables and ravioli in cans. There were no courgettes or aubergines for sale in H. Müggelberg's grocery store – only seasonal produce from Northern Europe.

Each time I look at these photos, they bring back tender memories of a lost era that was still alive during my childhood – the time of small neighbourhood shopkeepers who would greet you with a *How are you doing this morning, Ma'am?*, inquire about your corns or your uterus, or about the school grades of your son or daughter, and thereby weave the social fabric among the inhabitants of the street. It was while dealing with these merchants that we would bump into each other, chat, and gather the news of the street about births, illnesses and deaths, as well as scandalous titbits. It was a world of clear contours that was still simple and slow. No doubt a bit narrow, but on a human scale.

My street pulled itself together and looked straight ahead – and, above all else, it worked. It worked constantly. *When he got back from his imprisonment in Russia, my father worked his legs off*, a neighbour told me after I'd started a conversation on the pavement one morning. I'm getting ready to sympathise with her about how sad it must have been that her father was not able to take it easy, take better care of his health, be granted a little more free time, enjoy small pleasures and some tranquillity after all the horrible years he spent in Russia, but just as I'm about to sing my hymn in praise of indolence, my neighbour declares with proud conviction: *That generation went through so many ordeals, some of them got through two world wars – they were a lot more solid than this generation. What they went through built their character! People who work a lot develop a particular kind of energy and don't let anything get to them!* Six-day weeks, two weeks' holiday a year – no problem. All the elderly people in my neighbourhood vigorously defend that firm work ethic with absolutely no reservations. There is nothing worse in their eyes than layabouts and laziness.

My street is beginning to awaken childhood memories. In the 1960s I was still a little girl, but I would listen to the adults when my French family gathered at the table for Sunday meals. I heard their fascination, their perplexity and sometimes their anger – along with a large dose of envy and resentment – when they talked about Germany. I hear the voice of my grandmother, born in 1902, and her mocking almost aggressive tone, so contrary to her generally droll and generous personality, when she would declare, *And to think they lost the war, and now look at them, richer than us!* She couldn't get over it. And she didn't hide that she considered it deeply unfair, this undeserved *success story* that the losers of the war were in the process of writing for themselves. And when she got really worked up, she would speak of *les Boches*. In no time at all, Germany had become the second biggest economy in the world – and a dominant force in the areas of household electronics, machine tools, automobiles and chemical products. Germany seemed to be feeling good about itself – well-fed and nicely comfortable with its *Wohlstand* (affluence and prosperity). I recall hearing my mother close her *Spiegel* magazine, which she would read on the balcony while taking her coffee after lunch, and remark to my father, *Listen to this! Nearly two out of three Germans believe they are living through the happiest time in their history!* And I remember my father's reply: *After working themselves to exhaustion, they hardly think of the past any more. It's handy, all that work. For them, the Nazi time is no more than a bad dream and the war a mere interlude.* My mother, who had read the phrase somewhere, shoots back with *Work replaces the work of mourning.*

I remember Sunday excursions on the other side of the border – to the Black Forest, to Freiburg, to Karlsruhe, Offenburg and Baden-Baden. I remember being in the family car and everyone's snide remarks as we gazed out the windows and saw the impeccably rebuilt towns and mile after mile of advertising for Bosch, AEG, Miele, Mercedes, Volkswagen, Kaffee Hag, Dr. Oetker, Nivea, Sparkasse (savings bank) and Reisebüro (travel agency) – a veritable hit parade of solid, honest products and services. I remember the big cars parked along the pavements, the perfect red-and-white checked tablecloths at the inns, the syrupy *Schlager* music on the radio, and the people filing out of church after mass. An orderly idyll indeed. Everything clean, everything as it should be. *German economic miracle* was an expression I heard throughout my childhood. It was a sort of magic phrase that the adults would pronounce, wide-eyed, filled with a mix of genuine admiration and envious rage. Germany rebounded with such total and unexpected energy. And I'm not lying when I say that for a long time I believed the German people had special magical powers – a bit like what one hears at catechism about Jesus multiplying the bread and the fishes. The Germans knew how to turn horror into success, shame into the good conscience of a necessary job economically well done, depression into obsessional productivity, ruins into cute single-family houses overflowing with geraniums. Of course, Baden-Württemberg in the 1960s was not Berlin. Post-war conditions last much longer in the city located on the front than in Swabia with its *schaffe-schaffe-Häusle-baue* ('work-work-build-your-house', a quasi-anthem). Nevertheless, my street takes its place as a modest but genuine parcel in this wonderland of new prosperity.

12

The Revenants

John Ron returned to our street for the first time in 1957. Nineteen years earlier he had fled on a train leaving for Venice. This return was not to be a stroll down memory lane, nor was he going to allow himself to be engulfed by strong emotions. He returned with a precise objective: to consult with an attorney specialized in administrative matters about how to put together a dossier requesting reparations against the German Reich from the central indemnities office in Berlin – *an honourable gesture of Konrad Adenauer, who accorded me some financial compensation in recognition of the loss of my parents and the interruption of my studies.*

It's an expedited stay – fourteen days, not a day longer. John Ron rents a room from a very pleasant woman who makes him coffee and open-face liver sausage sandwiches every morning. They speak of the weather – wet for July. Not a word about the past. *Except the usual complaint about the air raids and the women raped when the Russians arrived. The Germans had the clear conscience of people who had truly suffered,* said John Ron. He is convinced that his landlady knows he's Jewish, *but even the word 'Jew' was taboo.* Moreover, he thought it *improper* to relate what happened to his family. In the evening, when he's in bed, the questions rise up: why come back to Germany? To meet an old kind teacher in a tea room? To pay a call on his mother's old Christian friend who returns to him Irma Rothkugel's white and yellow satin wedding dress and tells him that the last suitcase of his family's photos and letters burned in an air raid? To let his insides be eaten away with sadness and rage? Who is still alive? What had become of his classmates? He goes and knocks on doors. He asks neighbours. His parents, aunts and uncles are no longer there. No one asks what became of them. *People didn't show the least curiosity about my parents' fate or my own. Even my old friends asked nothing. Nothing.* This experience is unbearable.

Of the street of his childhood *there is nothing left but a sign naming a street that no longer exists. It was quite surreal!* John Ron does not dare to push open the door to his building. He stays on the pavement. And there, still attached to the garden fence, is the ceramic plaque of the office of Leon Rothkugel. He writes to his sister: *Ilse, it was a journey back to our childhood that was painful on more than one count. Our house is still standing, but there are only strangers there now. I spoke with a group of young students in order to counter the generally negative impressions that I have of the older generation of Germans. I believe I picked up certain signs indicating that these young people look at life in a more sober and less arrogant way than their parents' generation did.*

Don't play the magnanimous man, whatever you do! Ilse counselled him before his departure. John Ron has to fill out a ton of papers in triplicate. The tone of the instructions for filling out the forms is stupefying. *The examination of requests improperly formulated or unreadable will be deferred! Refrain from requesting any clarifications and from protesting! All erroneous information, whether intentional or due to negligence, may result in criminal charges but will also result in the complete disqualification of your right to reparations!* John Ron submits the pink form *Loss of life: Everything was rule-governed and divided into categories in the proper German manner. Loss of parents corresponded to a certain number of Deutschmarks according to a very precise chart. It's a bit awkward to quantify a murder in this way. It was necessary to prove my father's income and establish a list of all furniture and missing jewellery with, for each item, an estimation of its value at the time. All of these proceedings were of an indescribable brutality. Thinking of them today, I cry tears of laughter and anger. I deposited the money I received in England. But I was badly advised. The British pound declined so precipitously that I lost almost everything. Ilse was required to give her money over to the common account of the kibbutz. She was a little bitter.* John Ron was relieved when he boarded his plane back to the United States.

He returned to Berlin a second and last time with his sister Ilse in 1968. They stay at a hostel run by local residents in the Charlottenburg neighbourhood. The Wilheminian building has very high ceilings, big beds and thick down comforters. Young German people are doing 'sit-ins' and 'go-ins' as part of demonstrations against the American war in Vietnam and also protesting against the Springer publishing group for its *Hetzkampagnen*, or witch-hunts targeting all dissenters. The student leader Rudi Dutschke has recently been the victim of an attack on the Kurfürstendamm and the Berliner *Tagesspiegel* writes: *It seems the time has come for the country of the economic miracle, this welfare state saturated despite all the slogans for reunification, this country where one can live and demonstrate so magnificently, this bourgeois society with Berlin as its central nervous system, to face its grand moment of truth when it comes to domestic politics. Storms of violence are wracking German cities. The question is being asked whether we will meet this challenge or if the German tendency for radical political hatred will break our young democratic customs and habits that tolerate and respect the declarations of those who do not think as we do*. But above all, the German youth are demanding that their parents come clean: What were you doing during that time? *Auseinandersetzung, Aufarbeitung, Vergangenheitsbewältigung* – these are the key words of the day that occur in their verbal confrontations with the past. I do not know if the 1968 revolution actually disrupted life on my street – if, for example, in some of its flats there were any of those legendary meals where sons would goad their fathers, or if the local shopkeepers looked on shocked and appalled at the long-haired, coarsely shaven commune weirdos. But I am sure that the *Schöneberger Echo* was relaying the true preoccupations of the inhabitants of my street that year:

ABC Personal Credit: Fast and Easy ... for a modern kitchen, for new furniture, for a new television, for new curtains and rugs.

The present situation cannot continue! Road accidents are constantly on the rise! This is why you should be careful, respectful and understanding on the road!

Look for generous donors! We regret the continued shortage of public benches!

Not everyone can be a professional athlete, but everyone can go bowling!

The malady that costs the most is tooth decay, and an increase in the number of cavities is becoming ever more common!

Prevention is better than treatment! Vaccinate your child against tuberculosis, starting in kindergarten!

Then there are the advertisements: *VW automatic – no clutch, no need to change gears! Your new slimness will make others envious when you're wearing the Playtex-Lycra girdle – short and long models! Denmark, Norway, Sweden – Grand Tour of Scandinavia by Jet and Modern Passenger Trains! Housework made easy: If you like beating carpets, waxing the floor on your knees and dusting, you don't need a vacuum cleaner or waxing machine. But with our vacuum and waxer, you save time and energy.*

In the four issues covering 1968 that I examined, only one little article contained a reminder that the war had left traces: *The Schöneberg rail service will soon undertake construction work on the following lines ... In order to prevent accidents, people are encouraged to provide all available information about any remaining buried munitions or unexploded bombs dating from the war.*

John Ron and his sister stroll about Berlin. Ilse never stopped calling her brother Hans, and here in Berlin that first name sounds oddly enough like the right choice. *I wanted to feel my feet on the Berlin cobblestones once more! That's where a part of me is!,* Ilse confides in her brother, who replies: *If you said to me, 'My God, how beautiful it would be to live in Berlin again!' I would ask you, 'What's the matter? Are you unwell? Do you want an aspirin?'* Together they dare to do it – they ring the bell at the former Rothkugel flat. A stranger opens the door. They introduce themselves. The woman offers to show them around the property. Everything is mixed up. The flat is cut in two. Five or six renters live in the front part. All those names on the buzzers. A crowded flat-share. Only the kitchen's location is unchanged. The cupboards, the sink, the blue and white tiles. The smell has not changed since 1933.

It was their last visit. John Ron has never returned to Berlin since.

In 1946, Lilli and Heinrich Ernsthaft return to their street for the first time by taxi. Number 3 is one of the rare buildings on the street that's still standing. It's in pitiful shape. When he returns from his wartime captivity, the owner Oskar Lohmann hurries to undertake the most urgent repairs. With scraps of this and that to build with, they manage to construct an improvised roof and facade to at least protect the building's insides from the weather. The flats need to be inhabitable again. The rents need to come down month by month as the housing shortage subsides.

The once beautiful flat is chopped in two – a bit like the lives of the Ernsthafts themselves. The back of the flat is inhabited. The front one is in absolutely terrible condition but it has remained registered in the name of Heinrich Ernsthaft. *The parquet had dried and curled up like rose petals in the corners of the room, lots of furniture was missing, but fortunately the large, heavy pieces, many built into the walls, were still there. We were surprised by how much we ended up finding in the end. Since many people didn't even have a bed, it seemed fairly understandable that they helped themselves to stuff in a flat that appeared abandoned and carried off what they needed,* said Lilli Ernsthaft.

At first, the flat is uninhabitable. The Ernsthafts continue to live in a little room at the Jewish hospital. The proud businessman is now catalogued as *Opfer des Faschismus,* a victim of fascism. In the photo on his temporary ID card, Heinrich Ernsthaft has an indescribable sadness in his eyes. In the space for entering *Nationality* on Lilli Ernsthaft's displaced-persons identity card one sees *'undetermined'*. It was not until 1950 that she would recover her Austrian nationality. Their son Harry becomes an English and music teacher at the French lycée and enrols at Humboldt University.

Only after her husband's death on 21 April 1947 does Lilli Ernsthaft begin to renovate the flat, which had been assigned to a family made homeless by the air raids. *It should be said to their credit that they did not move in – the two women believed it would have been a bad omen,* Lilli Ernsthaft explains.

In a letter stored at the Brandenburg archives dated 25 March 1943 and nervously stamped *Urgent!*, the Reichstag service, on the authority of the recommendation of Reichstag president, Marshall Göring, who *wishes that all steps be taken as soon as possible to provide relief for this heavy loss*, implores the Brandenburg director of finances to supervise with particular care the housing reassignment of Dr Richard Schneider, a second-level attaché at the Reichstag, in an available Jewish flat of appropriate standing.

In 1948, Richard Schneider writes to inform Lilli Ernsthaft that *all of your flat furniture was purchased by the Neugebauer furniture company in a sales transaction that was unforced. It was from this specialized dealer that I was able in turn to buy some of the furniture in an entirely legal manner. As I learned at the time, the Gestapo most likely made a first pass and took valuable objects from the flat that were easily transportable. When your flat was severely damaged in an air raid in November 1943, and when it suffered significant water damage from leaks, I supervised the transportation of the least cumbersome objects by wheelbarrow and had them stored in the basement of the former Reichstag on Königsplatz.* Dr Schneider's letter includes a drawing of the Reichstag. *I have no knowledge as to who bought the other objects. In any case, when my wife entered the flat for the first time, all the armoires and dresser drawers were empty. My wife suspects that the president of the Neugebauer company may have taken these possessions for his daughter who was getting married at the time. We did not use the things we purchased and we have no intention of using them. We would like to leave them all to you, and we suppose that the department in charge of paying you your indemnity for material damages will also reimburse us the sum that I paid to buy them.*

If one day things get bad, remember the prosthesis! Lilli Ernsthaft did not forget her husband's admonition. Thanks to the sale of his platinum dentures, she was able to repair the wood floors and there was even a little left over for two armchairs. *Good friends had kept safe the bed and table linens, some cushions and the grand piano. Of course, it was only a temporary solution, but most people in those days were making do with makeshift solutions of all kinds.*

How could she return to live there – she who had only escaped deportation by extreme good fortune, whose son had lived in a cellar for two years like a cornered animal, and whose mother was murdered at Theresienstadt?

No Jews from my street who emigrated in the thirties give any thought to returning to live in Germany after the war. Lilli Ernsthaft was the only person who decided to stay. In the 1950s, the new state of Israel harshly condemns those Jews who continue to live *on the German soil gorged with blood*. Lilli Ernsthaft returns to the same street and the same building. What was to become of this decimated street? How would a Jewish survivor get on there now? How did neighbours who passed her on the street react? Did they lower their eyes? Or did they stare at her like one might stare at a ghost? *This flat was the place where she belonged, her haven, her refuge,* her niece Elga tried to explain to me.

Anti-Semitism did not disappear overnight – nor was the street de-Nazified with one wave of a magic wand. How could Lilli Ernsthaft return to buy her bread from the same baker who only a few years earlier had refused to serve her, snapping, *And I have every right not to, according to the law*? How can she return to the Kaiser-Barbarossa pharmacy run by Ludwig Guercke, a Nazi party member since 1935, who wrote to the prefect of police requesting a flat near his establishment: *I would be very appreciative, Herr Prefect, if you could issue me as soon as possible an attestation that would help me acquire one of the Jewish flats recently requisitioned in the neighbourhood by the inspector general of construction, Herr Speer. I am sixty years old and work alone with my wife in the pharmacy with no other qualified personnel. Because of the distance of my flat in Spandau, I cannot return home for lunch and thus spend the whole day at my shop from eight in the morning until eight at night. These long hours and the problem of not getting a proper lunch have significant repercussions on our health. Heil Hitler!* How could Lilli Ernsthaft engage in conversation with the same neighbours across the hall who from their balcony window had witnessed an early dawn round-up of thirteen Jews in the building? Lilli Ernsthaft was a troubling witness. People carefully avoided asking her how she survived. And she was careful to keep the conversation from sliding down slippery slopes. Was she perhaps afraid to hear what they might say? Did she hope that by pretending nothing had happened she would be able to pick up the tenuous thread of her life as it was before? After all, what's not talked about doesn't exist. But what did this rather frivolous but genuinely kind lady manage to do with her sadness, her fear, her bitterness and anger, and perhaps her desire for revenge?

As soon as she was back in her street, Lilli Ernsthaft jumped back on the grand merry-go-round of social obligations. *Alas,* she notes in passing, *I only have two Jewish acquaintances left.* Herr and Frau Kutschera return from Theresienstadt in 1945. In 1946 they reopen the Kaffee Wien. Karl Kutschera tries to forget that he was one of the first businesses to attract the attention of the *Stürmer* – the weekly magazine published in Nuremberg had launched a virulent campaign denouncing *the Jewish Eldorado* of Kurfürstendamm that belonged to *the despicable Jew* Kutschera. He tries to forget that in 1937, in order to avoid being shut down, he was forced to sign over his lease to two non-Jewish associates. Every day he's overcome with vertigo when he thinks of his children Karin and Gerd. A broken man, he died in 1950 from heart failure. His wife Josephine would take over and run the place until the early 1970s.

But the Ernsthafts also renew ties with friends *who sympathized with the Nazis and then discreetly took their distance.* Immediately after the war, while still living at the Jewish hospital, they go out to dinner with *our friends Fritz Aschinger and the business consultant Lohnert.* What did they talk about at the restaurant that evening? Fritz Aschinger, Lilli Ernsthaft's ace in the worldly game of cards, had so compromised himself. To shore up his empire that was teetering on bankruptcy, he took advantage of the Aryanization of Jewish businesses and was able to acquire the Kempinksi hotel group in 1937 at a price well below its true market value. Did he continue to offer caviar and crêpes Suzettes to Heinrich Ernsthaft and his wife on Saturday evenings after 1933? Or did he prefer to change pavements when by chance he crossed paths with his former business associate?

The grand hotels and the gourmet restaurant Rheingold were destroyed by bombs. On 8 February 1949, the Aschinger businesses, which were situated in the Soviet zone, were expropriated without an indemnity of any kind and re-baptised as state-run food companies called *Aktivist,* a name without savour or sensuality that marks the end of the Aschinger pleasure palaces. Fritz Aschinger and his sister Elizabeth commit suicide in Berlin in August 1949.

In May 1949, Lilli and Harry Ernsthaft go to the government offices in Berlin to file their request for reparations from the German Reich. This is the beginning of an interminable bureaucratic ordeal that Lilli Ernsthaft will obsess over for more than ten years. She has kept the mountain of correspondence relating to it. After aunt Lilli's death, her niece Elga places the large folders into a travel bag and stores them in the basement between some wicker chairs and boxes of books. One afternoon when I went to see her, she handed over to me the entire dust-covered sack. It was reading these piles of letters that allowed me to understand the hell that Lilli and Harry Ernsthaft went through all those years as they tried to restart their lives and move back into number 3.

Lilli Ernsthaft begins by conducting a complete inventory, piece by piece, down to the smallest teaspoon, of her lost possessions: *Very elegant bedroom with a large dresser with marble sink bowl, two night tables, a vanity, two large chrome mirrors, and a large armoire with glass front filled with suits, coats and underclothes. A dressing room with twelve feet of shelving filled with women's clothes, coats, hats, handbags, assorted fine lingerie, all of the finest quality.* She describes the Meissen porcelain angels in the glass case in the living room: *One is stirring chocolate, the other is playing the flute.* She makes a list of phantom objects that haunt the naked flat: an exquisite coffee and mocha machine with gold detailing of the brand Hutschenreuther that can serve eighteen people, the 500 books in the study, the collection of very valuable musical scores and records. She even lists the two mattresses in the bedroom made with real horsehair, all of the window blinds and curtains, the large stocks of food and soap in the pantry. The authorities spent years dealing only with the oriental room. This little folly out of *One Thousand and One Nights* that was now entirely gone had contained *a Kilim canopy held by two crossed weapons, piles of genuine Persian carpets, hand-made Smyrna cushions, small ebony tables with mother-of-pearl inlay, various saddlebags, a real water pipe, an authentic samovar, two octagonal ivory stools with mother-of-pearl inlay, and eight or ten valuable silver and nielloed silver cigarette cases with dedications by famous singers and actors like Caruso, Giampetro and Massary, offered as gifts to their friend Heinrich Ernsthaft.*

She collects sworn affidavits. Klara Knospe, a seventy-three-year-old, unmarried, retired housekeeper who worked eighteen years for the Ernsthafts and who was forced to abandon her position in 1933, writes: *It was a very well-kept household.* Magdalene Lied, a ninety-year-old divorced woman and Harry's former music professor, describes *a very well-furnished flat with many rugs. Some pieces of furniture were of very exquisite styles.* The German state comes to pass its finger on the surfaces of the furniture to detect any dust.

Harry finds this administrative hoop-jumping humiliating, with all the requests for detailed proofs of the claims made and of the arbitrary confiscations, and the demands for insurance policy histories and bank account details. He is disgusted when his mother is asked to furnish proof establishing that the claimant belongs to the category of persons persecuted for racial, religious or political reasons. He can't stand any longer the pleading letters she's required to write: *My husband was forced to hand over a coat entirely lined with sealskin also with a collar of sealskin.* To which the furrier replies: *The devaluation compared to the value new results from the natural aging of skins and furs.* Harry cannot believe his eyes when, in 1955, still their lawyer is still obliged to remind the administration that *the disposal of property belonging to Jewish owners of the time was in no way done as a regular sales transaction, the true value of objects being several times higher than the sums actually paid in the case of these forced sales.* How many times would antique and furniture dealers organize auctions in the flats of people deported from my street, selling their furniture at prices well below market value! It was a veritable Easter-egg hunt for the rest of the population seeking bargains. Harry is outraged. His parents were plucked like chickens and here they are having to do endless somersaults for years on end to recover some money which in the end will be a small fraction of the value of the goods stolen from them. Reading these files, one has the impression that for the state it's a case like any other. There isn't the slightest indication of any moral obligation or the admission of fault in any of it. The state used all available means to minimize the size of the indemnities that were paid out.

The trial in the 1950s that pitted Ernst Siemann against Lilli Ernsthaft is a nightmare that involves years of claims and counterclaims. On 6 June 1938, Ernst Siemann, for twenty-five years one of the most faithful employees of Ernsthaft & Co., purchased all of Heinrich Ernsthaft's shares in the company as well as the five-storey building where it was headquartered in the Trebbinerstrasse. The companies of several Jewish residents in my street were 'Aryanized' in this way – to the advantage of non-Jews, often former employees, and at bargain basement prices. The written correspondence between the widow and the former employee after the war testifies to how mean the trial was:

I cannot get over that you've stabbed me in the back in this brutal way. (Ernst Siemann, 27 October 1949)

I regret the polemical tone that you think you are able to use toward me. I hope that we will find within the framework of the current legal proceedings a satisfying solution for the two parties, and kindly request you remain patient until we do. (Lilli Ernsthaft, 8 November 1949)

If we were to have recourse to negotiations before the reparations commission, I would not hesitate to point out, concerning the value of the company, that Ernsthaft & Co. only kept its head above water during the period just prior to Aryanization thanks to cheating and food frauds. Perhaps you thought I would remain silent on this subject? If you want to preserve your reputation and that of your husband, you know how you ought to behave. (Ernst Siemann, 29 November 1949)

The decline in sales after 1933 and the withdrawal of certain brasseries, which had to put some distance between themselves and Herr Ernsthaft because he was Jewish, are entirely consistent with the methods employed by the Nazis. It was therefore Herr Siemann's responsibility, after Aryanization and his rise to director of the company, to prove his competence by restoring it to its previous level of activity. If he believes he's able to push Frau Ernsthaft to conclude an arrangement to his advantage by insulting her former husband, he is mistaken. Herr Siemann's proposal is refused. *Frau Ernsthaft will not go forward with any transaction with Herr Siemann after the latter's recent declarations. He has definitively cut all ties between himself and the former Ernsthaft & Co. We are requesting restitution.* (Lilli Ernsthaft's lawyer, 8 March 1950)

When one sees the mentality of Frau Ernsthaft on display, one is not surprised at the extensiveness of anti-Semitism at the time. (Ernst Siemann, 28 December 1951)

I would like to underline finally that I suffered more at the hands of the Nazi regime than Herr and Frau Ernsthaft, because what I endured as the manager of a Jewish company between 1933 and 1938 can only be conceived by someone who has endured it himself. The fifteen or so employees of the company harassed me whenever they got the chance calling me behind my back the valet of Jews. (Ernst Siemann, 14 June 1952)

In 1956 Harry emigrated to New York, where his future wife Rita, a cleaning lady at the Jewish hospital, had gone two years earlier. For Lilli Ernsthaft her son's decision is very wrenching. As she sees it, America *abducted* her son. He will no longer be coming home to number 3 for lunch at noon – her son who gave such fantastically popular lectures to audiences of hundreds at the recently inaugurated *Amerika-Haus*, and who was named the classical music selector for the RIAS radio station. She would try to console herself by exaggerating her son's successes in New York, such as his position as a bookseller with the famous publisher Doubleday. In similar fashion, she tried to get excited when he got a promotion and worked in the office that some years later would be occupied by Jacqueline Kennedy. When she travelled to New York, she would try and take pleasure in visiting her former classmate Ruth Mittler, who *had an elegant apartment on Park Avenue, the most distinguished of all the streets of New York, and who had invited five other girls of our class – nearly forty years later and after all the ordeals we had lived through – to an enormously moving reunion at her place.* While there she ran into Else Meyer, her neighbour from number 28, who was working as a waitress in a restaurant, whereas she had been living a life of silk and velvet in Berlin. When she finds herself alone again in her grand flat in Berlin, Lilli Ernsthaft is inconsolable. She misses her son. And yet, she did not for a second seriously consider joining him.

In New York, on 28 April 1978, Harry dies of cancer aged fifty-three. His mother is convinced that it's the damp cellar where he hid during the war that ended up killing him. The funeral service takes place in Forest Hills. Lilli brings her son's ashes back to Berlin. In the plane, sitting up straight in her seat, this tiny little lady frozen in anguish hugs her son's urn, now inside a handbag, against her chest throughout the entire flight. She places Harry's ashes in the family tomb at the Jewish cemetery, Weissensee. It's Sonya Rönnfeldt, the sister of Harry's former governess Grete, who picks up Lilli in her Trabant to drive her to the cemetery during the years living with the Berlin Wall. The night the Wall falls, Sonya rushes to number 3. Aunt Lilli is the only acquaintance she has on *the other side*. On 10 November 1989, the two women go out walking on the Kurfürstendamm. And when near the end of her life aunt Lilli could no longer get out of bed, Sonya comes once a week and helps her take a bath.

When I used to go to see Lilli Ernsthaft in the mid-nineties, I wondered how her building could still be standing. Number 3 is the only original building in its part of the street. A survivor just like its occupant. *Number 3 came through it*, we two neighbours say to each other. *A loner*, said Lilli Ernsthaft. Not to contradict her admiration for it, but number 3 was hardly the radiant diamond set among lesser stones in our street. It looked more like a big pumice stone with its black porous facade. The old elevator, covered in cobwebs and a thin layer of grime, had stood immobile since the war. The owner had some nerve leaving the place in such a state! Lilli Ernsthaft had often complained about it. Her building was the most worn-out looking one on the street. A crying shame! And when one thinks back to what it had looked like before the war! A distinguished dwelling. *For years we've been promised a runner for the stairwell*, she writes indignantly to the owner in 1958, *but instead of having one installed, you allow the very resourceful Frau Bandekow to place ancient threadbare little carpets on the steps – carpets she scrounged from other buildings. The new wall lamp and building map might not be out of place in the northern neighbourhoods of Berlin, but are hardly suited to what remains of this building that used to be so well maintained and absolutely splendid with its beautiful mirror and marble walls which are still intact.* Lilli Ernsthaft expresses her most vehement contempt when mentioning these *northern neighbourhoods* of Berlin. By north, she means Wedding, the working-class neighbourhood where the elegant haute bourgeoisie of the south-west would probably have never set foot if the Jewish hospital had not been located there. But the owner, Oskar Lohmann, does not want to take out a bank loan. And in any case, renovating would have been a money pit, especially since the rules in force during the time of the acute housing shortage prohibited raising rents in any significant way. Renovated or not, the rental income would have been the same.

I don't know if Lilli Ernsthaft was aware of the long trial that number 3 was at the centre of after the war, a conflict that hindered investment in the building. A heated correspondence is stored in the archives of the Berlin Land Offices. In 1950, the inheritors of an influential Jewish banker file a claim for reparations. Before their emigration at the end of the 1930s, the inheritors had signed over the building to Ida Lohmann and her son, Oskar Lohmann, a businessman. It was a forced sale like many that had taken place in my street. The Jewish owners were made to sell their property *for a pittance.* The inheritors' lawyer claims that *the transaction was concluded amid threats and under duress! The deal would never have taken place outside the context of the National-Socialist regime!* The inheritors demand a compensatory indemnity. Oskar Lohmann's lawyer objects and affirms that his client paid a correct price. In the wrestling match that the two lawyers become engaged in for years, there are a few low blows symptomatic of the climate of the time. On 5 April 1951, Oskar Lohmann writes: *The other party will concede that the fortune of the group of inheritors was entirely the fruit of speculative ventures, and principally the outcome of exploitation during the years of high inflation and distress for the German population which resulted in considerable economic benefit to the Jewish banking establishment.* On 4 May 1951, the lawyer for the group of inheritors replies furiously: *We categorically reject the accusations of property speculation and exploitation of distressed populations which are only too clearly recycled reiterations of Nazi regime propaganda.*

Then come the piles of bills and expert testimony proving that *extensive reconstruction work was contracted by Herr Oskar Lohmann to prevent the building from literally falling into complete disrepair. The goal is to determine the appreciation in value of number 3.* For years, Oskar Lohmann carefully kept the bills and receipts from building contractors. He makes a meticulous list of the expenses he has incurred: the number of bricks, the cubic feet of mortar, cement and plaster, the pounds of nails. He even counts the cost of hauling off rubble, and the number of hours worked by masons, carpenters and other artisans. He claims that during the blockade of Berlin when everything was in short supply he paid astronomic prices on the black market to obtain building materials.

The current owner of the building remembers that his grandfather would talk at the dinner table about the jousting between the two lawyers. *Herr Lohmann had only to remove one ring from his finger to purchase that building,* according to the inheritors' lawyer, repeating over and over that the price paid was a small fraction of its actual value. *This Jew turns up one day in Berlin with his shabby suitcase and buys up whole streets!,* replied Oskar Lohmann's lawyer, thus reviving the spectre of the stereotypical Jewish speculator who profited massively from runaway inflation. The grandfather said nothing more: *It wasn't his style at the end of a long evening and a few bottles of red wine to begin talking endlessly about the past. He only gave a few biographical details. But he wasn't a Nazi. Someone proposed that he buy the building. So why shouldn't I, he said to himself.*

For my grandfather, affirms the grandson, *this piece of property was simply an entirely ordinary way to invest his money. He was not wrapped up emotionally in the decision. The whole thing needed to work and generate rents that were more or less adequate – everything else was all the same to him. During the last fifteen years of his life, he never set foot in the building.*

Lilli Ernsthaft died too early to witness the belated restoration of her residence. In 2009, the facade at number 3 disappeared behind a green screen tarp stretched across scaffolding. For many weeks the building was closed in on itself, isolated from the rest of the street – in a sort of quarantine. Number 3 received a total makeover. The grandson, a post-war German, chose a challenging facade, not just a superficial quick-fix. Reviving the style of 1904 was out of the question however. *The old facade seemed too massive to me, too thick and heavy in that typical Wilhelminian way. I found those colonnades too pompous. It was the display of the great invincible Germany. No, no, what I wanted –* and he raised his arms to the sky with enthusiasm like some large bird preparing to take flight – *was something light, a bit playful, with a few Art Nouveau touches. A few elements are pre-fabricated polystyrene creations manufactured industrially, but all the floral pieces were done in the traditional mortar method by a Polish stucco specialist. With the naked eye you can't tell the difference. When someone walks by it today, he could believe that he's seeing the original facade.* He chose, he says, *a historicized interpretation, but a purely imaginary one that is not derived from any historical model.*

13

Finally, Glory!

Who would have believed that, one day, fate would string a thread between the street of my Berlin exile and the upper-floor maid's room under the eaves where, as a weightless, contemplative teenager, I lay stretched out on the bed listening to the same vinyl record for hours? I don't know where it ended up, but I remember the album cover showed a large drop of water splashing into an oily blue puddle. I didn't know it at the time, but the electronically assisted hang-gliding of the mind that I indulged in on those afternoons was actually preparation for the journey to the street of my adult life.

I recently spent a frenetic evening surfing aimlessly on the Internet. Entering my street name into Google just for fun, I stumbled accross a blog in French that recommended making a musical pilgrimage to it because an electronic music group had for many years used the former bakery at number 7B as their studio. The fact that, as the blogger affirmed, *the first sparks of Cosmic Music* were ignited at this dull blocky house built after the war seemed like some kind of joke.

I few clicks later and I discovered that the group in question was Tangerine Dream. I had also thought that they were

English, like Pink Floyd. I had never tried to find out more about the identity of those almost perfectly still silhouettes standing at their giant synthesizers. Along with Frederik, alias Reinhard Mey, Tangerine Dream was, as far as I know, the only German musical act popular in France at the time. They reigned alongside Jacques Brel, Maurice Béjart, Boris Vian, Monty Python, Greta Garbo and John F. Kennedy on the Olympus of my adolescence. They were a diverse group of deities, and, as I see now, ideologically incompatible. Discovering all these years later that one of them lived in my Berlin street was a revelation. So I decided to do some further research.

I came upon a video on YouTube. For one minute and twenty-five seconds, the camera does a panoramic travelling shot of my street as it looked in November 1974. Grey, silent, obscure, with its black facades looking as though they'd been carved out of a massive lump of coal. The sadness of the postwar years still sticks to the walls. The street looks like East Berlin before the fall of the Wall. I imagine the odour of the coal stoves and the pallid light of the streetlamps at dusk. Along the pavements there are a few cars old enough to be in a museum. The chestnut trees have not yet been planted. The street ends at the intersection with the major road. The large block of council flats that obstructs the way today has not yet been built. *Tangerine Dream, the emblematic group of German rock music abroad,* says an off-camera voice during the video. *For the last two years the records of the 'orange dream' have sold by the millions. The three founding members have achieved a success that most of their fellow musicians can only dream of: sold-out concerts abroad and a full calendar of projects for movies and television. In England the Berlin group is the focus of an ad campaign with the slogan* 'Tangerine Dream Rules!'

Then one sees a group of bearded men with long, stringy,

slightly greasy hair parted in the middle – symmetrical curtains hanging either side of a bunch of pale faces. They're sitting in a semi-circle, backs arched, eyes looking down, slumped in chairs amid a thick fog of cigarette smoke. On a low table in front of them are bottles of beer and an overflowing ashtray. *Our concern is to remain honest*, affirms one of them in a monotone voice. Feeling virtuous, he lashes out against the entertainment industry: *Shit, it's easy to let yourself go musically, just working the system. The whole music business is one big whorehouse. If you want to just be turning tricks, OK, it's your choice.* Instead of provoking joy, pride or a shiver of excitement, their remarkable success seems to have plunged the group into an inextricable crisis of confidence. *We don't want to act like stars!*, one of them explains. *We're trying to preserve our spontaneity!*, blurts out another. *We're expensive, but there's a good reason for that! It doesn't at all mean that we necessarily think of ourselves as part of an elite or anything very special!* One of them, particularly sinister looking, then mumbles almost to himself, *What do you want exactly?* It would seem he's become obsessed with this awkward introspection of his own mind. He says he's trying to live with *complete consciousness*. And that *man needs to realize himself.* All these tortured words spoken by Germans in the seventies and eighties. I don't understand much of what they're saying, except that life is an accumulation of unsolvable problems. They seem to be suffering, and preoccupied by the painful contemplation of the human condition. They resemble those teenage Germans on school field trips who would gather in small tight groups on the steps of the Cathedral in my home town Strasbourg. Serious, argumentative, unwashed, and not at all sexy. I confess I never had the patience to watch this video all the way to end, despite several tries. I'm disappointed. The gods of my teenage years have no panache – they're grey and sad! Every sentence they speak seems to require so much mental effort. Not a single smile, not any spark of passion in their voices. I just want to shake them and shout, Life is beautiful! Enjoy it! You are stars! Girls are at your feet! A young woman, a pretty brunette, the only female in this group of men, is the only one to let out a peep that almost resembles a burst of laughter – but it's quickly squelched. So Tangerine Dream turns out to be a bunch of preachy types obsessed with remaking the world? I admit I'm a bit sorry that it wasn't Monty Python who'd been my neighbours instead – life in my street would have been a bit funnier.

I end up finding an email address for Edgar Froese, the group's founder, and screw up my courage to write to him. Edgar Froese divides his time between Los Angeles and the outskirts of Vienna. He has made more than 120 albums, and was friends with Salvador Dali and Andy Warhol. He has composed music for sixty-four films in the United States and Europe, including three with Tom Cruise in the leading role. Tangerine Dream was once the warm-up band for Jimi Hendrix, and was nominated six times at the Grammy Awards. The group played at the Tiergarten, at the ice-hockey stadium in Warsaw, at the Bois de Boulogne and Palais des Sports in Paris, and at the Royal Albert Hall in London. In 1980, they were the first Western group to play at the Palace of the Republic in East Berlin. In the 1970s, Edgar Froese and his fellow musicians even participated in two initiatives of rapprochement between peoples. They played at the cathedrals in Reims and Coventry. The latter performance is said to have provoked an old bitter Englishman, probably a veteran of the Royal Air Force, to exclaim, *They came to bomb the place. Today they come with synthesizers.*

Edgar Froese was now living in other cosmic spheres. Was he

going to want to remember this little insignificant street where it all started? His reply to my email was not long in coming. A few days later, the abstract of a dense dissertation in sociology filled my screen: *Having moved into number 7B in 1970 and in 1976 into number 7 amounts to – given the context of the time – possessing extremely detailed knowledge of the cultural and social changes. Of course I don't know if your research takes up both the macro-sociological and the micro-sociological levels, but I suppose that in any case you must have gathered together much information concerning this 'central core' around the shadowy cultural practices of the Schöneberg bourgeoisie.*

Edgar Froese agreed to meet with me. I was over the moon, and also very intimidated. I imagined our 'reuniting' – my heart would stop beating as I held out my hand; the wine we'd share at the little Italian place at the end of the street; our visit together to number 7. He had moved into an old flat in the adjacent building in 1976 and established his *administrative and audio-technical headquarters* – in other words, his studio. In the twenties and thirties, Edgar Froese told me, it had been a bar called Tam Tam, which served as the meeting place for avant-garde Berlin artists in those days. It was the place to go for those who, at four in the morning, wanted to stylishly complete an evening that was already awash in alcohol. I was beside myself. But then Edgar Froese had to first go and record some film music in New York. It was only supposed to take a few weeks. We would agree later on a meeting time. He used to torture me with his messages: *We are going to meet, but where?* And he would sign them *007****. But I was not going to give up. Loyal groupie that I was, I waited.

After several months, an electronic season's greetings message arrived at Christmas: *Merry X-mas & Happy Holiday and a prosperous New Year! Warmest regards from Tangerine Dream.* Then the band, dressed in multi-coloured wigs, played a Christmas song in a hard rock style.

I remained patient. I was ready to jump on the next plane for Vienna or New York, or walk the short distance that separated me from number 7. The pleasure of anticipation kept me afloat. Until the day his wife informed me that Edgar Froese, back in Vienna for a few days, had fallen flat on his face in the street: *broken jaw, emergency operation, hospital stay, meeting unfortunately put off for now.* Our conversation could not take place in person, she wrote. It would have to happen via email.

Stumbling so close to the finish line, argh! I imagined my god mute and disfigured with a big bandage wrapped around his swollen bruised jaw ... and I watched him vanish into darkness and distance. My heart tightened when I walked past number 7 the next morning. Edgar Froese called it 'binary coding', the emails that we would exchange back and forth practically in real time. I sent a long list of questions beginning with 'Did this street have a particular meaning in your life?' His answer popped up on my screen some days later. To console me, Edgar Froese sent me a picture of him in an attachment. In a narrow Vienna street, a white-haired older man, still cool in his black shirt and white linen pants, is pointing out something to his wife in the distance. He had made a real effort. I had found an accomplice: *One doesn't get attached to streets – you leave them, you go back one day, or you abandon them forever. Streets can leave almost imperceptible traces in the life of a human being, or else deep impressions, memories, yes, even scars in one's soul. One needs to remember that a street is always a curved or straight line where hundreds of lives coexist, each with its cares and concerns. Beauty, ugliness, tragedy and drama are often separated from each other by the mere thickness of a*

partition wall. Streets spring up from the blueprints of some elite plan-
ner, but they are inhabited by people with the most diverse set of lives
and states of consciousness. In the past, streets were uninhabited arable
land, and they would re-become just that in a far off future. Everything
is cyclical. In my memory, I know every piece of pavement in that street
which for thirty years was the landmark I always returned to. And yet,
aside from that perception, no particular relation links me to it.

Then, suddenly, his message became meticulously precise.
He had moved into 7B, on the second floor at the corner of the
building, on 1 July 1970 – two and a half rooms in the new flat
of his in-laws. His wife was pregnant. He had come here grudg-
ingly. *Since I had grown up on the outskirts of Berlin, in the rural area*
of Rudow, I was not especially attracted by Schöneberg and this street.
In 1970, as the social and moral inheritor of the spirit of '68, this street,
which was mostly inhabited by civil servants, was deeply repulsive to
me. All the customs and habits that we had prejudices about, concerning
conservative petit-bourgeois codes of behaviour, seemed to have origi-
nated in this street and to have been cultivated there for years and years.

Here he was denigrating our street, deriding its dullness,
mocking its narrow-mindedness. No, one did not feel the winds
of the vast world here. No, it was not here that marginal types,
conscientious objectors, decadents and deadbeats of every kind,
eternal students, theorists, potheads, artists and agitators, leftists
and feminists, flaming homosexuals, sons and daughters of small
provincial West German towns in exile from their conservative
and narrow-minded families, sought a refuge wherein to live
their lives with some fragile modicum of freedom. My street was
a petit-bourgeois enclave within turbulent West Berlin. Edgar
Froese, a rare bird indeed, swept aside in one go all my illusions.
The movement of 1968–9 in no way affected our street which, due to the
composition of its population, took no part in the changing mentalities

in Berlin and other metropolitan centres around the world. The residents of this street in the 1970s, from my admittedly subjective perspective, were above all civil servants, or nearly so, whose mental universe consisted exclusively of tending to their little gardens and flower boxes and dreaming of their material security. The young people who grew up there would wait to become independent and then leave.

My street was divided into two camps. Number 7, the lone standout, chanted 'Ho-Ho-Ho-Chi Minh', while everywhere else the petit-bourgeois majority fought to see that the building regulations were respected. My street totally side-stepped the 'events' of May '68 and later those of the German Autumn, *Deutscher Herbst,* marked by attacks carried out by the Baader-Meinhof group that rocked the country. Edgar Froese seized the first opportunity to get out. *When in 1980 we got our first invitations from America to work on film scores, we began living and working all over the world. We never experienced our departure from Berlin as a loss.* He also wrote to me that he possessed *the intellectual passport of a citizen of the world.*

One Sunday evening, having spent the afternoon strolling along my street, I told Edgar Froese of my discovery of the 'labyrinth mirror' in the hallway entrance to number 7. When you place yourself exactly between the two mirrors hung on opposite walls, your own image is multiplied an infinite number of times to dizzying effect. *This goes so perfectly with your music!* I wrote. His reply arrived that same evening. I could tell that Edgar Froese had really enjoyed composing it. It left me stock still. *This mirror is not interesting just because it happens to be there, but because David Bowie, Brian Eno, Iggy Pop, George Moorse, Friedrich Gulda, and many other contemporaries glanced at themselves in it and observed how much the passage of time had marked their faces.*

Then these icons of a time out of time would come up to the second floor to our place and sit down to a nice hot meal. It was hospitality among us birds of a feather.

David Bowie at number 7! I was speechless. I now suddenly saw my street as a meeting point of global stars and punk rockers. To my knowledge, no celebrity had ever chosen to reside in my street. The psychoanalyst Wilhelm Reich, famous for his research on sexual orgasm, and the composer of light operas Walter Kollo, who wrote some unforgettable songs, were its only notable trophies. While the former, at one end of the street, was exploring the heights of human ecstasy, the latter, at the other end, composed a hymn to our neighbourhood in 1913, *Es war in Schöneberg im Monat Mai* ('It was in Schöneberg in the Month of May'). And yet that neighbourhood, the *Bayerisches Viertel*, was home to many illustrious names. I have always been jealous of the other streets just around mine, and I'm sure in fact that they look down on it, bragging to themselves: Gottfried Benn lived here! Gisèle Freund lived here! Billy Wilder! Erich Fromm! Alfred Kerr! Albert Einstein! And on and on. My street alone was unable to be decorated with those plaques dedicated to the memory of great men and women. Physicians and Nobel Prize winners, poets, filmmakers and actors all seem to have agreed to take a detour around my street. And yet here was David Bowie who had lived at number 7! My neighbour!

David Bowie arrived in Berlin in the summer of 1976 and left in 1978. He didn't stay long. He wanted to get away from the spotlight and get unhooked from cocaine. Berlin was his last chance. There's no doubt that he found in my street the sanatorium atmosphere he seemed to be so ardently seeking. It certainly doesn't have the *overwhelming and caustic Berlin energy* that

Bowie would later speak of. He came often. He even lived two and a half weeks at number 7, in the flat of Edgar Froese and his first wife. One morning in 1976, the Froeses receive a call from Bowie's manager asking them if they can help David find a flat in Berlin: *The city had a magic attraction for him, he wanted to live there for a while. When Bowie and his close circle arrived in Berlin, his new flat had only been half-renovated, and that's why we offered him a room at our flat, which he ended up using for a time. Even though we tried everything to keep the news from getting out, after three days we started seeing the same shapes standing behind parked cars with a telephoto lens. Some particularly impudent ones even bribed residents in the street to observe the entrance to our building from behind the curtains in other flats. Thus the only thing to do was to leave our place at dusk, hidden under a hat and scarf, so that we could at least go out to a restaurant or to meetings. After two more weeks, the renovation work on his flat at 155 Hauptstrasse was completed and everyone moved there (including Iggy Pop, among others). Bowie's stay in Berlin lasted almost two and a half years though – it was a time of many adventures and there were also many interesting, stimulating conversations amongst us. I devote an entire chapter to Bowie in my upcoming autobiography.* And then Froese turned off the faucet to his stream of consciousness.

My street, I don't mind putting it this way, saved David Bowie's life. Perhaps we ought to consider putting up a plaque above the entrance to number 7? We could engrave in marble the memory of this brief symbiosis between a modest Berlin street and one of the greatest legends of rock music. This fetishism of memorializing the names of illustrious residents on the facades of buildings is all the more absurd when one recalls that, as with Bowie, many of these individuals may have only passed a few days within the celebrated old walls. But he really did, honest to god, sleep at number 7, drank his glasses of milk, ate his peppers, smoked his Gitanes, satisfied his keen nostalgia for Weimar-era Berlin only a stone's throw from the home of Christopher Isherwood, suffered like a dog through the delirium tremens that occurred during his drug withdrawal programme, and, one hopes, wrote some of the songs of his Berlin trilogy. His feet walked along the pavements in front of number 7 and up and down its staircase. His hand held the banister and, yes, his handsome androgynous face was reflected an infinite number of times in the two oval mirrors in the downstairs hallway. Why is it that the proximity of those who were truly great honours us so much? Why are we, the current residents, so flattered by the phantom-like presence of our predecessors? Here is number 7, ennobled, despite the paint peeling off its facade, the disorderly and foul-smelling rubbish bins in the back courtyard, and the electric wires hanging indecorously from the walls in the stair-well. And we, the little people of this street, find ourselves ele-vated too – and so proud! Between Bowie and us there is a deep affinity, and frankly I'm a bit saddened that neither Tangerine Dream nor David Bowie thought of paying homage to this street of their youth that gave them so much. Just imagine a hymn to our street! Penny Lane got one, and of course so did Broadway and the Champs-Élysées; and then there's Pigalle, the rue de Blancs-Manteaux, Unter den Linden, Telegraph Road, and so many others. Over a hundred songs evoke in their title the name of a street, avenue, boulevard or lane. Ours is not among them. I find our musicians rather ungrateful.

14

Frau Soller Moves

Here's how I imagine the surreal collision that took place, I'm certain of it, at the end of the seventies on the pavement of my street. At nightfall Frau Soller leaves her flat and crosses the street to go up to the U-Bahn station. When she passes in front of number 7, Frau Soller narrowly misses bumping into David Bowie, who's turning to enter the building. Their shoulders touch slightly. He steps aside and murmurs 'Sorry' or perhaps even *'Tschuldigung'*. He bows and gestures with his hand to yield the way to Frau Soller. She stares for a second at this wan ephebe in his Borsalino and black leather coat belted at the waist who has appeared out of the shadows. She does not recognize him and each continues on their way.

Bärbel Soller and David Bowie? An employee in the women's clothing department at KaDeWe and a global rock star? Two lives that one would think were never destined to cross paths. But the laws of probability care not for the laws of space and time. It's the magic of neighbourly proximity in the same street – fleeting chance encounters between two beings with nothing in common. The only grass that Frau Soller has ever held between her fingers are the weeds among her petunias in the flowerbox on the balcony. And besides, whenever she's anxious or agitated, Frau Soller prefers passionflower pills over cocaine, and she would certainly prefer the songs of the crooner Rex Gildo over those of the Thin White Duke.

Two years ago, Frau Soller moved out of the flat on the first floor of my building where she had lived forever. At least that's what I had come to believe, so much had her crepe soles on the faux marble linoleum in the entryway, her sonorous *Guten Morgen!*, her doormat announcing *Willkommen*, her three strong-smelling cats in the stairwell, and her bike locked to the waterspout become part of the décor of the building. Since her departure, there's been a hole that our little community, deprived of one of its pillars, has had difficulty filling. Luckily I'm able to get a grip on myself, otherwise I could easily go on thinking that the newcomers on the first floor, perfectly nice people really, were a horde of brazen intruders. Sometimes I'm startled when their door opens as I'm walking past. I glimpse a well-lit flat in pastel colours and everything new. In other words, nothing like the obscure place with its brown wallpaper and cats that welcomed you when you called on Frau Soller.

Frau Soller comes back regularly to visit us. She parks her bike at the usual spot as though nothing had changed, gives a joyful double push on the doorbell to announce her arrival, and ascends in the lift thanks to the special key that she's kept on the end of a piece of orange ribbon. She first rings twice at the ground-floor flat of the former concierge, Brigitte, who knows her signal. Two rings: It's Bärbel! The two women exchange their back issues of the magazines *Freizeit Revue* and *Funkuhr* while chatting for a good long while in the smoky living room. Then Frau Soller goes upstairs one floor at a time.

On the second floor she loops around the doorknob a plastic bag containing homemade jam and jellies (elderberry or blood orange, depending on the season); she lingers a bit on the landing of the third floor to hear news about the sick and the children; and she finishes on the top floor with a small cup of coffee with the wife of the tax consultant in the last flat on the left. Their mutual sympathy dates from the time when the consultant's wife had fallen off her bike and broken her foot – as she was immobilized in an armchair for weeks, Frau Soller had offered to do her shopping for her. Though they're no longer neighbours, the two women never forget to wish each other happy birthday and they might mark the occasion with a card, a bouquet of flowers or even a homemade cake. Sometimes Frau Soller stays quite late, so that in the stairwell going back down she can meet the talkative hairdresser returning to his flat on the top floor to the right. *Ah, my dear Frau Soller! You're here today! What a pleasant surprise!* The two hug each other on the stairs and I hear peals of laughter. Frau Soller is a privileged customer at the very chic Salon situated in a street perpendicular to the Ku'damm. To thank her for having watered the thirty bonsai plants on his terrace with fresh water and tender words of encouragement for countless summers, the hairdresser treats her to a cut, stylish bangs and a large cappuccino ... for life. She only has to call to make an appointment at this *Salon* where – as their webpage announces – *everything is done with one goal in mind: to create complete harmony between the coiffure and the personality of the one wearing it. We take inspiration from the precision of English fashion, French finesse, and classic Italian elegance.* Frau Soller had trouble accepting this kind neighbourly gesture. She never fails to bring the staff a crumble made with apples from her worker's garden at the foot of the Insulaner, and jars of jam for their boss, *a little gourmand who would never dream of going without his dose of morning jam.*

Frau Soller was our fairy godmother. Since 1973, when she arrived in the building, she had seen all the renters come and go as well as the new owners when some of the flats went up for sale in the 1990s. The Wall had fallen, Germany was reunited, and Berlin was becoming a normal city – ideal conditions for investing in property. Gone were the days of being a little island with an uncertain future, walled off and subsidized, and therefore cut off from the law of supply and demand. Property prices, it was hoped, were finally going to start climbing. The new arrivals from *Western Germany*, as the people in my street would designate 'mainland' Germans who came from the areas of Munich or Frankfurt, and civil servants in the Bonn government would want to put their money into property, up until then still a bargain, in the city that would soon become the new capital – a metropolis like London, Paris and New York. If the property boom was slow to ignite, it was still from that moment that the social mixture of some of the buildings in my street began to change once again. Renters with modest incomes, often retirees or single mothers, were gradually replaced by owners with more money who were more preoccupied by job obligations, social commitments, their children, friends, business and pleasure trips, and, it's true, were less inclined to build neighbourly relations with the people across the hall.

When this or that person was on holiday, Frau Soller, who had spare keys to all the flats in the building, would water the plants, empty the letter boxes and feed the cats, canaries, goldfish and rodents. She cried real tears when Frankie, the gerbil of the children on the third floor, devoured Johnnie, his cage companion of many years. Frau Soller was relieved that this odious act of cannibalism did not take place during the holidays while the two little beasts were under her supervision. From her balcony she surveyed the bikes, the cars and the comings and goings along the pavement. Sometimes when you'd return in the evening, she would smile at you from behind her flowerboxes and you'd at once feel enveloped in a peaceful cocoon. Yes, Frau Soller was there, we had arrived safely home and all's right with the world. Frau Soller was always there – at her post, rain or shine. You could count on her. She never went on holiday – just once a year a steamboat ride on the Havel with her former colleagues from KaDeWe, and sometimes a day excursion by bus to the area of Spreewald.

Having taken care of the little needs of various residents for so long, Frau Soller ended up feeling somewhat responsible for everyone's collective happiness. *I am the way I am. If we can't help each other out as neighbours!,* she'd cry when someone would scold her for again placing the newspaper along with a slice of still warm fresh cake in a plastic container outside the door on Sunday morning. Cakes, cookies with icing, Christmas cookies, all homemade! Frau Soller got up at dawn to start baking. She didn't dare ring the bell. She didn't want to disturb anyone – her only wish was to create a little happiness.

Since Frau Soller left, Christmas has not really been the same in my street. The new neighbours stick felt stars on their windows that have probably come straight out of the Manufactum online catalogue for bourgeois bohemians with irreproachable taste. No, it's just not the same. Every year on 1st December, exactly one month after All Saints' Day, once it was dark outside, there'd be a garland of plastic Santa Claus lights with the bulb in each one's belly blinking on Frau Soller's balcony above the mini-refrigerator against the wall – on-off, on-off. It was Times Square on the first floor above the bicycle parking area. In the days when she was still working, Frau Soller would call her husband from KaDeWe at four when she got off work. *Light the lights, I'll be right there!* Kurt Soller did as he was told. He lit the garland of lights, and the star that would shine between the branches of the fir tree and the holly on the balcony, then each of the nine pyramids, one in each window. When Frau Soller turned into her street, she saw her flat sparkling from far off, like the star seen by the Shepherds in the sky of Bethlehem.

For a few years now property prices in Berlin have been climbing. Old tenants who still pay a ridiculously low rent impede the speculation stampede. The company that owns the building wants to sell, so it has proposed to Frau Soller and her husband that they trade their old flat for a brand new, ground-floor one-bedroom place in another neighbourhood. *It was our last chance*, argues Frau Soller, and when she brags about now living just two streets away from Daniel Barenboim, I'm sure she's actually trying to convince herself that she didn't get swindled in the deal. By a strange coincidence, it was just a few weeks before Frau Soller's departure that our little community began to get a little friendlier. The facade of our building had just been redone, and the scaffolding and tarpaulins that had smothered us for an entire summer were now gone. We could breathe again. At the owners' assembly meeting it was decided this needed to be celebrated. Therefore, we united for the first time all together in a room marked 'reserved' at the Italian restaurant in the street. Seated at a large table of people happily chatting, Frau Soller was in heaven. She looked at us tenderly like a mother hen who has finally managed to gather all her chicks under her wings. Everyone came. The medium who lived on the third floor – according to what I had been told in strictest confidence by several neighbours – had already been consulted by several of us and to each she had given her professional opinion about marriage problems, depression and other oscillations of the soul. Her husband was a retired 'traveller'. This poetic term, which I had found in a directory from the 1960s, did not refer to some Thoreau figure walking the trails of the world with a wooden stick; rather, he had been the sales rep for a big American cosmetics firm, *in charge of twelve assistants, each one prettier than the next*, as his wife never missed pointing out. There was the retired football coach who you'd meet each morning wearing his track suit and wool cap, in summer or winter, his blue eyes bloodshot and his ruddy face perspiring. He would be coming back from his morning jog in the Pennerpark, the 'tramp park', carrying a bag of small bread rolls. Each week he would slip some issues of the sports magazine *Kicker* into the letter boxes of the boys in the building who idolized him. When I'd meet his wife – the last hippy in the street, with her Indian tunics and long brightly coloured scarves – near the bicycle lock-up area, she was always returning from some grand spiritual voyage in regions of the globe where the karma was far superior to what circulated in our materialistic street. Her habit was to go out early in the morning to the playground of the Pennerpark long before her husband, and especially before the arrival of any of the street's boys, and do her slow, circular Tai-chi movements, which, she congratulated herself, *ground her so wonderfully to the earth*. There was also a professor-diplomat who was venerated because he moved in the high circles of government and because a chauffeured Mercedes was waiting for him outside the building every morning. Then there was a whole array of new people who came up and presented themselves one by one. At a separate table near the buffet were the children – all boys.

The tranquillity of this wonderful evening was almost disturbed by a little competition over who had lived in the building the longest. The winners, thank goodness uncontested, were the travelling salesman and the seer, who had arrived in 1960, followed by Frau Soller in 1973, and then the former concierge who had arrived some weeks later that same year. Then each person bragged about the local historical events which, either before or after moving to the street, he or she had witnessed: the Berlin blockade, the airlift, the riots of 17 June in the DDR, the inauguration of the Philharmonic, the building of the Wall and the haggling at the border checkpoints, and of course the event about which everyone has their little story to tell – the spectacular fall of the Wall and the puff-puff, cough-cough arrival of a few Trabants in our street during the night of 9 November 1989. It was only some time later that Frau Soller shared with me that she had been present under the balcony at the Schöneberg town hall when Kennedy made his *Ich bin ein Berliner!* speech in 1963. Her employer had given her permission to leave her post temporarily to cheer on the president. Tiny Bärbel Soller in the middle of this enormous crowd had always had a sweet spot for this *smart* and *easy-going 'Mister President'*. A few months later, in November, she knocked at the door of the concierge in the middle of the night to share the news that Kennedy had just been assassinated.

The travelling salesman and self-appointed spokesperson for our little community made a nice speech. We applauded heartily and lifted our glasses to toast the good health of our building and the longevity of our street. The hairdresser was the most extroverted of us all. Before the dessert, he rose and proposed that we all convert to the familiar '*Du*' form of address. He intended this as a way to seal our community's common destiny, as he explained a little choked up and on the verge of tears. It goes without saying that the reaction to this proposal was not exactly enthusiastic. Some people visibly stiffened in their chairs, others pretended not to have heard and continued to move bits of food around on their plates. Only a little group who were already quite soused jumped spontaneously into using the more intimate pronouns. It was late when we all said goodnight, promising each other to do it again soon, by Christmas time at the latest.

The day of the move was approaching. For many weeks Frau Soller had been tidying, sorting and emptying her *verwohnt* flat. This nice verb, untranslatable into French or English, perfectly describes the tired-looking appearance of a flat that's been lived in for thirty-eight years by the same renters – fatigued and a little out of breath, like at the end of a long life. Frau Soller gives away her curtains and books. A charitable organization comes to remove a few pieces of furniture. *Ah, Frau Soller, it's always up to you!*, she mutters occasionally, talking to herself. Her husband is far too sick to be of any real help. After finishing one box and before starting on another she allows herself a break and comes up to my place for coffee and some storytelling about her life. Frau Soller is a true 'flower of Schöneberg'. She sprouted and grew out of the soil of my street one might say. She was born in 1940 in the maternity ward of a small paediatric clinic close by, and baptized in May of the same year in the church at the end of our street. She lived with her parents and brothers and sisters in an adjoining street, *where now there's the beverage merchant Hoffmann – the building is new.* She remembers the day she moved into our street like it were yesterday. It was in December

1972, during an incredible storm in Berlin. There had been a warning to not go outside, but it was precisely the day when the owner of our building, an acquaintance of the Sollers, telephoned: *I have a flat for you!* The gentleman on the first floor had died. *The opportunity came up just like that and we took advantage of it. In those days there was such a bad housing shortage in Berlin.*

The Sollers moved in on 8 February 1973. The flat looked nothing like it had when it spanned the entire and most noble floor in the building, inhabited by the developer who had constructed the whole thing. It had been cut in two just before the 'grand Berlin room'. Frau Soller hid this amputation at the end of a hallway behind a thick velvet curtain in an area she used for storage. Most flats in my street were mutilated in this way in the early 1930s. During those years of economic hardship and inflation, no one had the means any longer to continue living spread out in seven rooms. Owners subdivided flats into units of two or three rooms. Sometimes the layout that resulted in these smaller spaces was not the best. They would add a small bathroom and kitchen wherever they would fit, sometimes in a corridor or in the miniscule maid's quarters, which were always available since no one could afford a maid any longer.

At the time Frau Soller moved in, the street had taken on more relaxed habits. In the morning, women in dressing gowns and hair curlers would go down entirely unselfconsciously to purchase their bread at the bakery. Gone were the days when the woman of the house might receive two dozen guests seated around a large table in the grand Berlin room. The new tenants didn't know what to do with such a gigantic room, which had only a single window looking out onto the back courtyard. In my Berlin room in the past there had lived an electrician, his young wife Edith and their baby. They shared a kitchen and bathroom in the 'tail' (the name for the three rooms of the flat that linked to another wing) with the Baron Leonidas von Barkow, *a half-savage in a checked coat*. He would say *Dear Madame* to his young female flatmate, and barely kept from kissing her hand when they crossed paths in the hallway in pyjamas on their way to or from the toilet. I also remember having been told that my Berlin room was once the home, I don't know exactly when, to a four-by-eight-foot electric toy train installation.

Flat ceilings in my street have also been lowered. Who wants to live in rooms impossible to heat with their twelve-foot-high ceilings? Border mouldings and circular or oval centre mouldings disappear under lower false ceilings. Who still has time to wax the wood floors on their hands and knees once a week? Worn wood is coated with polyurethane or else covered with carpeting for easier upkeep, and linoleum is placed down over the granito tile in the kitchens. Sliding panel doors are gotten rid of. The flats lose some of their generous spirit.

Gone are the interiors that were as congested as the facades were complicated. It was around the time the Sollers moved in that the first rubbish collections for large items began in Berlin. The city's sanitation services offer to collect at no charge any objects that residents want to get rid of. One morning in the middle of summer, people on my street pulled open their curtains to discover piles of stuff on the pavement. In front of each building there was a good-sized mound. People were chucking out old dusty furniture that was hard to clean, too heavy to move easily, and especially that reminded them of an unfortunate time they'd rather forget. People go for what's new and light and preferably made of plastic and formica. Instead of armchairs upholstered in brocade, they want fake leather and acrylic. Instead of heavy horsehair mattresses, they want ones with springs and special support for the lumbar region. People want build-it-yourself shelving made of teak, short pile nylon carpeting that's easy to clean. In short, modern comforts. Advertising copy in an issue of the *Schöneberg Echo* from 1973 praises the easy and fast installation of a tiny bathtub, explaining that *the layout of dark, humid old-fashioned flats with their toilets on the landing and a true bathroom nothing more than a dream must now be relegated to the past. In only three hours you can feel as fresh as if you had just returned from a holiday at the seaside.* Buffets and headboards, night tables and fancy gold frames, curtain rods and old taps, old suits, kitchen cabinets from the twenties, standing lamps with their metal brackets and shades, leather-bound books, and on and on had all been deposited discreetly on the pavement in the middle of the night. The street looked like a flea market. All day long people strolled and poked and picked at all the junk-treasure. Some people carted off coveted pieces of furniture using wheelbarrows. Others went down the street in their cars filling up the trunk. It was a windfall for the low-income flat-sharing residents. Repainted bright red, this Biedermeier armoire would be great for storing jumpers, they thought, without any respect for the beautiful old cherry wood. The greatest find in my street was a Biedermeier-style sewing box with elaborate marquetry.

When Frau Soller moved into my street, the postman still delivered mail twice a day, in the morning and again at noon. The guardian of every building still felt personally responsible for the cleanliness of the portion of pavement out front and for the safety of passers-by. As the first snowflakes fell, you could hear them shovelling snow and spreading sand at dawn. Tenants would take turns cleaning the stairwell once a week; now that chore is outsourced to a private company. In those days there were only a few cars, practically antiques, parked next to the pavement. The chestnut trees had not been planted yet and the street still joined up at the end with a major artery because the low-income housing estate had not yet been built. Where there's now a passageway through the building, a circular staircase led down to underground public toilets.

In those days there was also still a shop assistant who acted like a pharmacist, and a pharmacist who acted like a doctor. There was a soap merchant and a colour merchant – two wonderfully old-fashioned names for product lines that don't exist any more – and there was the little cinema near the entrance to the park that I so regret never having known. There was still the *Pension Clausius* on the first floor at number 5 with its six smoky rooms and its licence to serve beer. Residents of my street would put up their West German parents in these rooms when they were having family reunions. It was a simple guesthouse, clean and well-maintained by a war widow with her spitz who constantly circled about her barking. There were many such women, anxious and alone, renting out a room filled with old furniture draped with needlepoint covers and telling the gentlemen that female callers were prohibited. After the death of Frau Clausius, the guesthouse was turned into a flat.

A little grocery stayed in business until the early eighties. Renters would have their purchases delivered by the shop's apprentice. He would receive a tip and the bill would be entered into a large accounts ledger. One could pay later at the store when it was convenient. Each child would receive a cookie wrapped in a large piece of paper. The owner Christa Liedtke had serious troubles in the 1970s. Marta Schreiner, the manager of the tobacconist's situated on the ground floor of the same building, complained that the grocery was using the small garden plot to display its merchandise. Christa Liedtke defended her practice: *For twenty-five years, in other words since the founding of this store, each owner has displayed their merchandise out front. Every Berlin greengrocer does the same, as you well know, because that allows the customers to see fresh produce and allows the owner to sell those items before they spoil.*

Frau Kubeth, the ironing lady that John Ron spoke to me about in Berkeley, seemed to have been there forever. The day that Baron von Barkow got it into his head to iron his shirts himself, he went down to Frau Kubeth's, positioned himself behind her ironing board, and watched her technique. The housewives on the street tapped their foreheads to indicate that he was crazy.

Frau Soller described to me the dizzying merry-go-round of businesses that came and went in our street: the tobacconist's and newsagent's that was replaced by a plumber's workshop, and then by a brothel. The drugstore that then became a mini-mart. The cobbler who gave up his lease to a wallpaper seller Schulz, who in turn sold it on to a dental prosthesis maker, and he sold it to a tax consultant. A small market reopened as an Edeka supermarket, which later become a used motor parts supplier. In the back of the printer Beyer, near the underground station where today there's a winter sports equipment shop, there was once a typesetter who assembled his lead blocks to print church bulletins. Frau Beyer was an artist – more precisely a gymnast and trapeze artist. This oddly paired couple lived on the first floor above the print shop. Next door was a religious bookshop, a little dairy products store, and 'the Mansard', an alternative-type bar that the police ended up closing down because there was too much pot smoking going on there. Old uncle Willie, an inveterate chess player, faced off against a bunch of regular partners in a corner of the bar. He always won. Today the Mansard is home to a cooperative nursery. The Copyshop displaced the Neugebauer paint and wallpaper shop. Schraubenschmidt, an Ali Baba cave for the do-it-yourself crowd, also went out of business eventually. The wife of the taxi driver who lived at number 17 was for years the head secretary at Schraubenschmidt. And only a few years ago, the antique dealer at number 12 turned over his lease to a kitchen supplies specialist. In front of the antique shop were piles of books priced at one mark each. Out back were porcelain dolls and little silver cases for this or that customer. When the American soldiers came across its treasures, they parked their big cars out front and hauled off enormous Westminster clocks in their trunks. Then they'd drive off in the direction of the brothel at Viktoria-Luise-Platz. Seated at the Italian ice-cream stand on the square, the mothers of my street would keep one eye on their children and the other on the GIs who would come and go at the entrance to the brothel. *One's just come back down, another just got back in his car. They come and go. It never stops.*

Our street as Frau Soller would describe it to me has not existed for a long time now. Back then everyone knew each other. Starting around ten in the morning, people would routinely greet one another with *Mahlzeit!* – a combination of 'Hi!' and 'Bon appetit!' They would attend the same funerals and exchange news about what this son or that daughter was doing now. Frau Soller was forced to make the damning observation that *people today live more and more isolated from each other and the everyday kindness of people has declined.*

I don't know if I have accurately related the succession of

changes in the business community in my street over the years. It's quite likely that I have mixed up or forgotten a few things. But whatever the case may be, the present reality is undeniable – these little independent businesses all ended up disappearing one by one.

Frau Soller worked at the giant department store KaDeWe for thirty-eight years. *Kaufhaus des Westens* was the great pride of her life. On the eighth floor was the labelling area for the women's ready-to-wear department. There the merchandise as it arrived from the manufacturers was prepared for display to customers. This involved verifying the kind and amounts received, recording packing slip information, attaching prices, etc. In 1998 – four years after the takeover of Hertie and KaDeWe by the Karstadt group – Frau Soller was laid off two years before retirement with *an unemployment benefit that was worth peanuts.* Her biggest regret was that she would have so liked to celebrate forty years of service for KaDeWe. *Oh well, too bad it didn't work out that way.* She remembers her tenth year with the company: *I was given a bonus of 600 marks which was enough for me to pay for driving lessons.* She also remembers her twenty-fifth anniversary: *I received 1,200 marks and a gift package of assorted cold cuts. My colleagues didn't stay long though and only drank a little orange juice because it took place during store hours.* The personnel director made a speech and bestowed on Frau Soller, who was feeling a bit timid in her navy blue skirt and jacket, white stockings and blouse, a bouquet of flowers nearly as big as her and also a beautiful certificate on which was written: *To Frau Bärbel Soller in special recognition of her fine and loyal service.*

During the years of the Berlin Wall I have the feeling that my street was host to one party after another. The street was dizzyingly alive. My neighbours were thrilled by this period of expansion after the grey drizzle of the 1950s and were trying to forget that they were living scrunched together on a minuscule parcel of contested no man's land fought over by opposing Cold War rivals. My building vibrated with activity – parties, receptions, birthdays, anniversaries and carnival celebrations. The Soller photo albums suggest that life then was one endless surprise party. The wedding album shows Bärbel and Kurt Soller marrying in a civil ceremony at the Schöneberg city hall just like all the residents of my street did both before the war and still today. One sees the same photos taken on the same steps, only the couples change. Lilli and Heinrich Ernsthaft in 1922, Klara and Herbert Fiegel in 1929, Liselotte and Wilhelm Wagner in 1942, Bärbel and Kurt Soller on 1 July 1966. It rained the day before and the day after, but they had splendid weather for their wedding day. The religious ceremony took place at the little Schöneberg church in the Hauptstrasse, the same street where a few years later David Bowie would live. The old village church was decorated from top to bottom with rosebuds. That day at least Frau Soller could fully exercise her talents. The wedding couple arrived in a horse-drawn carriage with a driver in frockcoat and top hat and the two horses decked out like in the tales of princesses. Herr Soller appears tall and distinguished, a handsome man, and Frau Soller looks so sweet and blushing behind an abundance of white lace and muslin.

The wedding reception took place at 'The Black Porker', across from the Nollendorfplatz underground station in a space that's now a pizzeria. The 'Our Wedding' album shows the guests seated at long tables with pictures of hunting scenes hanging on the wood walls behind them. On the tables are steins of beer and glasses of red wine. Bärbel and Kurt Soller exchange a discreet kiss on the cheek. And then suddenly as one turns the pages one clearly sees a jovial party atmosphere take over. An accordion player appears among the guests. A large jolly-looking man has put his arm around the bride's waist and led her to the dance floor. This wedding meal is turning into a real Bacchanalia. The bride and groom, now wearing night caps, pass under a lace dais while holding hands. They're squeezed and hugged. People cry out, clap, and sing at the top of their lungs, their eyes closed in ecstasy. The women appear out of control. One can glimpse the unshaved hair of their underarms and see their swollen ankles crammed into pointy heels; their artfully constructed hairstyles are beginning to flop despite the stabilizing efforts of tons of hairspray. Frau Soller's suspender belts fly up to the ceiling. The guests dance wildly, twirling like dervishes between the tables. A heavy-set couple do their best to hold each other in the traditional way and dance a normal waltz together. In the middle of all this tumultuous festivity, seated and dressed in a black dress down to her ankles, is the grandmother. I was expecting to see her tip over and fall among the dancers in this dizzy atmosphere; but no, she holds tight to her chair, her eyes vacant and her chin protruding because she has no teeth in her mouth to hold the shape of her jaw. She is one of those fabulous old ladies who were still a part of the cast in every family in the seventies but who no longer exist today.

The party continues in the Sollers' later photo albums. Tables of guests at carnival time with sparkly paper necklaces, pointy party hats and Venice-like gondolier outfits. Here is Frau Soller smiling uproariously and sandwiched between two friends as they descend on a wooden sled. It was taken at the *Sportpalast*, five minutes from my street, the place where Joseph Goebbels gave his famous 1943 speech on 'total war'. Until it was demolished in 1973, it hosted sports and a wide programme of entertainments, including a Viennese figure-skating show, six days of indoor cycling competition, Czech puppet shows, beer festivals, and other parties that the Sollers would attend. Then there were the parties at the flat. Here's Frau Soller in a mini-skirt pretending to be a wheelbarrow. A friend holds her ankles and she's crawling forward on her elbows. Several women are seated cross-legged on the floor. You can see their white underwear. Kurt Soller and his friends are crowded together on the couch applauding. Flamenco, Kazatchok, Sirtaki, Rumba, Twist, French Cancan and on and on. At the Sollers' and at the home of the travelling salesman, they dance until they can no longer stand up. Since the wooden beams traverse the rooms, the floors and ceilings vibrate with the movement. Sometimes a neighbour from the floor below would ring the bell: *Hey stop it, your floor which is my ceiling is going to end up in my soup! – Well hey, what do you want, we just love dancing!*, the partyers would reply, and then continue dancing in the corridor instead. Even at KaDeWe every birthday was celebrated with a party. Display tables for blouses and cardigans would be cleared off to make room for little rolls from Lenôtre, *Katenschinken* (Holstein ham) and Tilsit cheese, all sent up on the dumbwaiter from the food floor below. *That cheese was strong but it was good. We'd eat standing and then tidy up and get back to work.*

Thirty-eight years living in the same street. Leaving the flat and the memories of an entire life spent in it is wrenching. There are the goldfish in the aquarium. There is the giant shelving structure in rosewood bought in 1966 from the Möbel Missling store with its greenish neon light, its tchotchkes here and there, photos of the children, and a few books on historical subjects. Like a fortress wall marked with black and yellow patches, this ten-foot high structure occupies the whole length of one room. Five movers are hired to extract it from the building laboriously, as though it were an extraordinarily large and deeply impacted wisdom tooth. There is the stack of wooden tables each smaller than the one above such that the smallest are more decorative than useful. There is the *Garnitur* – the sacred trinity of the German living room – a sofa with a matching bulky armchair on each side in reddish-brownish fabric that has been noticeably scratched by cat claws. *It's the fourth living room set we've had in forty-five years! But I guess it's starting to look tired,* Frau Soller apologizes. There's the Sputnik lamp in the living room, bought at the end of the sixties at KaDeWe, with its twelve or twenty-four crystal balls according to the lighting arrangement one chooses. It won't be going to the new flat – too imposing and too low. Frau Soller has been trying unsuccessfully to get rid of it. There's also the complete kitchen ensemble with pastel-coloured furniture and cupboards with sliding doors. The formica table covered with a wax-treated tablecloth is where Frau Soller would prepare her cakes and cookies.

One morning a few days before the Sollers' move, when the painters had already taken possession of the place to start on extensive renovations before the arrival of the new owners, Frau Soller came ringing at my door: *I have something for you! A real discovery! Come down quick!* The painters had torn off some flowery wallpaper in the Sollers' bedroom and discovered an older layer of linden-green coloured wallpaper and underneath that entire pages of the *Deutsche Allegemeine Zeitung* from 1941 that had been used as a base-layer. *I was born one year earlier,* Frau Soller reminded me breathless with emotion. She was trying to situate this archaeological discovery along the frieze of her personal timeline. I went back upstairs holding long strips of this rough-grained newsprint in my arms. In the stairwell neighbours gave me nervous looks. They didn't dare ask what I was planning on doing with these shreds of newspaper from the Nazi era.

That morning Frau Soller had accidentally stumbled upon a trace of earlier tenants who were renovating their flat in June 1941. On June 4th, the emperor Wilhelm II died in exile in the Netherlands, and on the 22nd, under the code name 'Operation Barbarossa', the Wehrmacht invaded the Soviet Union. On that day life on my street was perfectly ordinary and no one yet suspected anything. Bits of dried wallpaper glue are stuck to the surface of the newspaper, but it's still possible to make out the words of a few articles. An editorial indulges in a hateful analysis of the way the English are conducting the war. The Wehrmacht high command announces that twenty-six British planes have been shot down – *a black week for the RAF*. Daily life continues as usual, a surreal backdrop as the German *Einsatzgruppen*, mobile units advancing just behind the Wehrmacht, are beginning the systematic extermination of Jews, Communist Party leaders, gypsies and prisoners of war on Soviet soil. There are ads for summer clothes, poplin coats, pills to aid digestion, property offers to let empty or furnished flats. In the June 24 issue, the paper announces the *First Day in the East* and publishes obituaries and employment offers, mostly for women's work – governess, paralegal, babysitter, experienced telephone opera-tor, stenographer-typist. The latest currency exchange rates and stock market values are printed. And even though Germany is at war against most of Europe, the language school of a certain Dr Heil is proposing *a teaching method for rapid self-instruction in English, French and Italian*. On 25 June, the Wehrmacht high command announces that *great successes in the East can be expected* and readers are also told of *airstrikes over Liverpool*.

For years, rows of soldiers decorated with military crosses, captains, *Sturmbannführer* and parachute specialists all photographed at attention will watch over the sleeping Sollers, who never suspected that such military surveillance was happening in the intimacy of their bedroom.

Kneeling on the ground in my office, I pore over these little dusty strips of the past spread on my wooden floor. National Socialism seems to be indelibly tattooed on the buildings of my street. This is hardly a metaphor. What I observed on the walls of the Sollers' flat was all too real: the year 1941 had been stuck to the plaster for seventy years – layers of paper, one over another, creating strata of different time periods and their stories. One life replaced by another. One tenant replaced by another and another. And sometimes some vestige of the past would resurface.

Eventually the removal van would carry away Frau Soller, her husband, their cats and their rosewood armoire. They would leave only a few traces of their stay. There were the rectangular shapes of original wallpaper colour where pictures had been hung. A bobby-pin stuck in a crack between two floorboards. A metal spoon forgotten at the back of a cupboard. A few cobwebs hanging from the ceiling, a few dust balls roaming on the bare floors, and the marks of burned linoleum. There was an electrical cord hanging down, a hook in the bathroom, a couple of cracked flower pots on a shelf, a pile of old magazines in a corner, curtains with little fishes on them in the kitchen, a postcard from Majorca stuck to the frame of the bathroom mirror, a ring of kitchen grime on the ceiling above the stove, a dry, wrinkled sponge in the sink basin. A crown of forget-me-nots made of blue cloth embroidered with butterflies would stay on the front door for a few weeks, until the new arrivals removed it as they went about reuniting the two halves of the flat and moving into the larger space – now extra-large, as it had existed before the war – with their designer furniture and ultramodern kitchen equipment. They even succeeded eventually, I don't know how, in getting rid of the cat smell that had lingered about Frau Soller's flat for many months after her departure. On that day the Berlin of Frau Sollers ceased to exist in our street.

15

Gossip

Can one say about a street that nothing ever happened there? On a superficial level my street is so well-mannered. Its name rarely comes up in the human interest stories of Berlin newspapers that I've combed through scrupulously for hours. *On the night of 9–10 May 1961, unknown individuals broke into the Kaiser-Barbarossa pharmacy. At this stage in the investigation it appears only some cash was stolen*, says the pharmacists' newsletter. Great Caesar's ghost! This is the only gritty story I've been able to find about my street. But so what? When I stitch together archival records, bits of neighbourhood gossip, and more or less reliable legends that have circulated, I'm able to reconstitute dozens of volatile little events that over the years make up its lively history.

A very useful tool for reconstituting the history of a street over time is the neighbourhood complainer. This resident is upset and needs to make his or her upset feelings known. Complaining is their reason for being, one could even say their all-devouring passion – so intense is the pleasure they derive from their self-appointed mission, namely getting others to see what's wrong and restore what's proper and right. What's wrong is dog excrement and pee on the pavements, mice and cockroaches in the cellars, humidity and cracks in the walls, toilets that don't flush properly or gas lines that leak, excessive noise at night, secret subletting, and so on and on. From 1904 to today the catalogue of complaints has been roughly the same. They're perhaps too conventionally boring to be replaced by more exciting ones. A complaint gets passed from one whiner to the next, from generation to generation, as though each witness were handing on a baton in a relay race. Usually, the person doing the complaining is not whining alone in his corner. On the contrary, the complainer usually makes an official complaint, in writing, and often. Take the case of Julius Poppelauer, with his ridiculous name, his brow furrowed in rage, his coldly polite turns of phrase, and the aggressively deep pencil marks that cover the stationary he sends over and over to the police. Julius Poppelauer is the champion complainer of my street, the record-holder when it comes to making a noticeable stink over the past 100 years.

His first freak-out dates back to 1930, in the middle of the economic crisis. The owner of his building, number 2, decided – probably because coal was so expensive – to do away with central heating and revert to individual stoves. In almost every building in the street, the radiators were shut off in every room, as well as in the common areas and entryways, and a stand-alone stove was installed in the living area where people spent the most time together in winter. For weeks the neighbourhood's two chimney and stove specialists, Oswald Wabner and H. Flick, would leap from one rooftop chimney to another as though they were young mountain goats in a springtime pasture. Together with other artisans they installed the new stoves. Of course, it didn't take long before some breakdown was reported. Herr Direktor Julius Poppelauer fired the first shot and led the charge of the furious renters. The nuisance of the smoke! Toxic fumes! Unbearable odours! Bedrooms uninhabitable! An intolerable situation!

In all, the complaints stretch out over the entire century. Read today, most of them appear wonderfully ridiculous. In 1917, at number 8, the director of housing services orders the owner to eliminate rats on the premises, and suggests that he apply a phosphorous paste to some piece of bait – *preferably fish (sardine or herring) or pieces of ham hock, because experience shows that phosphorous paste spread on bread will not be eaten by rats unless there is absolutely nothing else available to eat.* In 1929, at number 3, a renter asks the landlord to install an electric lamp in a pantry to replace a dangerous oil lamp. In 1930, the ministry councillor Doktor Westphal, a big cheese who lived on the top floor, reported a roof leak and an outbreak of fungus on the walls. After the war, there are recurring reports of stolen bread rolls. Many complain that the main entrance is not locked at night and the building is not guarded! In 1936, at number 8, Frau Kaufmann's son is sleeping in an attic space that he has no right to use as living quarters. *As there are no toilet facilities in this attic area, all the lapses in proper hygiene on the part of Frau Kaufmann's son have been reported,* notes the denouncer.

Sometimes on my street there have been little explosions of rage. In 1947, at number 5, a workman is *rudely insulted and physically attacked* by the interior decorator on the ground floor. The plaintiff requests that *the maximum penalty be applied.* In 1973, in my building, the war veteran and 90 per cent invalid Alfred Konrad – a renter living for twelve years on the same floor as an elderly woman with limited mobility, a man suffering from cardiovascular problems, and another paraplegic war veteran – complains that the lift has been out of service for several weeks. I learned later that Frau Konrad had *severe oedema that caused her to become completely swollen.*

What a pleasure when, starting in the sixties, the stories of my neighbours corroborate the information found in the municipal archives. The Konrads, who are having such a hard time and are deprived of their lift, suddenly live through something truly dramatic – being confined to their apartment, weak and helpless, like their invalid neighbours.

The complainer is always in need of some new axe to grind, and therefore always on the lookout for new conflicts to serve as whetstones. Take the person who, incognito in the middle of the night, placed on my doormat the wilted flower I had thrown from my balcony down onto the pavement – yes, intentionally, because I thought it was silly to put these few biodegradable petals in the garbage pail! One can only imagine how much the petal-picker-upper must have stewed in anger, fulminated over the filthy state of the street and over my audacity, congratulated himself for this little act of anonymous vengeance and taken pride in his own courage. Then there are the ones who spy on everyone's trips to and from the garbage bins, and who lift the lids at night to make sure the rules on which type of waste material goes into which container are being respected. A street throbs furiously with these mean-spirited denunciations, undeserved slights, inter-neighbour warfare, jealousies, quarrels, claims and counterclaims of all kinds. The tragedy of the chewing gum spat out on the pavement directly in front of the entrance to the building! The nerve of whoever lets their dog do its business in the front garden! All these threats, all these *If you don't stop, I'll call the police!*

*

Another unavoidable figure in any street is the pariah. The pariah and the complainer form a perfectly complementary and united couple. One might think that the pariah had been set down on the checkerboard with the express purpose of heating up the bile secretions of the complainer. On Sunday afternoons during nap time, the pariah will be stubbornly throwing bottles into the recycling bin in the back courtyard, seemingly gleeful at the noise made by each one as it crashes against the others. For months he allows his cat to pee in the dark alcove under the letterboxes at the base of the stairwell. Also gifted at provoking rage are children who do not greet their elders, who slide down the bannister, who play basketball in the hall and skateboard on the pavement. There are the insomniacs who listen to professional wrestling matches in the middle of the night, flush the toilet at 1 a.m., or who simply pace around on their creaky parquet at all hours to pass the time. There is the Rolling Stones fan who needs to broadcast his enthusiasm with windows always open and music blaring on summer afternoons. And there's the young fellow who tunes his electric guitar in the stairwell because the acoustics there are better than in his parents' living room. *The house trembled*, recall the neighbours.

First prize in this infinite decathlon of anecdotes goes to the former tenant of the flat across the hall from mine. People have told me so much about this woman that I'm almost a bit disappointed to have arrived too late to have known her. *I'm telling you, this woman could really push us to the edge!*, reports the actual owner. *She'd have her little aperitifs all by herself – half a bottle of cheap champagne and a dose of Valium, one after the other.* And when the elevator starting moving in the middle of the night, the concierge knew what was up: *Ah, ah, there she goes out on her rounds!* He burst out of his porter's lodge to catch up to the woman in her nightgown and take her back to her flat. One day, smoke appeared from her kitchen at the back of the building. It was the football coach who alerted everyone: *It's coming from her kitchen!* Through a crack in the door the doctor who had been called in to help could see her prostrate body in the middle of a large puddle of alcohol in the hallway and her dentures lying nearby. The firemen were called. *Six vehicles arrived. What an affair!* They knocked down the door and dragged the body out onto the landing. She was still breathing!

I had to dig a little, it's true, to find all these stories. I might pry a little during a bit of light conversation and see if someone would cough up an anecdote. My street is located in Northern Europe. This isn't Naples or Marseille with life overflowing onto the pavements, noisy and bossy, as is typical in so many Mediterranean cities. My street is much too buttoned-up for the bourgeois residents to allow themselves to set out their folding chairs in public, their camping tables, their chess sets, their bottles of rosé … and their evening conversations. Even in summer during the hottest days, people stay at home, curtains drawn, doors and windows shut. Life happens inside. My street is introverted and shyly formal as well. There are no public benches on the pavement, no outdoor cafés where one might rendezvous with a friend in the evening, no neighbourhood bakery where people might meet every morning while buying the bread. Neighbours are rarely seen standing on the pavement together just chatting. In fact, it can happen that one's not entirely confident of recognizing all the people in the building opposite. Only when the windows on the back courtyard side are wide open on summer evenings does one get a glimpse into the intimacy of these grand flats. George Haberland, the developer who built my street in 1904, had a noble conception of this back courtyard: *Particular attention was paid to the details of these interior courtyards. The housing lots were conceived so that all the free space there remained a common area and harmonious plantations could be possible. This was how it happened that, instead of the typical plain squares of pavement, the Bavarian Quarter was the site of pleasant courtyards cultivated with flowerbeds.* In fact, the back courtyards in my street never fulfilled this sublime vision. My neighbours have told me that in the 1930s these spaces were purely utilitarian, including a bar for suspending carpets, the beating of which was only allowed on Saturday. The WGs, *Wohngemeinschaften* or communal living arrangements, were the first to transform the courtyards into public open-air living spaces. At number 26, the tenants on the ground floor let a jungle grow. A mini-Amazon forest grew lush and tall between the bins and the cellar windows. There were cactuses and other succulent plants, some bushes, a rabbit hutch, and even a large plastic container that served as a poor man's swimming pool and was enjoyed by a solitary little girl who splashed about on very hot afternoons.

Spend an entire day in the back courtyard and you'll experience the intimate side of a street. The clink of silverware being put away or the sound of knife and fork against porcelain plates, the gargling, the undefinable ablutions, domestic disputes, toilets flushing, the noise of vacuum cleaners and other household electrical items, snippets from television shows, and the sounds of love-making emanating from bedrooms – all these noises bump against the back wall in the courtyards and get amplified. I have even noticed that after long years of living in close proximity with each other, some of my neighbours have synchronized some of their daily motions, including several who brush their teeth at the same time. And when someone on an upper floor flushes the toilet, suddenly the one below has the urge to go pee.

The brothel on the ground floor at number 26 could be considered the diamond in the modest jewellery box of stories about my street. When speaking of it, my neighbours pause slightly, savouring the moment. They prefer the word *Bordell* – more evocative of erotic refinement – to the childish word *Puff* or the functional *Absteige* (flophouse) that sounds too sordid. It's true that *Bordell* – especially with the German spelling and pronunciation – is more stimulating to the senses. My neighbours get a kick out of seeing my jaw drop, my mouth hang open, and my eyes go out on stalks. What! A *Bordell* in our street! Here! *Ach nee*, not possible! And yet such an establishment truly did exist in our virtuous street. My neighbours speak in a somewhat indecent tremolo when presenting the *principal protagonists* – something they do with the gusto of a movie producer announcing his cast.

At first it was a modest, ordinary brothel – just two or three girls, *that was about it*, plus the Madame who lent a hand, so to speak, on busy days. She lived with her pimp husband and a gigantic bulldog (or two German Shepherds in some versions) in a sombre one-bedroom flat at the back of the courtyard. They often fought at night, waking up the whole block. The television was always on loud from morning 'til night, and they consumed enormous quantities of alcohol. It is said that on the day of the pimp's funeral, a guest threw a bottle of vodka into the grave which broke when it hit the coffin. *A family tradition*, it seems.

The brothel took out ads in a local paper and was never lacking customers. It could happen sometimes that a little embarrassed man, worked up into a high state of libidinal distress, would get confused and ring at the door of an honourable mother on the first floor who would slam the door in his face. The plumber's visit remains legendary in the history of the street. The innocent artisan had been called in to repair a shower fitting. He rings at the door of the brothel. The Madame opens the door and says, *What rate do you want, the fifty mark or the eighty mark job? – I was called by you,* he replies, *I'm looking for the shower.* Certain renters in the building, and even residents in the adjacent buildings, had seriously thought about asking for an 'orgasm nuisance discount'.

Later Asian women were employed. They were thin and graceful, wore lots of make-up, and jumped out the windows onto the flowerbeds in the back courtyard when the police made their occasional raids. Wearing only their canary-yellow lace underwear and a transparent nylon negligée, they would scurry like frightened deer behind the line of rubbish bins and escape through the adjacent building. People also say that customers, regulars mostly, would cross the ground floor hallway half naked to sip a cold beer in the porter's lodge. Taking advantage of the strategic location of his quarters, the concierge ran quite a profitable little side business that was completely illegal. In secret and at jacked up prices, he would sell beer and hard liquor to thirsty customers who needed a little fortification before offering themselves a second go in some original Asian style, a little erotic extra before putting on their beige socks and zipping the fly of their Dacron trousers in time to get back for *Abendbrot*. It's rumoured that since the local police and civil servants at city hall were themselves regulars at this well-known establishment, the concierge's backroom bar was never shut down.

When my neighbours tell me the story of the brothel, they usually do so in a tone of high indignation. *Ein Bordell!* In our

street! The shame of it! But I have no trouble detecting the tremolo in their voices – perhaps a slight ache of some unsatisfied
desire. A regret at having been so silly not to have ridden one of
the adorable little deer in their yellow lacy underthings at least
once before a doctor's office and the virtuous Sylvia became the
next tenants on the ground floor. The *Bordell* was then forced
to close down. Today it's the exhalations of the members of a
meditation circle that rise up the stairwell in the evening.

16

Rebel Rebel

Suddenly an event, a real big event. All of a sudden in my street there's a public spectacle.

The curtain went up one morning at dawn. Cloth banners were draped over the facade at number 4 on the square with their angry demands in red ink: *Schöneberg does not belong to the powerful! Against the destruction of affordable housing! Protect the tenants from the Far West!* That morning we learned that the building consisting of 106 low-income housing units opposite the entrance to the Pennerpark was slated to be demolished.

This dilapidated housing estate, built in 1964, was such a familiar part of the patchwork of my street that I had hardly ever paid any attention to it. I had never seen anyone enter it or exit. Sometimes an ambulance or a police car parked out front hinted at the human dramas unfolding on its many floors. Several fires there had been put out before it was gutted. And there was once a cadaver that was finally removed from the mattress where it was decomposing after a pestilential stench had begun to spread throughout the stairwell. A neighbour had called the firemen. No one had noticed that the little old man on the second floor had not been seen in two weeks. People on the street made a big story out of it, imagining all kinds of plot twists and inventing juicy details at will – a hungry rat, a sadistic burglar and on and on. For weeks, no one talked of anything else. Even today, older residents are happy to launch into retelling the whole thing from the beginning without leaving out a single detail and adding new ones whenever possible.

It had the reputation of being a sinister building. Little by little signs of life inside disappeared behind tiny sombre windows. I thought it was deserted. How could anyone still be living in such a wreck?

The giant builder Hochtief AG had recently acquired the building and lot, and had received approval for its urban renewal project. The neighbourhood council, encouraged by a general tendency in favour of economic development and its own desire to *unblock the situation*, had voted to demolish the building and construct on the same footprint a block of luxury flats whose spaces would sell at top prices per square metre. Its other feature would be an underground car park – the ultimate symbol of the moral corruption that would soon spread throughout the neighbourhood according to local residents, most of whom were militant cyclists. *A number of remarkable projects throughout the world are proof of our company's dynamism*, asserts the group's website. *We moved the Abu Simbel temples, linked Europe and Asia with a bridge over the Bosphorus, contributed significantly to the Frankfurt skyline, built rail lines and roads across large expanses of Australia, and drilled the Gotthard Base Tunnel*. And at the very end of this splendid catalogue of accomplishments, the Hochtief group mentioned number 4 on our square. My little street had been admitted to the company of global players.

This was all anyone spoke about now. The most outrageous rumours were circulating. The future of our street hung in the balance. This sudden wealth was going to provoke burglaries, bicycle theft and the stealing of children's toys! The luxury sedans of the new owners would be torched! At night, silent silhouettes, their faces covered in black stockings, were going to deface the walls of the *Fortress of the Powerful* with human excrement! Our square was going to become the ground zero of May 1 labour riots! A target for anarchists, extremists, alternative globalization activists, graffiti artists, vandals and riff-raff of every kind. They would come to shock the bourgeoisie and vandalize the capital! Our peaceful existence on our dead-end street was over.

Very quickly the call went out and a citizen's brigade was constituted. A first demonstration on the steps of Schöneberg town hall took place. It turned out to be more a thinly attended get-together than a real demonstration. Still, a police car had been dispatched – you never know – to secure the area. A policeman supervised the event with a barely veiled yawn on his face, in his right hand a cup of latte macchiato, in his left a buzzing megaphone. A few speechmakers took turns making their point on the town hall steps. *I apologize for also speaking*, began a hippie, only to be nudged aside before she had hardly finished her sentence. A young woman with sad eyes came forward brandishing a sign that read 'Stop violating my house!', accompanied by a picture of a squirrel and a bat, and a quotation from Mahatma Ghandi: 'The more helpless the creature, the more it is entitled to protection by man from the cruelty of man.' She informed us that more than twenty-nine healthy old trees were to be cut down in the adjacent park, and blurted out the good reasons not to do this in the voice of a scared little girl reciting her lesson by heart. *The trees capture carbon dioxide and have a positive effect on the human psyche!* What was happening on our square, she reminded her audience, went against all the commitments made by the government to fight global warming. On a small scale, Germany was in this instance breaking all the promises made at international summits and authorizing the destruction of an ecosystem. Fortunately, leaders from *Die Linke* ('Left') party, who took it upon themselves never to miss a barricade, arrived to whip this amateur agitation into shape. The most ardent of the speeches followed. Their representative denounced *social misery* and *the sale, slice by slice, of every Berlin neighbourhood.* Comrades from the DKP, a small Marxist-Leninist party, proposed a little insurrection in the neighbourhood, a mini-Revolution without blood-letting or risk-taking. All worked up by this second spring that they sensed coursing in their veins, these folks had hurried over armed with a multi-page pamphlet for distribution. It was a lame little document that intended to place this improvised skirmish within an ideological framework in the 'History' of class warfare – capitalists on one side, the oppressed on the other. The comrades deployed the heavy rhetorical artillery, denouncing *evictions, the folly of urban renewal, social rigidity, heavy-handed manoeuvres to expel renters and in particular those who have only recently immigrated, such that there is almost a racist dimension to these proceedings that will certainly damage the reputation, including the international reputation, of Berlin-Schöneberg!*

My street was caught in the vortex of large-scale *gentrification*. This English word made the rounds in Berlin, more stumbled over than stated. So many unspoken threats and fears were half-hidden behind this noble epithet. Too bad for seniors living off their small pensions, the unemployed, students, artists and all the penniless folks that number 4 had sheltered. Too bad for social diversity. Our street was going to become *socially homogenized*. The poor would be relegated to the outskirts of Berlin and their dwellings would be taken over by the *Zugezogene*, newcomers from the four corners of the globe – high functionaries in the Federal civil service, a rich dentist from Düsseldorf or successful lawyer from Munich, some rich person's son going through his Bohemian phase, Swabian ad men living off vegetarian ravioli and fair-trade muesli, speculators from all parts including Ireland, Spain, Denmark and even Israel, as well as wealthy American retirees. Maybe even some Hollywood star, a colleague of Brad Pitt and Angelina Jolie who live nearby, would buy an upper-storey loft with hanging garden in our neighbourhood and attract a procession of paparazzi. Our street would become Sunset Boulevard-East. These new arrivals were the incarnation of the class enemy contemptuous of the human race and only interested in parking his wealth in the swingingest city in Europe with the hottest property boom. They were going to disfigure our street and divide it into two entrenched camps: the poor, innocent, gentle victims on one side, and the guilty, no good, stinking rich on the other.

Twenty-five years ago in the former West Berlin, no one would have ever considered buying such a building. Who in their right mind would have wanted to protect their savings by investing in property in a frontline city of the Cold War with such an uncertain future? It was a poor city that lived off subsidies from the old Federal Republic. But after reunification and the choice of Berlin as the capital of the new Germany, all those fears gradually disappeared. Investing in property is not a bad idea in these times of financial instability. One often sees estate agents wandering about the neighbourhood looking for buildable housing lots, perhaps a little empty space left over from the war that could be filled in. The post-war buildings labelled 'fit for demolition' that had generous and buildable front gardens were particularly desirable. These locusts, as they were called in my street, were eager to exploit every available square metre. *But who will pay the bill?* the local paper complains. *The remaining West Berliners who survived the strange and difficult times of the Cold War? We have our doubts. More likely people from elsewhere for whom Berlin, like it or not, is 'in' and 'trendy'. People from dynamic new demographic areas who are absolutely in need of a second, or third, pied-à-terre with underground parking in the heart of Europe. People who consider the ascendency they have over others as their free-market right. People who, for purely business reasons, will alter the time-honoured logic of our neighbourhoods with a new building project.*

For several months, eleven rebels were still holed-up in their little flat. A red-haired lawyer who had grown up on the corner of my street was leading the counter-offensive and calling for the issue of a *Red card to the building lobbies!* He was assisted by Hannah, a young sad-eyed ecology activist whose letter to the Bundestag contained 2,000 signatures; a carpenter; an apprentice police officer of Greek origin; a Turkish cashier at Woolworth's; an old lady over ninety who'd been a tenant for thirty years and who some wanted to *send off* to a retirement home where *her soul would never be at peace*; a doctor of physics who was living off unemployment benefits; a twenty-five-year-old Polish woman; a young woman with a difficult personality living on welfare payments and alcohol; a retiree; and a few others who all refused to leave their bastion. They had asked for an injunction and demanded that their fifty-year-old building be *renovated and made more attractive*. I had trouble imagining how to revitalize such a shabby-looking building. By repainting the facade some bright colour as had been done at number 27?

Or by sticking on some new steel balconies? No, in this case it seemed like a losing battle.

A billboard announcing *Exceptional Location – Come Live Here!* was soon erected in front of the building. It was very big, brightly illuminated at night, and well-anchored in the ground with supports lodged in cement. With the first snowfall, the rebels picked up gravel that had been spread on the street and threw it at the billboard, which then for a few days afterward looked a bit like a Jackson Pollock painting. Next came a barrage of graffiti. Each week a new slogan: *Down with the neighbourhood assassin! Speculators out!* And many times the classic, one-size-fits-all *Fuck you!* – obviously much more edgy in English than in German. No sooner were they erased than they appeared again.

The eleven mutineers were forced to walk the plank – they were expelled and the building was emptied. Only the barest signs of extinguished life remained: a grey tulle curtain at a fourth-floor window. A string of little lights on the balcony on the sixth floor. A tuft of dried grass in a flowerbox on the third floor. A few green stems were growing right out of some balconies – hardy vegetable life emerging from this stone block in agony. On a ground-floor wall there was a torn wedding photo of an oriental bride wearing a diadem and veil that highlighted her large doe eyes. There was an empty red wine bottle stuck between the bars of a banister, broken glass, rickety shutters, a laundry line, an upside-down toilet, the salmon-coloured wallpaper of a kitchen. Also on a ground-floor wall, an orange heart with no initials, no name, no I Love You or Forever. Just a little unhappy heart that would soon cease to beat. On the gates surrounding the building were pieces of thread and ribbon tied by those opposed to the project – the last vestiges of the grand days of revolt when everything was still possible. Now only three sunflowers out front, their heads held high, were all that remained invincible.

The opening day for the pre-sale of the new units was scheduled for a Saturday. Hochtief laid on some music and gave away petits fours. They presented their project and then let the sale begin: flats, lofts, duplexes for top professionals, families, dynamic young managers and others aspiring to acquire an address that *allows one to give free reign to the blossoming of one's personal life.* People say several limousines drove around the square, and that on that first day twenty-five units were pre-sold. We saw for the first time images of what was to come – generic designs by ordinary developers, an old-fashioned looking facade tacked onto a high-tech interior. The architect paid no attention whatsoever to the historic building that the businessman Carl Graf had constructed at the beginning of the last century, from designs by the architect Paul Wiesener. The only historic building intact on the square is the school – the former Chamisso-Schule that Lilli Ernsthaft, Ilse Rothkugel, Hannah Kroner and her friend Susanne Wachsner all attended, and that today houses a primary school and adult education classes. The other buildings are all post-war. They're positioned half-facing the square, thus destroying the harmony and play of symmetries. The new investors were responding to the growing nostalgia since the fall of the Wall for the old pre-war Berlin. They were trying to blot out everything that happened on the street after 1939. This housing block, a testimony to the destruction our street had experienced, would be eliminated. It made me nervous. Was our street going to let itself be wrapped in retro kitsch?

The sleek brochure boasted of *a charming neighbourhood in a metropolitan area with heart. Here you will find the aura of a big city and the romantic ambiance of a village, surprising diversity, and open people. A unique mixture of bourgeois atmosphere in residential neighbourhoods of high quality and high energy.* It described *the homes of the powerful dating from the foundation of the Empire* that give the neighbourhood its signature. My neighbours and I look at each other perplexed. We have trouble recognizing our street in this razzle-dazzle advertising copy. Where exactly is this *meeting point between history and modernity?* Where are *the attractive cafés and bistros that invite one to linger over an espresso, latte or croissant?* Is everything about us really *kind and seductive?* Where is that *refined spirit* they speak of? And precisely what location do they have in mind when they mention *a seductive square, without a doubt one of the most representative squares of Schöneberg's entire urban landscape?* Do they mean our roundabout with its abandoned centre circle given over to unkempt grass and dog poo? The 'jewel square' conceived by Georg Haberland has not lived up to its name in a long time. The mythical scene where one would visit it, like an Italian piazzetta, to see and be seen, while strolling idly around surrounded by magnificent architecture, collides with today's reality: a tangled knot of six streets where cars barrel into each other and spin chaotically around the central roundabout. The question of priority is not easy to resolve and several times a day one hears shouting and swearing between cyclists and car drivers who have cut them up. Far from being that verdant oasis of silence where time stops and tensions evaporate, our square is really a crucible of stress and conflict. Moreover, there isn't the least accommodation for a moment's respite. No benches, no inviting piece of grass to stretch out on. The edge of the fountain with its bronze figures is too uncomfortable. For twenty years, city planners have scratched their heads. No money, few ideas. Granted, city street sweepers still pass by and pick up rubbish, but the wear and tear continues. When it rains, local dog owners who don't want to go all the way to the municipal park let their pets add fertilizer to the plane trees. Foxes roam at night.

It was about this time that one of the park benches disappeared overnight. The craziest rumours began to circulate up and down the street. My neighbours were really letting their imaginations run wild. Some even suspected Hochtief of having organized this nocturnal raid in order to eliminate a drunkards' hangout before the arrival of potential customers. Reading the Hochtief brochures, you'd almost think that our Pennerpark was going to turn into a mini Jardin du Luxembourg. Instead of the two wooden huts and the dinky slide, there would be a carefully designed playground with an *educational discovery circuit* for children. And when I call anonymously as a potential buyer and pretend I'm nervous about the park, the promotor promises me it will be an *oasis of oxygen with no quarter given to layabouts who have no business there and only want to drink beer and have private barbeques in secret.* The units sold will all be owner-occupied, and 95 per cent German! he assures me, paying no attention to my French accent. The DKP even proposed renaming the park. In their flyer, the comrades pull the old knock-down argument out of the drawer. *Given the fact that under the Nazi regime Hochtief benefitted from the large-scale exploitation of forced labour performed by prisoners from different concentration camps, one should, in order to preserve the memory of the Jewish founder of the first primary school for social workers, rename the park to which she gave her name, if, that is, the company goes forward with its destructive project. The Gestapo forced this Berlin Jewish woman to emigrate in 1937.* To provide even more fuel to the comrades' jets, maybe they should be told that the Führer's bunker in Berlin, 'the Wolf's Lair' in

Eastern Prussia and the Berghof in Obersalzberg were all built by Hochtief AG, as the company's website duly notes.

Once the building was evacuated and the facade blocked from view, the demolition work could begin. Lorries and skips encircled the central roundabout. The building was shaken down with a convulsion at its inner core. Pneumatic drills began their relentless chiselling. Tiles were split apart, partition walls were destroyed, roof beams were dismantled, piping and other metals were removed. Then came the bulldozers and the children with their teachers from the school next door, who watched in awe as these giant crabs delicately took hold of entire pieces of facade in their claws. Prehistoric monsters out of some science-fiction movie levelled the old rebellious building. Every morning at 8:15, a green Land Rover would park on the edge of the pavement and a father, mother and two young boys would step out to witness the progress from the day before. And every morning the two kids shouted in protest when the parents forced them to get back in the car. I could hear the soft voice of the mother, *But my little lambkins, we'll come back tomorrow.* And sure enough, at exactly 8:15, the two kids had their faces pressed against the chain-link fence. On the fire-wall adjacent to number 4 there reappeared a large advert for Bakery & Pastry that had been hidden for several decades. A thin coat of dust covered the trees, balconies and cars on my street. My neighbour the hairdresser with whom I often take the morning ride in the lift asked me where the large white cloud at the end of the street came from. When he goes to his *Salon*, he always walks down the street in the other direction. He was the only one to have missed everything.

The demolition lasted three weeks. During that time little talkative groups formed around the building site, each person giving their opinion on the whole thing, sharing their consternation. It united us and new supportive ties were made. Gisa at number 12 spontaneously invited others over for coffee. Monika offered to share the photos she had taken. Never had the Pennerpark been visited so often and never had our street experienced such solidarity around a shared destiny. Passers-by, seeing the demolition, also volunteered their opinion: *If it's like the Willy Brandt airport, you're not moving in tomorrow!* clucked a cynic in the direction of the workers. *To think how long it takes to build something like that, and in no time it's a pile of rubble. Impressive! That's how Berlin must have looked after the war!* remarked an older man who perhaps had an odd feeling of déjà vu. Number 4 did resemble pictures of post-war ruins. *You don't see that every day. I wanted to take some pictures too.* A photographer came every day with his tripod. Onlookers took souvenir photos with their smartphones. The street cleaners allowed themselves a mid-morning break and added their commentary in their Berlin accents: *For the same price, I tell you, you could buy a nice family house!*

Who will come to live here? Young families earning good salaries who will shop at organic food stores, patronize sushi bars, attend yoga classes and enrol their children at bilingual preschools. I imagined people bidding at prices per square metre like at an auction. 3,000 euros, says one. 4,000, counters someone else. 5,000! Our street would echo with the little dry knock of the auctioneer's hammer.

A little Polish man bundled up in a big coat stopped me one day, pleased to have someone to listen to him share the good news from the Jehovah's Witnesses. He offered me a booklet in French: *Is this what God wants for me and the family of man? Where can I find help to resolve my problems? Can one hope to see peace on earth one day? The Bible has convincing answers to these questions.* I found in these writings some maxims that would unsettle the conscience of more than one visitor to our Pennerpark: *Reject what Jehovah hates – the use of tobacco, alcohol and so-called mild drugs.* And when a passer-by started predicting turbulent nights because our street was about to become the epicentre of Berlin nightlife, the sins of *sexual immorality and inappropriate words* spoken of in the texts of the little Polish witness suddenly took on the air of something out of Dante's *Inferno*. Only one of my neighbours, an influential gentleman, dared to say in an aside destined for my ears only that the new building would finally improve the standing of our street a bit. He intended to send off a letter to the neighbourhood's city councillor with some suggestions for the renovation of the square – a little café next to the fountain, for example. While he was indulging in visions of croissants and café au lait after his morning jog, I noticed the shocked looks on some faces, so I gave this dreamer a little tap on the shoulder and advised him to pipe down if he wanted to avoid being lynched.

I spent hours wandering near the crater dug in the middle of my street. Here once again was the passing of an era. The vestiges of the war were disappearing. Sometimes a feeling of quiet sadness came over me. I thought of those who were dead, of those who had fled to the other side of the world, of those who had moved to another neighbourhood. And I asked myself if I had the right to slide into such sweet nostalgia, to cry over a building that I had in fact always considered ugly and undignified. I was feeling a certain tenderness and absurd attachment to my street that had been so roughed up by the history of the last 100 years. It had never found peace. What would it be like in a few decades? Rumours circulated that 7A and 7B were to meet the same fate. Surveyors had already measured the lots and an investor had filed for a building permit.

In a way things have come full circle. My street is in the process of returning to its initial grandeur when, at the beginning of the century, it was an exclusive address, *a privileged location* in the lingo of today's property developers. For a long time after the fall of the Wall I thought it was too run-down to be returned to normal. I had watched it resist defiantly and raise its fist. But was this just a blind underestimation of the forces of property speculation? Was my street now going to capitulate? What was to become of the man of dubious hygiene who sat all winter in his sleeveless T-shirt looking out of his window at the construction site? And what of the retired concierge leaning on a cushion at the window of her ground-floor lodge? For decades she had witnessed the street's continuous theatre and watched the sliding panels of different decors and the distribution and redistribution of different roles throughout the various buildings. What of the homeless people in the park? The retirees of another era? It's true these little people, *poor but sexy*, were going to clash a bit with the airbrushed *House & Garden* look that the new builders had in mind for us. Will my street allow itself to undergo this total beauty make-over? Will the vulgar be turned into the charming? Will the half-broken become the coquette? The rough-edged the picturesque? Will it soon be a cool street with vintage furniture stores and other fashionable shops, clubs and bistros? I have trouble believing it.

Photo Credits